Hull's Victoria Dock Village

Colin McNicol

Foreword by
Rt. Hon. John Prescott, P.C., M.P.

Highgate of Beverley

Highgate Publications (Beverley) Limited
2002

In conjunction with

Kingston upon Hull City Council

 KINGSTON UPON HULL CITY COUNCIL

and

Bellway

Acknowledgements

Over the years in researching the history of Drypool and Victoria Dock, I have read all the material I have been able to find about the subject, which must amount to hundreds of articles, leaflets and books. One avenue seemed to lead to another in the quest for pieces of the jigsaw and all the while a more complete picture of the area built up. I cannot pretend for one moment that what I have written has not been influenced by what I have read and as a result I have quoted widely from many sources in the preparation of this book and wish to acknowledge with grateful thanks those from which I have drawn most freely. It has proved very difficult to attribute sources for all the information used, which has, in some cases, been absorbed almost unwittingly and there are, therefore, some that I am unable acknowledge, although I am no less grateful for them.

Particular thanks are also due to Howard Dawe, Chairman of Bellway p.l.c., who provided the initial encouragement for me to carry on writing this history, to John Prescott, M.P., the Deputy Prime Minister, for kindly agreeing to write the foreword, to Councillor Tom McVie, Deputy Leader of Kingston upon Hull City Council, for his unstinting support for the book, to John Markham, for correcting the manuscript, to Arthur G. Credland, of Kingston upon Hull City Museums for his observations, to Bellway Homes Limited (Yorkshire Division) for their assistance in having the book published, to John Bates and Simon Green, both of Hull City Council, for moving things along, just when it seemed that progress had come to a halt and finally to my wife, Lesley, for her patience whilst I sat tapping away.

British Library Cataloguing in Publication Data.
A catalogue record for this book is available from the British Library.
© 2002 Colin McNicol
Colin McNicol asserts the moral right to be identified as the author of this work.

ISBN 1 902645 24 3

Published by

Highgate of Beverley
Highgate Publications (Beverley) Limited
4 Newbegin, Beverley, HU17 8EG. Telephone (01482) 886017

In conjunction with
Kingston upon Hull City Council

and

Bellway

Bellway

Produced by
Highgate Print Ltd.
4 Newbegin, Beverley, HU17 8EG. Telephone (01482) 886017

Contents

Foreword

by
The Rt. Hon. John Prescott, P.C., M.P.

Victoria Dock Village tells a remarkable story: how a marshy site on the east side of the River Hull became a military base, then a thriving dock and shipyard, before its new phase of life as a unique housing development.

The building of Victoria Dock Village has attracted nationwide, even international, interest. All those involved in its creation – developers, architects, planners, councillors and, of course, residents – have been determined to achieve a vibrant community of people living in surroundings where they feel at home, enjoying the amenities and atmosphere of a real village, though not far from the City centre. All very different from the stereotyped image of an anonymous housing estate.

It has been a pioneering project involving co-operation between the public and private sectors – a true partnership – and I was extremely happy to be invited to open, first, Victoria Park and, later, the school. This is a good example of a community working in partnership with local and national government where the community commitment and voice make a real difference.

I am proud that Victoria Dock Village is within my East Hull constituency and I congratulate Colin McNicol, the enthusiastic first Chairman of the Residents Association, on producing a book which will have great interest for people in Hull and beyond.

Introduction

Two events encouraged me to write this book. One was moving house to Victoria Dock in September 1989, which gave me a motive; the other was my retirement from the Fire Brigade in December 1991, which gave me the time.

Moving here came about from reading the media and sales hype that surrounded the creation of a new 'Riverside Village', with new houses, the promise of open vistas of the Humber, from a mile-long promenade, new shops, a marina with individual landing stages for yachts, a school, two pubs, bistro's, a restaurant, a new public park, other landscaped public spaces, etc. It seemed an opportunity too good to miss. It never quite lived up to the hype but then these things seldom do. A national recession and the subsequent loss of political and economic confidence deflected slightly from the original aims. Still, what remains of the dream is mighty impressive by the standards we had become used to in Hull.

Having moved to 'The Dock', I discovered how little I really knew about the area, despite being an east Hull lad and having served for many years at the East Hull Fire Station. What brought that lack of knowledge to the fore came about as a result of a chat with one of the archeologists of the Humberside Archaeological Unit, who were carrying out an excavation at the site of the former Citadel, digging just to the rear of our new house. They had revealed, merely by excavating in one small corner, just how massive a construction it had once been. I quickly realised that what I knew about the Citadel could be written on my little fingernail, with room to spare.

Then I recalled memories of my school-days, at Maybury Junior School, when there were occasional tales of lads who had drowned in the timber ponds at Victoria Dock, usually caused, so the grapevine had it, because they were sailing about on home-made rafts that fell apart. The stories, told in hushed tones, swept around the playground of our school and, when I repeated them at home, brought forth dire warnings from my mum about the dangers of playing on, or in, deep water. I also remembered that my dad, (who was also a fireman, during and after the war) had been called to many a spectacular blaze among the tons of pit-props which were stored on the dock, telling us at home of the magnificent efforts that were carried out by his colleagues and himself to confine the fires. I knew I needed to find out more about this place, but where to start?

The encouragement I needed was actually more of an inspiration. When I finally retired from service with the Fire Brigade after 31 years, my wife and I joined the Local History classes at the Hull College, where it was my good fortune to meet Christopher Ketchell, who was head of the Unit at Park Street. Chris really fired my imagination by surprising me with just how much information could still be found about the times, places and events in our city, if you only knew where to look. He taught me how and where to enquire, to seek out visual clues, to look up, as well as down, to note detail, to find out its meaning and to question everything, particularly other people's long-held assumptions. In short, I owe him a great deal.

However, when I first started to look at Victoria Dock Village and the area surrounding it as a subject to study, I thought I would be lucky if I could find enough material for a notelet. In fact that later stretched to a leaflet, later still a pamphlet, then it got to, well, perhaps, a booklet. I was to be surprised.

Perhaps not surprisingly, the history of Drypool is bound up in the history of Hull to a close and fascinating degree and, although the majority of historical detail lies on 'that side' of the river, the eastern side, too, has its story to tell. More than anything, I wanted, if possible, to tell the story of this area and its place in the history of Hull over the period of the last millennium. In that way it would encompass a time-scale which began even before the existence of the seven or eight mud huts that originally formed Drypool, through to the end of the Millennium and the creation of a new village, comprising the 1,500 homes at Victoria Dock – and all that had happened in between. It's a long journey in time that never travels much further in distance, than one mile or so from the Victoria Dock Village.

Finally, I remembered the wisdom that Chris Ketchell had imparted to me long before, which was: 'If you ever do decide to write a book, at some stage you'll have to decide to freeze it, otherwise you will go on and on finding new bits of information and never stop.' Well, I've finally reached that stage. I hoped that it would coincide nicely with the end of the 700th anniversary of Kingston upon Hull and, who knows, perhaps the 900th anniversary of Drypool. Most important of all, I hope that you find as much enjoyment in reading it as I have found in writing it and that it unravels some of the tangled threads of the history of this area. It's not intended to be a work of great scholarship but rather a book which will give the reader a sense of the place and time of this little corner of our great city.

The Victoria Dock Story – A Chronology of Events

1000 Probable date of the establishment of Drypool as a small settlement of huts used by shepherds and turf cattle sheds.

1070 Drypool suffered 'lamentable destruction' in attacks to avenge the Norman Conquest, by Swayne, King of Denmark.

1080 Lands in Holderness, including Drypool, awarded to Drogo de la Beuvrière.

1086 Drypool recorded in the Domesday Book as the berewick of Dridpol.

1193 Earliest mention in official records of Wyke as a port, when used as a gathering place for the wool collected as a part of the ransom for Richard I.

1211 Sayer de Sutton altered the course of the River Hull by widening and increasing the depth of Sayers Creek between Charterhouse and the Humber.

1265 Disaster struck when a major breach of the embankments allows the waters of the Humber to flood land as far north as Beverley.

1266 Earliest written record of St. Peter's Church, Drypool.

1292 Wyke reached the position of Third Port in England. Population around 300.
August, Edward I visited Wyke upon Hull and recognised its importance as a strategic port of supply for his military campaigns against the Scots.

1293 Meaux Abbey granted all its right in Wyke and Myton to Edward I in exchange for other properties in the area.

1299 Wyke received a Royal Charter on 1 April, making it a free borough.

1303 The road to Holderness approved, from Hull, 'through the middle of Dripole to Somergang', via the new North Ferry over the River Hull. Population of Hull around 1000.

1321 Hull merchants petitioned the King for greater protection of the town. The King issued a Royal Charter authorising work to be undertaken to improve the defences of Hull.

1356 The town walls, built of brick, were completed, enclosing the town to the south, west and north.

1378 First defensive works sited on the east bank when a tower built to secure the floating chain which was hauled across the mouth of the River Hull at dusk each day.

1382 Richard II granted the River Hull and Haven of Sayer's Creek to the burgesses of Hulme or Hulmo and their successors forever.

1539 Dissolution of the Monasteries. Drypool ceased to be subject to the Nunnery at Swine. The land is taken over by the King.

1542 22 February, foundation stone laid at the fortifications on the east bank of the River Hull which were constructed by the command of Henry VIII.

1551 The Great Plunder, when the Crown confiscated valuable property held by the Church. St. Peter's Church, Drypool, was despoiled as a result.

1574 Earliest recorded entry in the St. Peter's Church, Drypool, Register.

1603 The Great Plague arrived in Hull, The Bench met at the Castle and the markets moved to Drypool.

1642 23 April, Charles I refused entry into Kingston upon Hull, by the Governor, Sir John Hotham.
3 July, Hull placed under siege by Royalist forces.
27 July, siege lifted.

1643 2 September, Kingston upon Hull again placed under siege by Royalist forces.
11 October, siege lifted. Celebrated in Hull as a day of Thanksgiving and marking the date of the commencement of Hull Fair ever since.

1680 Martin Beckman arrived in Hull to inspect the defences of the town. Charles II ordered the construction of the Citadel.

1681 Work began on construction of the Citadel. Reported complete in 1685.

1715 Citadel repaired and refurbished.

1743 Population of Drypool around 100.

1775 October, foundation stone of 'The Dock' was laid, excavated by manual means. Opened September 1778.

1785 Drypool Feast thought to have started this year, thereafter held annually on second Monday and Tuesday in August, with exception of war years, until 1958.

1793-1815 Napoleonic Wars. Citadel manned by up to 15,000 troops.

1801 Population of Drypool, 671. Population of Hull, 22,161.

1809 June, The New Dock opened. Entry was from the Humber. The Dock renamed as the Old Dock.

1814 October, *Caledonia* became the first steam-powered ship to be introduced on the Humber.

1821 Population of Drypool recorded as 2,207.

1822 15 April, medieval Church of St. Peter demolished.

1823 New St. Peter's Church, Drypool, opened 20 June.

1827 Parish School of Drypool opened in west gallery of St. Peter's Church.

1829 June, Junction (Prince's) Dock opened. Linked the town docks together, by following the line of the former moat.

1831 New road to Hedon constructed through Drypool, established by a turnpike trust.

1846 Citadel transferred from War Department to Department of Woods and Forests.

1847 Asiatic cholera arrived in Hull. Became the worst affected town in Britain.

1850 July, East Dock opened, later renamed Victoria Dock.

1851 Charles and William Joel Earle rent out land at the eastern end of Victoria Dock to lay out as a shipyard.

1853 March, Earle's first ship named *Minister Thorebeck* launched from their new shipyard into Victoria Dock. May, York and North Midland Railway open the Victoria Dock Line to rail freight traffic and in June to passenger traffic. Reverted to freight only in October 1854.
Victoria Dock Railway Station became passenger terminus for the Hull and Holderness Railway.

1854 Queen Victoria and Prince Albert visited Hull. Docks renamed, the Old Dock as Queen's Dock, the New Dock as Humber Dock and Junction Dock as Prince's Dock. Hull and Holderness Railway Company opened the Hull to Withernsea line.

1857 Martin Samuelson opened his shipyard at Sammy's Point.

1858 Drypool School opened, sited between Church Street and Raikes Street. Citadel offered to the Corporation for use as a Public Park.

1862 *Dido* became the last vessel to be launched by Earle's into Victoria Dock.

1863 Earle's first launch directly into the Humber.
Martin Samuelson launched four ships into the Humber on one day. Last recorded firing of the guns at the Citadel.

1864 Citadel demolished by Department of Woods and Forests. Martin Samuelsons' shipyard sold to Humber Iron Works and Shipbuilding Company.

1865 South Bridge across the River Hull opened (Ha'Penny Bridge).

1866 Citadel Isolation Hospital opened.

1872 Bailey and Leetham, shipbuilders, acquired Sammy's Point.

1893 Dock strikes in Hull. Military assistance called in to support the police in restoring law and order.

1900 Earle's placed under voluntary liquidation.

1901 Population of Hull, 240,259.
Earle's shipyard sold to Charles Henry Wilson.

1903 Thomas Wilson and Sons took over Sammy's Point and close shipbuilding yard.

1917 Earle's shipyard sold to Sir John Ellerman.

1931 Earle's shipyard closed.

1934 South Bridge closed to pedestrian traffic. Demolished 1944.

1964 River Hull entrance to Victoria Dock sealed off. Passenger services on the Hull to Withernsea line ceased.

1968 Goods services on the Hull to Withernsea line ceased.

1970 February, Victoria Dock closed to commercial traffic.

1987 Victoria Dock acquired by Hull City Council from A.B.P.

1988 Bellway commenced house building at Victoria Dock.

Chapter One
In the Beginning – Drypool and Hull

Victoria Dock Village is often referred to as 'the village within the city' and is tucked away in a corner of Kingston upon Hull, just to the east side of the present course of the River Hull. It is built on the site of what was formerly a busy shipping dock but its story is far older than that. It falls within the Parish of Drypool and there is strong evidence to show that Drypool is even older than Kingston upon Hull. So let's go back to its beginning and find out why that is and where the story of the village began. To help us on our journey just imagine for a moment that a time machine has been invented and that it's possible to go back in time to take a look at the area where Victoria Dock Village now stands. To test your imagination even further, let's pretend that it is a clear dawn, on 1 January 1000. It's to be hoped that there's a boat to meet us on our arrival, since, even at low tide, we'd be surrounded by the muddy brown waters of the Humber, which could be chest deep, so we'd probably not be able to see a great deal. But even had we a higher vantage point, there would be very little to be seen that could suggest the conditions that might have led to the establishment and development of either the village of Drypool, or the town that was to become Kingston upon Hull.

This is because the area where the present city is sited was formed by a huge, shallow depression, badly drained and liable to flooding. However, centuries of such flooding had raised the level of the land until, by the end of the tenth century, there was some cultivable land that showed above the shallow water as green patches, or 'holms,' which even at high tide were relatively free from inundation. The whole area would have presented a dreary prospect for any visitor, with the waters too shallow to navigate and the shores too swampy to walk on, although the whole district would have been alive with the cries of seabirds. We might also see some smoke rising from a few settlements around the fringes of this wide, shallow tidal lagoon, such as at Hessle, Kirk Ella, Cottingham and Sutton, which occupied the higher ground that even the highest tides could not reach. Their history dates from the earliest period of the Anglian occupation of this area.

Around that time, Sutton would have been a long narrow island near to the eastern shore of the lagoon, the western shore being formed by the foot of the Yorkshire Wolds. At normal tidal levels the island was attached at the northern end to Waghen, or Wawne, as it is now known. It stretched for two and a half miles (4 km) to the south-east where, beyond Risholme, it was similarly attached to the southern part of the main isle of Holderness. The ridge of this low island was set out in arable, open fields, farmed according to a well-organised pattern. Later settlements, such as Myton, Newland, Dunswell, Stoneferry, Marfleet, Southcoates and Drypool, could only have been planted and inhabited after a system of embankments had been raised, which, in effect, narrowed and thus limited the course of the freshwater stream known either as the Wyke, a name derived from the Scandinavian word 'vik' meaning a creek, or the Hol, after the great hollow into which it drained. The embankments also limited the incursion from the Humber estuary and thus allowed land to be recovered from the water. The recovered land steadily transformed the great hollow waste of mud and brackish water into something which, over a fairly short period of time, turned into meadow, or pasture, or improvable marshland. Drains were cut to carry the upland waters to the new channel of the river, and eventually Sutton was no longer an island and found itself surrounded by thousands of acres of green meadows called 'ings' and marshy pastures known as 'carrs'. The mud flats would have required time to become fairly solid and covered with grass and, even then, would not be very valuable until a lot of hard work in ditching and weed clearing had been carried out. The labourers who were employed in cutting the ditches to drain the land also raised the embankments.

However, the drainage work was still incomplete by 1150, since even at that time there was a great sheet of water that lay between Sutton and Swine known as Sutton Marr. Between Sutton and Drypool there was another 'marr' called Stanmer, which drained into both the Humber and the river known as the 'Hul' by means of low marshy channels.

There is little doubt that the lion's share of this newly created territory went to whoever might have held the manor and thus caused the work to be carried out. The remainder of the meadow and pasture would have been divided among the free tenants of the manor and the holders of the old 'lands', according to their holding.

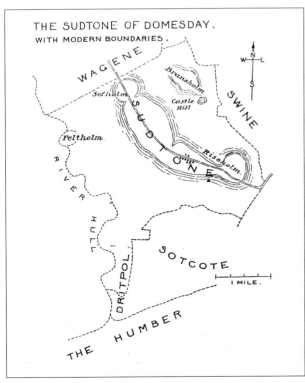

The Island of Sutton at the time of Domesday Book (1086).

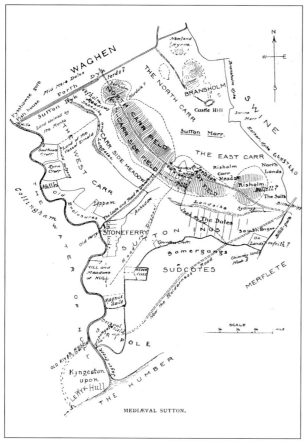

Sutton in medieval times.

Since none of the names of these later settlements are Danish in origin, it seems more than likely that they were formed at an earlier date than the Viking invasions and, due to their limited areas of occupation, the implication is that they were founded in the late Anglian period. It, therefore, seems reasonable to suppose that the villages and embankments were only recently formed when the Viking settlers first sailed into the Humber during the ninth century. It is more than likely that Drypool itself originated as a thinly scattered small number of – not more than seven or eight – rough, flimsy dwellings and perhaps some cattle sheds, built of turves or earth – as they existed in an area where there was no natural building stone – used by shepherds and herdsmen. There are two credible suggestions of the origin of the name Drypool: one is, as it indicates, from a reference to a 'dried up pool', but is believed to mean one which has been drained, rather than one that dried out under natural conditions; the other is that it took its name from a creek that jutted out from the Humber where the old harbour ran, later known as Sayer's Creek.

The story really gathers pace in 1042, when Edward the Confessor succeeded to the English throne. He was content to be a puppet king and the government of the land was in the hands of Godwin, Earl of Wessex, and on his death in 1053 his son, Harold, retained control over the government of the country, becoming, in effect, the most powerful man in England. Harold was shipwrecked on the coast of France in 1064 and fell into the hands of Duke William of Normandy. To gain his release, he swore a solemn oath, promising that he would do all in his power to help Duke William

to the English throne. However, shortly before Edward the Confessor died at his new palace in Westminster, in 1066, he named Harold as his successor. Harold then revoked his oath to Duke William, claiming it had been made under duress and accepted the crown.

William invaded and established himself as monarch, but things did not go easily for him in England. Resistance to his rule remained strong, especially in the East and North. Between 1068 and 1071 the North of England was devastated in what was termed the 'Harrying of the North', when the region, led by the Earls Edwin and Morcar by Grinchil, the latter who held the lordship of Holderness and the chief portion of Sutton, rebelled against the Norman overlords with disastrous effects.

Thousands of English rallied against William, and his problems became even worse, when in 1070 a fleet of 200 Danish ships, under Sweyn, King of Denmark, entered the Humber and lent support to the rebels. Drypool, Myton, Sculcoates and Ferriby are mentioned in Domesday Book as having suffered lamentable destruction, with everything valuable on both sides of the river destroyed. Domesday Book (1086) provided a census of the value and ownership of all land and property in England. The King's clerks described Drypool as a manor, with Ralph de Mortimer its lord, and the berewick of Dridpol, or Dritpol, described, together with the surrounding area as, 'a few settlements on the higher ground situated in a saltmarsh with embankments of mud and turves joining the island settlements'.

Whatever else the Norman Conquest may or may not have affected in England, it altered dramatically the political balance in Holderness. For here, where many laymen had held estates before 1066, the redistribution of the lands following the Harrying of the North and the confiscation of the Earl of Morcar's lands in 1071 led to the creation of a single powerful block of land in the possession of one man, a foreigner at that and a member of the victorious military alliance, who held all Holderness except for the church's land. The Isle of Holderness, including Dritpol and Sotecote (Southcoates), became the property of Drogo de la Beuvrière, who had accompanied William the Conqueror and had been rewarded in 1080 by the grant of lands in Holderness. Little is known about Drogo, except that he was a knight and a Fleming who most likely came from the village of la Beuvrière near Bethune. He was an excellent soldier experienced in fighting and was responsible for the building of Skipsea Castle. Allegedly he murdered his wife, a relative of King William. After her violent death, Drogo went to the King, pretending that he wished to return to Flanders with his wife and asked him for money, which the King gave. Drogo used the money to escape overseas and, although the King sent for him to be seized, when he found out what had happened, Drogo was never to return. The lands in Holderness were re-granted by the King to Count Odo, the dispossessed Count of Champagne who had married the King's niece and who was the first of the line of the Counts of Aumale. It was recorded by the King's clerk, that: 'Holderness was given to Odo of Champagne, who had the King's sister to wife . . . this land was exceedingly barren and unfruitful at that time, and brought forth nothing but wild oats', although this was little more than a ploy by Odo to gain more land.

Drypool extended on the eastern bank of the River Hull far into the parish of Sutton by the beginning of the thirteenth century and did so for many years after, covering almost the whole of the district that became known as the 'Groves', either side of the present Cleveland Street. The southern portion outside the parish of Sutton was in Swine, upon which Drypool was dependent. To the north of Drypool, by the side of the River Hull, were arable lands and meadows, extending to Stoneferry, in the area later known as Wilmington. These meadows were sometimes referred to in ancient charters as 'the meadows of Sutton extending as far as the water of the Hul' but they were also called the 'meadows of Hul', seemingly after the river whose banks they formed. Owing to the lack of efficient drainage and to the frequent floods of early times, the land at Drypool would be nearly valueless, until the great demand for wool brought every acre that would carry sheep into practical use as meadow and pasture. In fact the east bank of the river, north of Drypool and as far as Stoneferry, was largely unoccupied, but there is evidence to show that there was a landing place for vessels in a creek on the eastern bank where wine, corn, lead, wool and other merchandise were freely bought and sold without any further exaction than the payment of an accustomed toll which had long been rendered to Sayer de Sutton and his predecessors for the measuring and weighing of all goods brought into the river.

At that time Wyke upon Hull, which had been developed by the Monks of Meaux from the scrubland outside Myton as a point for gathering wool for export, was described as 'a farm at the confluence of the Hull and the Humber' and was considered rather unimportant, consisting of little more than pasture land on which stood a few houses and shepherds' huts, made of turves and mud, with sheds for cattle and a complete absence of roads of any kind. When vessels capable of crossing the North Sea came to the Hulmo, it was not on account of any hamlet at its mouth but because it was a harbour that gave access, through waterways, to the riverside ports of Beverley and York, where there might be some demand for their merchandise. However, the increasing profitability of sheep farming, due to the foreign demand for wool and the use of Wyke as the gathering place for the export of wool which was shipped from the harbour, increased to the point when it was ranked as the sixth highest trading port in 1203-1205, when King John imposed taxes on the merchants of the ports of the east and south coasts of England, according to their trade (known as the Quinzeme, because it exacted one-fifteenth of their income). Wyke paid the sixth largest amount at £344. 14s. 4d. At that time foreign merchants, who made about nine shipments to every one made by an English merchant, dominated the trade of Wyke.

None of the English merchants were described as originating from Wyke but as coming from such places as Beverley, Hedon and York. The main import through Wyke appears to have been wine for the Archbishops of York, which was shipped in earthenware containers.

Even so, at the beginning of the thirteenth century, the village of Sutton was of much more consequence than Wyke, being one of the larger villages in Holderness, and Sayer de Sutton the Second (1211-1269) was at one time the Bailiff of King Henry III, being placed in charge of the port at the mouth of the 'Hul' to be kept for the King's use.

It was Sayer de Sutton who, early in the thirteenth century, decided to alter the course of the River Hull, from where it used to flow into the Humber, to the present channel, in order to better drain his widespread but marshy lands, which at that time were subject to flooding. The original courses of the Hull ran westward from an area behind the present Charterhouse, called Sculcoates Gote (Gote being a Danish word for a stream or drain, derived from Dan Gjot), and then along a winding course through what were open fields to the end of Castlerow, where it entered the Humber. He created the new course by widening and increasing the depth of Sayer's Creek, which formed a straighter channel along the last few hundred yards from the Charterhouse area to its outfall in the Humber, and this new tidal estuary had a range at spring tides of 20-22 feet. The marr known as Stanmer, that lay to the south of Sutton Ings, was finally drained by the new channel. The old channel then became known as Limekiln Drain, taking its name from some lime kilns which stood in that locality. It remained for many years following the digging of the present channel and was frequently referred to in the medieval records of the town. In fact, as late as 1303 the current in the old Hul, as it was already called, was thought to be still strong enough to power a proposed water mill.

Despite changing the course of the River Hull and continuous effort in raising the embankments of the Humber, there were several occasions when they were breached and low-lying land was flooded. However, in 1265 disaster struck when a major breach of the embankments took place and a huge area, including Drypool, was flooded. The villagers again had to drain the land and rebuild the embankments once the waters had receded.

The third Sayer de Sutton (1269-1289) in a charter thought to be dated 1269 granted the nuns of Swine a 'freeway for carts and wains, men and horses, and for driving the rest of their animals over a path, or road, reaching from the bridge at Bilton through the midst of the meadow at Sutton and through the pasture of Summergang as far as Dripole, and to their sheepfold,' thereby giving the nuns the same right of passage as the men of Sutton and Dripole who used it. This track later became Holderness Road. This was an important concession as then there were very few public rights of way other than those by which the free tenants reached their scattered lands. He also granted the nuns a further right of way from Swine, through the parish of Sutton, to their new properties at Wilmington and to their pasturage and sheepfolds in Southcoates.

Edward I spent three weeks in East Yorkshire during August and September 1292. During his stay he took the opportunity to visit Wyke, which by that time had developed into a place of some importance, although, in size, it comprised little more than two long streets running parallel to the River Hull on the west bank, with four short cross streets providing the only public access to the river, the remainder of the bankside being occupied by 29 properties. The total population probably comprised around 300 persons, or some 60 households, who dwelt in a built-up area of less than 60 acres. However, it was the flourishing trade of the port, mainly in the export of wool, that caused the King to recognise the possibility of Wyke becoming one of the great commercial centres of his kingdom and also of being of great strategic importance in securing a port of supply for his military campaigns against the Scots, who were hostile to his claims to the Scottish throne. His stated objective in developing Wyke was 'to increase the fitness of the port for ships and traffic'.

Meaux Abbey granted all of its rights in Wyke and Myton to the King at the end of January 1293 in exchange for other lands and properties in Lincolnshire, and he took formal possession on 19 March the same year. It was now a royal town, Kingston upon Hull, governed on behalf of the King by a 'Keeper'. The people of the town petitioned for a Royal Charter in December 1298 and officials were received by the King in person at Baynard Castle, Cottingham, where he was spending Christmas at the family seat of Lord Wake. The town received its charter on 1 April 1299, through the payment of 100 marks. Wyke upon Hull received a royal designation, becoming officially, the free borough of Kingston upon Hull, giving the burgesses (townsmen) and those who wished to build and reside there the status of freemen, with no feudal dues owing to a lord.

They also gained the important rights to buy and sell property, to elect a coroner, to build a prison and erect a gallows. More importantly, they gained freedom from customs dues and from all tolls throughout England, except London. Having founded his new town, Edward was keen to foster its trade. This necessitated the construction of proper roads which would help commerce. On 8 June 1300 the King granted the mayor and aldermen the right to impose tolls, the money raised from which was to be used to pave the main streets of the town. The people living in Drypool must have noticed the gradual increase in the groups of houses on the holm where central Hull is today. In 1303 a writ was issued at Westminster to William de Carleton and Geoffrey de Hotham to enquire into the matter of a new road, a King's Highway, into Holderness. It was suggested that the road be made from a point on the River Hull just to the north of the town to Bilton Bridge. This road was not entirely new, as it roughly followed the right of way earlier granted to the nuns of Swine. It was to go 'through the middle of the town of Dripole to a pasture called Suttecotes Somergang' and from there straight to 'the cross standing in Somergang'. Although the exact site of this cross is unknown, the description suggests that it was somewhere in the neighbourhood of the old Mile House, where Holderness Road takes a decided bend. From the cross the road was to go to 'the west of the vill of Suttcotes, to a ditch between Sutton Meadows and Somergang, where a bridge is to be made, by a place called Lambholmesikes', which is where Holderness Road is now joined by Ings Road. From there the road was to be built, at a breadth of 40

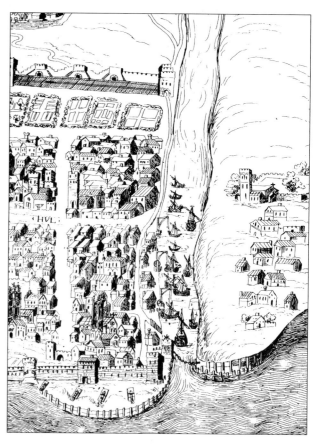

The undated Cottonian Manuscript plan of Hull showing Drypool.

feet, to Bilton Bridge, where it would join the ancient road through Sutton towards Hedon, to link up with such roads as then existed in South Holderness. The road effectively divided the northern part of Dripole from the rest. The traffic on the road can only have been light, most likely consisting of a dozen or fewer packhorses on an ordinary day and only a little more on a market day or during a fair. Carts would rarely be seen and were, at some times of year, even prohibited because of the damage caused by their wheels to the soft roadway.

These momentous events did not leave Drypool totally untouched. For instance, Sir John de Sutton the elder, was aggrieved, not only by the building of the road through his land in Drypool but also by the fact that goods were now landed and loaded on the west side of the stream, whereas for the first half or more of the thirteenth century one or more landing stages had been utilised on the east side of the river, and so he felt the loss of his trade and the tolls therefrom quite keenly. However, his greatest grievance appears to have been caused by the loss of his ferry across the River Hull, which at that time had no bridge crossing. The burgesses of Hull had now decided to provide their own ferry, shown in the detail from the undated Cottonian Plan of Hull. The new ferry was situated less than 60 feet (18.3 m) away from the old ferry and as the burgesses made no charge, Sir John's ferry went out of use and he calculated that he had lost 40 shillings per year in revenue. In the light of this situation, Sir John thought fit to show his power, which he expressed by refusing passage to the people of Hull on the new road to Bilton, which terminated opposite the North Ferry. The King replied by having both him and his brother, Nicholas, carted off and thrown into the town gaol until they had paid a fine of 100 marks, which was probably around his total income for one year.

Following the end of the Roman occupation, brick making had died out as an industry in England and it was probably the import of bricks from Holland that stimulated the revival of the industry locally. As previously noted, this area lacked good quality stone for use as a building material, and to import it would have doubled the cost. However, it was well endowed with clay and by 1300 Hull had a brickyard, situated between the Postern Gate and the Humber, where bricks, thinner than modern bricks, were made and became the major building material in the town. This gave the town a charming and distinctive appearance and a certain claim to national fame as 'the one brick built town of the Middle Ages'.

As long as the town of Kingston upon Hull remained under the guardianship of a Keeper, the Crown undertook to keep the banks of the Humber under repair. In 1311 the Crown appointed Commissioners to maintain the flood embankments and drainage of Holderness, spending, for example, 40 pounds during 1313 on the work. But, despite the Corporation imposing a levy for water bailiff's dues on all shipping and cargoes entering the port, it did not give enough attention to maintaining the depth of the channel. Eventually, a proclamation of 1321 directed that no ships should discharge their ballast, usually consisting of gravel, chalk, or large rocks, into the Haven, thus causing obstacles to the navigation of the River Hull. The order proclaimed that anyone caught dumping ballast into the Haven, as the port of Hull was known, had to remove it at their own expense. However, as much of the waste proved impossible to recover, increasingly heavy fines were imposed on those who did not heed the proclamations.

Maintenance of the Haven was made more difficult by the fact that the town could not exercise any real control over the east, or Drypool, side of the river. Since Sir John de Sutton had both lost the revenue from his ferry and been thrown in gaol, he can hardly have been disposed to exercise any control on behalf of the town. A petition to the King, dated 1321, from the merchants of Hull, asked for greater protection for the town, which by now was becoming quite prosperous. Edward II replied by issuing a Royal Charter authorising work to be undertaken to improve the defences of Hull. Walls of 'stone and lyme' were to be raised on the inner side of the town moat, or more accurately, ditch, which itself was to be cleaned and widened. The timber palisade surrounding the town was gradually replaced by a brick wall, the first, completed in 1339, being that along the Humber front. The remaining defensive works along the north and west sides were built after 1350 as funds permitted and were completed in 1406. The walls were built of brick and were constructed to an unusual Byzantine design, with square towers in a style reminiscent of the Eastern Islam Empire and were thought to be unique in England. They incorporated four main gate towers (North Gate, at the northern end of High Street, Beverley Gate, at the west end of

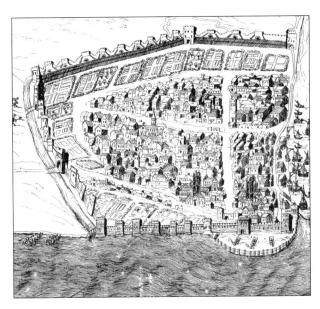

The defensive wall around Kingston upon Hull. (Cottonian Manuscript).

Whitefriargate, Myton Gate and Hessle Gate, near the Humber) and 25 others at regular intervals and linked by walls, which were 2,610 yards in circuit. The records reveal that the number of adults paying Poll Tax in Drypool and Southcoates combined was 73.

Further consideration of the eastern defences, which were formed solely by the River Hull, there being no walls here, was made in 1378, when there was a threat of foreign invasion from the French, who had allied with the Scots. Sir Thomas de Sutton of Holderness granted to the mayor of Hull, Robert de Cross, a strip of land on the east bank of the River Hull, ten yards in length, (9.14 m) from north to south and 100 yards (91.4 m) from east to west, on a ten-year lease for the nominal rent of one rose per year, 'on it to construct a tower for the safety and defence of the town'. The proposed site for the tower was north of Drypole Gote, where the Summergangs Dike had its outfall, near to the entrance that later formed Drypool Basin, and between there and the old North Bridge, but there is no evidence to show that it was ever built.

It was intended to have been used to secure a heavy chain, fastened to logs, to be hauled manually across the mouth of the river at sunset each day. It would have been the first means of defence on the Drypool side of the River Hull.

Some men moved up the social and economic ladder of success in the growing town of Hull, faster than others, one such family of note being the de la Poles. They were merchants typical of many who were to be found in Hull, handling a variety of cargoes, including wine, wool and corn. Richard de la Pole founded the dynasty and was given custody of the town in 1326, due to the ill health of Robert de Hastang, who then was the sworn 'Keeper of the Town'. William, the son of Richard de la Pole, became the first mayor of Hull in October 1332, when Hull ceased to be a Royal estate administered by the 'Keeper' and gained the right to elect a mayor and four bailiffs. He was given the Lordship of Holderness, the King's Manor House and the banking house of the Bardi Company as tokens of Royal esteem for their financial assistance.

He held the office of mayor until 1336 and in 1337, as a result of a royal favour, he founded a consortium which secured a monopoly over the export of wool, which was channelled through Hull and left him much the richer.★

Sir Michael de la Pole, the son of William, married an East Anglian heiress and later became mayor of Hull in 1376. He rebuilt the great Manor House, sited opposite St. Mary's Church in Lowgate, which became known as the Suffolk Palace. Later he became the Lord Chancellor of England and first Earl of Suffolk. In 1385, however, he made enemies within the Court and was exiled to France, where he died in 1389, aged 55. His statue can be seen in the Guildhall. Suffolk Palace was a huge building, with over 20 rooms, a hall, a chapel and summer hall, set in large grounds which consisted of three gardens, each with a pond, the whole occupying a nine-acre site and with a three-storey brick tower.

The frontage facing Market Street measured 719 feet (219 m). It remained the official residence of the descendants of William de la Pole. After a chequered history (fairs were held in the grounds during the 17th century, then the Methodists used the tower as a meeting house), the house was finally sold in 1663 to a prosperous merchant, Robert Broadley, although it was later demolished to provide clearance for street building in the 18th century. However, the stables survived until 1899.

In December 1460, during the Wars of the Roses, 100 people in Hull subscribed to the cost of an iron chain, which was provided with a windlass to ensure its speedy operation, to close off the mouth of the River Hull. The chain was secured to a small round tower built on the east bank of the river. In 1469 a small jetty on the east side was taken down to reduce the chances of an assault from that side of the river. The entrance to the Haven was secured on the west side of the river by a battery of four guns sited on reclaimed ground at the South End.

Following the dissolution of Meaux Abbey, Thornton Priory, the Charterhouse in Sculcoates and the Nunnery at Swine, all of which occurred during the period of the Reformation under Henry VIII, much of the area that formed Drypool was taken over by the King. The monks of Meaux were dispersed on 11 December 1539, and Swine, which had formerly exercised control over Drypool, was surrendered on 30 September 1540. The nuns held Drypool Grange with the lands that belonged to it and this property was granted to Sir Richard Gresham in the first place, but by the year 1553 it was once again in the hands of the Crown, for in that year it was granted by Queen Mary to Sir John Constable.

During the Pilgrimage of Grace (1536), rebels, who were bitterly opposed to the religious reforms of Henry VIII had laid siege to the town, surrounding it on three sides. They had subsequently been allowed unopposed entry to the town by the Corporation. This act of treachery roused the King's fury and he ordered that fortifications be constructed on the east bank of the River Hull to make the town more secure. The east bank of the river soon took on a different aspect. *(See Chapter 3 – A Notable Fortress)* Work on the fortifications began in the spring of 1541 and Gresham was compensated with an exchange of land. On completion of the works the remaining land was let to Thomas Alured, who had been the Paymaster of the Works.

He had been Member of Parliament for Hull in 1557 and again in 1559 and in 1561 he was mayor. An inventory of his property, dated 21 September 1562, includes his holdings in Drypool, 'One Grainge in Drypole – 36 Oxgangs of land – fifteen and one half acres meadow – in one close called Armescroft. Five acres in Sutton Ings, in a place called Grym together with all manner of Tenths, Annuities and other Commodities, and three cottages', which the deed of Henry VIII described as being 'near to the churchyard of the parish church'.

In 1564, Thomas Dalton, three times Mayor of Hull, a 'Merchante of the Staple and Venturer,' bought from Thomas Fairfax and Thomas Boynton, their shares in the Manors of Sutton and Rowstone, with 20 messuages and 20 cottages in Stoneferry and Drypool. He died in 1590 and is buried in the chancel of Holy Trinity Church. He was a man of wealth and position and his descendants continued to hold a substantial estates in Holderness.

In 1565, Henry Curdeux acquired from Thomas Grey 20 messuages and 14 cottages in Sutton, Drypool

The iron chain across the River Hull: details from the Cottonian Manuscript plan of Hull.

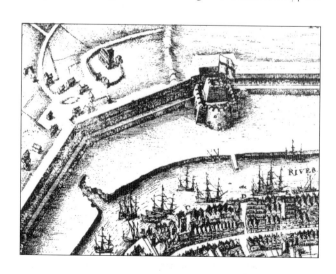

Drypool 1640. (Wenceslas Hollar).

★A statue of him was commissioned in 1868 by Sheriff Robert Jameson and was made by the Hull sculptor W. Day Keyworth the younger. It was formally presented in 1870 and placed in the Town Hall, where it remained until 1901; it now stands at the pier.

and Stoneferry and free fishing in the Sutton Marr. The engraving made by Wenceslas Hollar (1640) shows the castle walls in close proximity to some of the houses in the village of Drypool. The village now lies completely to the north of St. Peter's church and an embankment had been placed to the south of the church, in Kirkfield. A later drawing by Joseph Osbourne, dated 1668, does not show any housing near to the walls.

Hull took the side of Parliament during the English Civil War and was besieged twice by Royalist forces, the siege of 1643 being the most severe, as Charles I tried to capture the town and its vitally important magazine, which at that time was said to be the largest in England.

The fortifications on the eastern side would have been strong enough to repel any attack made from that direction, especially as the ground outside the walls was intersected by numerous deep ditches which ran east to west and would have prevented an orderly attack. It seems more than likely that those houses in Drypool lying closest to the walls would have been destroyed to prevent their use by the besiegers of the town. However, in September 1643 the Garrison Commander of Hull, Lord Fairfax, ordered the Humber banks to be cut and this flooded a huge area. It was recorded that 'Drypool's meadows and grounds were quite spoiled'. The roads were covered, the hay crop spoiled and the grass lands lay waste for a long period after the waters had drained away. In the winter of 1643 the soldiers quartered in the blockhouse had made matters worse by breaking down and stealing the wooden defences to make fires, whilst a 'hideous and mighty winde wrought further devastation by causing a high tide which carried away what was left'. These actions later resulted in claims to Parliament of compensation, for the damage done, which seems to have been drastic, as in 1647 it was reported that 'they have laboured still to keep out the waters from breaking in upon the country'.

In fact the carrs and other low-lying land near the Humber were no better than marshes, except in dry seasons and depended on the upkeep of the banks and drains to discharge the waters into the Humber and the Hull; otherwise they were always liable to flooding. However, there had been several serious floods caused by the breaches in the banks of the Humber in the recent past. The engraving by Hollar shows the earth bank parallel to the Humber, just south of the church. The people of Drypool had been made responsible for keeping both that and the river banks in repair. Any neglect was visited with penalties proportionate to the seriousness of the offence. The inhabitants felt they should not be entirely responsible for something which benefited the whole community and, as a result, dissatisfaction was in the air. In 1647 those who were responsible for the collection of the taxes for this purpose refused to act. They were brought up before the Court of Sewers, where they were found guilty and sentenced to a stay in York Castle. This gave them time for a period of reflection and, when they realised that they were missing the hay harvest and the corn harvest was fast approaching, they petitioned for their release. Once again they were brought before the

Court, where they confessed 'they were sorrie for their forwardness and former obstinacie' and were acquitted.

The men of Drypool also protested against having to bear the cost of maintaining the riverbanks. This case dragged on for some time and the Court threatened a fine of £1,000. Eventually, the Court compromised, taking into account the 'unhappy warres' and 'the mighty power of God', levying a rate on the inland townships, to make a loan to the men of Drypool.

There were 23 families recorded as living in Drypool in 1743, which probably consisted of around 100 people. During this century, however, there were two events which completely changed the face of the parish. The first change was agricultural. From time to time there had been a number of small enclosures, but not until the closure of Summergangs in 1748, followed by that of Southcoates in 1764, were medieval farming methods finally abandoned. For generations the owners and occupiers of the best land in the country had been fettered by a system that had long outgrown its original purpose, and at last a long series of Acts of Parliament ensured that the old open fields with their bundles of strips disappeared. They were replaced by farmsteads surrounded by neat, trim hedgerows. The prime mover in both enclosures was Charles Poole, the Lay Proprietor of the Tithes, and his monument in Sutton Church expresses the best opinion of his day on the subject of the enclosures. It tells of 'his spirit and example opposed to the prejudice of ages against improvements in agriculture, by draining, enclosing and planting the adjacent country'.

The second profound change in the parish during this century was industrial, as gradually ship building, rope-making, seed-crushing, soap-making and sugar-refining, which had first been established on the Sculcoates bank of the river, expanded into the Sutton portion of Drypool. It's important to remember here that early in the 18th century, while the fortifications built by order of Henry VIII still stood along the east side of the Old Harbour, the North Blockhouse stood right in front of the North Bridge until it was taken down in 1801, so that traffic had to go partly around it and along a short piece of road called Bridge-foot. Beyond this lay Blockhouse Lane, now known as Witham, which was then a country road between grass fields, with a few agricultural buildings at either side. At the furthest end of this wide road the great open common of Summergangs stretched out into the distance.

Blockhouse Mill stood near its corner, opposite the centre of the wide road. Lime Street was then known as the High Road to Stoneferry and Sutton and ran close to the raised banks of the River Hull, leaving a width of some 30 to 40 metres of grass between the bank and the stream. The local name for this place was the 'Growths' or 'Groves,' which was only covered at the very highest tides. The High Road ran past the old enclosed lands to the east that extended back in large strips as far as Summergangs Dike, where Dansom Lane was later made. Seed crushing and shipbuilding were established in Sculcoates on the west bank of the River Hull early in the 18th century and similar industrial development soon began on the 'Sutton Side'

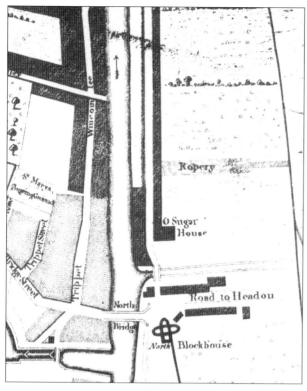

Drypool 1791. (Hargrave).

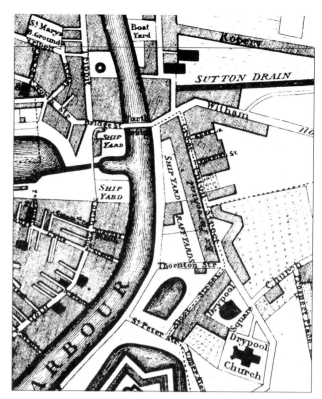

Drypool 1817 (Craggs).

as it was sometimes called. One of the first industries to become established was brick-making, and the area became known as the Brick Kilns. In 1726 a rape mill was built. A notable rope-maker on the east bank early in the century was John Spyvee, who still has a street bearing his name.

The Thornton Sugar House was built in 1732, on a plot consisting of six acres of grass that extended along the wide part of Witham as far as Dansom Lane. At one time there was a draw-bridge across Lime Street which had to be raised to let a high-sided vehicle pass and an upper bridge where men could be seen wheeling sacks in a long procession. In the following year Wilberforce and Foster built their soap house, with warehouse for smelting tallow. Some of these early industrialists were buried in the Drypool churchyard. There would be a few houses thinly scattered in that neighbourhood and the district known as The Groves was then mainly an open field.

The population of Drypool had risen to 671 in 1801 but, in the main, Drypool was little affected at first by the expansion of Hull. However, change was at hand. When the Government abandoned Garrison Side in 1801, 37 acres of land were granted to the Corporation of the town and the Trinity House, in return for money they had laid out on the building of Humber Dock. A road known as the Causeway ran across the land from near the North Blockhouse, along the eastern rampart, to the ancient gateway in the north wall of the Citadel. On Monday, 3 January 1803, the Committee appointed for the management and disposal of the Garrison ground met at the Guildhall to receive proposals for pulling down the wall, extending from the North Blockhouse towards the New Cut on the Garrison Side, and for the forming and making of a new road

from the Blockhouse to the Garrison. On Wednesday, 16 February 1803, the ground from the North Bridge southwards was sold. The old Blockhouse was sold for upwards of £800.

A new road was made, 51 feet wide, including a flagged pavement of six feet, together with another road 40 feet wide branching from it at Drypool, across to the harbour, which it reached about 247 yards from North Bridge. A quay was also formed 15 feet wide. In 1803 this street was named Great Union Street. Another parcel of land was later sold to Mr. William Gibson, who created a shipbuilding yard on it in 1805. His firm produced a number of wooden warships there, including the frigates *Hyperion, Aurora* and *Coelus*. These have given their names to some of the small streets which link Church Street and Witham to Great Union Street. The Gibson family confined themselves to wooden shipbuilding and repairs until the yard closed in 1897. Small carvings of ships could be seen until quite recently on some of the propped-up, weathered gravestones of the shipwrights, sailors and shipbuilders, in what remains of the churchyard of St. Peter's church.

The population of Drypool had trebled by 1821 when it was recorded as 2,207. The Rev. Henry Venn became Vicar of the Parish in 1827 and in 1828 promoted the establishment of a school which was to be affiliated to the National Society. It opened in 1829 and was housed in an unremarkable two-storey building that amazingly still stands in Great Union Street at the beginning of the old Hedon Road. It is now used for commercial purposes by a firm of photo-lithographers but it is still possible to determine the original use of the building.

Another, in Prospect Place, off Church Street,

replaced this school in 1863. In one of his letters, written probably around 1830, Henry Venn describes his view of Drypool: 'Drypool is not a place where everyone could, or would undertake . . . the population is altogether of the lower ranks, with an overwhelming mass of surrounding poverty, about 6,000 and none but poor.' Venn must have added the population of The Groves, then at around 4,000, to make his total. Although this area was actually in Sutton, Drypool was then the nearest church, until St. Mark's was built in 1843, when Drypool lost the portion of the parish lying in Sutton.

In 1831 the new road to Hedon was constructed through a turnpike trust established the previous year, which gave the right to charge a toll for the use of the road. The road passed through Drypool and shortened the old and circuitous route along Holderness Road, then through Wyton and Preston, to Hedon. The following year, Drypool was incorporated into the Borough of Kingston upon Hull. Sir Thomas Aston Clifford Constable granted Drypool Green to the Parish in perpetuity in 1836. This piece of land lay in front of the church and was partly occupied by an area of stagnant water, known as the Green Well, which was progressively being filled in. Gradually, over the years, parts of the Green were sliced off for road widening but the last remaining part, on which the Drypool Feast was held, was only built on as late as 1958.

Drypool Feast was held yearly on the second Monday and Tuesday in August. The date of the event was, allegedly, associated with the dedication of the parish church of St. Peter. The feast is thought to have commenced c.1785 and is said to have begun as a charitable fraternity, or club, which held its annual carousal at a public house and tea garden in Drypool, which usually attracted large crowds. It was later considered to be quite ribald, with many sideshows, and was described in 1851 as being increasingly productive of drunkenness and riot. As a result the inhabitants of Drypool asked for it to be suppressed

and made many complaints to the magistrates. However, it continued, in later years as a fair until 1958, with breaks only for two World Wars.

The increase in Drypool's population by the middle of the 19th century, resulting from the influx of workers who found employment on the docks and the railways, also meant that more burial space was needed. This pressing matter was further complicated by the requirements of the Dock Company, which in 1843 requested a portion of the churchyard to create the lock pit for the proposed Victoria Dock. The negotiations took four years to conclude and finally a sum of £1,800 was accepted. The Dock Company agreed to build 'a sufficient wall with iron pallisading' and also undertaking 'All expenses and responsibilities attending the removal of the bodies, vaults etc'. These were the days of the body snatchers' and the railings replaced the former high walls so that their activities could be more easily observed. The loss of the churchyard meant that a new burial ground was needed. Eventually, it was decided to accept an offer from Hull Corporation, 'of a close of land to the north side of Hedon Road'. The land was secured and in September 1848 it was decided to build a sacristy and lodge. Several disputes attended this piece of land during the ensuing years. The ground was finally closed in 1929 and the sacristy was demolished two years later. It now forms the garden where the modern statue of Peter was placed in 1989.

Drypool had seemingly not improved in the 20 years following the description given in the letter of the Henry Venn. Overcrowding was rife. Medley Square, Drypool contained a particularly nasty area, as a report by doctors on the Sanitary Committee of the Hull Medical Society, dated November 1847, records: 'Closed in on every side there are at least 20 tenements or rooms for as many families. One poor woman cannot open her sitting room window because a walled-up pigsty is close beneath it. Beneath her bedroom window also there is a stinking rabbit warren.' Many working class families kept pigs to ease their lot, their

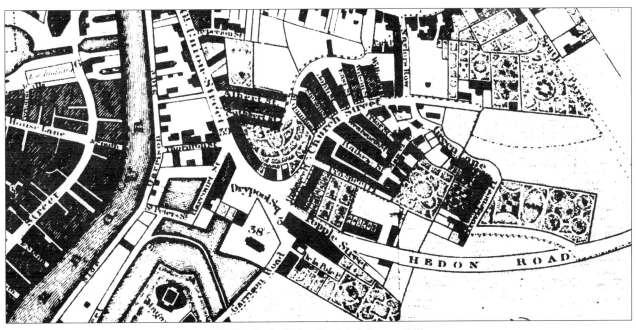

The New Road to Hedon. (Goodwin & Lawson, 1842).

houses stinking, filthy and squalid. Plaster fell from roofs and walls, doors hung from their hinges, broken windows were stuffed with rags and often people slept on straw strewn over the floor. The report noted: 'The unpaved streets of Drypool have accumulations of foetid water . . . masses of filth in profusion and disgusting variety.' The report stated that nothing could be worse than 'the conditions of the poor operatives of a ropery in this locality, which is surrounded on every hand by stinking ditches and smoking dung hills.'

A parish school, known as St. Peter's School, which at some stage was held in the west gallery of the church, opened in 1827. A person of superior education, in this case probably the vicar, did his best with the poor materials available to him, since interesting books were few. The school was condemned in a report of 1858 as being 'ill-lighted, ill-ventilated, ill-arranged and altogether inefficient'.

This report spurred the closure of this school and the National Society school, both to be replaced by the building of a new one in Prospect Place, off Church Street, sited between Church Street and Raikes Street. The site cost £1,000, which was donated by a lady from Welton, and the building itself cost £1,500, towards which the Committee of the Council granted £688. The architect was William Kirby and the Archbishop of York laid the foundation stone on 27 August 1863 whilst building work was underway. The new 500-place school was a handsome building which formed a quadrangle and comprised three large schoolrooms with a playground for each. The three schoolrooms provided accommodation for boys, girls and infants, under the charge of Mr. Richard Carner, Miss Jessie Londen, and Miss Caroline Bampton, respectively. It was built of red brick with stone dressings, relieved by black bricks; the gable ends had three light-tracery windows, with bellcotes in the roofs, and porches at the entrances to each schoolroom. It was described as being of the geometrical, Gothic style.' Some of the stone used in its construction came from the magazine of the Citadel, which was being demolished at this time. The school opened its doors in 1864 and survived until 1942 when it was destroyed by enemy action.

Drypool, in common with other parishes in Hull, also had a workhouse, established as a result of the Poor Law Act (1834). It was sited at the junction of Thornton Street and Great Union Street. The institution was

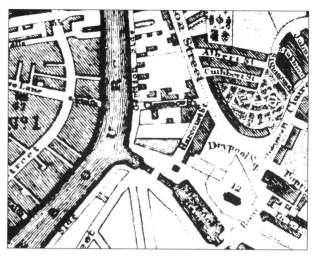

Drypool Workhouse. (Goodwill & Lawson, 1869).

designed to provide for the genuinely destitute, while at the same time acting as a deterrent to the scrounger and serving a general warning to the poor about becoming dependent on the Poor Rate. A further handicap to the poor was the constant increase in house rents as property became scarce due to the great influx of immigrants and unemployed agricultural workers into the town. The consequence of this was manifested in the appalling level of overcrowding in the urban slums.

The 1847 report of the Sanitary Committee noted that in Liddle's Buildings, Sutton Bank, 'the houses were overcrowded, there being in one 16 inmates, in another 15 and in a third 21. In a fourth, three married couples live in one room. Fever of a dangerous and often fatal character has prevailed in almost every house.' The report also noted that dry privies were shared by whole courts of 50 or more people.

Hull Flax and Cotton Mill Company was formed with buildings in the Groves on the east side of the River Hull and spinning, begun in 1838, continued until 1876, when the building burned down in a disastrous fire. Voyages were made to both Bombay and New Orleans and for some years after 1845, when a second company, the Kingston Cotton Mill Company, was formed. The 1851 census revealed that 6% of the total working population was engaged in cotton spinning or weaving. The second mill closed down in 1894, due to the handicap of paying excessive freight rates for bringing American cotton to Hull instead of Liverpool. Many hundreds of Lancastrians and Irish immigrants were attracted to Hull, and most moved into The Groves, where the flax and cotton mills were situated. Additionally, unemployed farm labourers and many hundreds of other Irish immigrants also arrived, looking for work in building the docks and added to the pressures of overcrowding in the town.

The census of 1851 revealed much overcrowding, with over 300 people squeezed into 20 four-roomed cottages, creating a squalid ghetto, in narrow, crooked rows and lanes. So many immigrants were squashed into the Hodgson Street area that it became known as 'Little Ireland'. Life in the Irish quarter was rough and tough. Policemen patrolled in twos and often went in fear of their lives from well-known ruffians. According

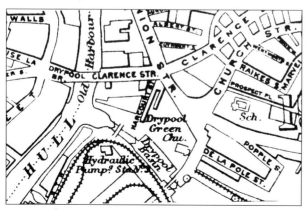

Drypool School. (Bacon, 1906).

to one journalist of the day: 'the police constables' frequent remedy was to take a posse of police with drawn batons at the double through the streets where the tumult was most in evidence'.

When Alexandra Dock opened in 1885 social chaos came to East Hull. The dock construction had provided badly needed jobs. When the work ceased, over 1,000 men had no jobs, many of them skilled tradesmen with families. To help them survive many small shop keepers gave credit to hungry families, who lived miserably, mainly on a diet of bread, rice and oatmeal. Children suffered particularly badly, especially in winter. Reports from the 1880s in the *Eastern Morning News* told of a family with five children which had to exist on a pittance of just 1s. 6d. (about 7.5p) for six weeks. They had no fire, no bed, no bed clothes. The reporter found an eight-week-old baby wrapped in a coat and the other children huddled together for warmth in a room said to be almost bare. It was a common sight to see people carrying small, improvised coffins by hand – a practice deemed by some to be a nuisance. At one time a soup kitchen was set up in the Williamson Street Primitive Methodist Schoolroom. It provided 1,000 loaves and 800 pints of soup. The food value was, however, extremely meagre as each pint had no more than $1^1/_{10}$ ounces of meat and just over 1½ ounces of vegetables.

The Corporation recognised the tremendous problems and went ahead with the building of East Park, which opened in 1887, providing work for many of the unemployed. But records tell of men being so weak from hunger that they collapsed while they worked. Their place was taken by young single men who had fewer mouths to feed and also by labourers who came into Hull from the rural areas of the East Riding, since they too lived in hardship and squalor and Hull offered the chance of a better life. However, efforts were being made to try and improve matters. Under the provisions of the Housing of the Working Classes Act (1888) 602 homes were demolished between 1891 and 1898 and another 127 closed until alterations had been made to bring them up to a higher standard.

Squalid overcrowding persisted for many years, as demonstrated by an article in the 1921 issue of the Drypool Parish Appeal, which commented on the 'congestion of population in parts of the parish: 'In one street alone there are no fewer than 570 houses with a population of nearly 3,000. There are no tenements, no cellar dwellings, no back-to-back houses but in part there is a great deal of squalor and one saw in passing through the parish far too many ragged, unkempt and shoeless children.'

As late as 1933 malnutrition was common and the City's Health Department was seriously concerned about the problem, as there were scores of cases where family income was so low that food came at the bottom of the list of priorities. Poverty was still rife in the City and a Health Department report noted that many children were going to school without breakfast. Many had probably not eaten since 8.00 pm or 9.00 pm the previous day: 'As a result, they suffer from a sub acute gastritis, just as many adults do who have smoked or otherwise indulged overmuch.' That year Hull introduced the National Milk Scheme and more than 30,000 bought the milk which was available for a half-penny for one-third of a pint at school, and around 1000 pupils were given free milk. Many properties in Drypool were severely damaged by enemy action during World War II and several streets were cleared in various slum clearance schemes. However, some remain, since modernised, and now provided with gardens in the spaces once occupied by their neighbours.

Sources:

Thomas Blashill. *Sutton in Holderness and the Monks of Meaux* (Hull, 1896).
Thomas Blashill, *Evidences Relating to East Hull* (Hull, 1903).
J. R. Boyle, *King Edward I and Kingston upon Hull* (Hull, 1899).
Barbara English, *The Lords of Holderness* (Hull, 1991).
Bernard Foster, *Living and Dying. A Picture of Hull in the 19th Century* (1984).
Mary Fowler, *Portrait of East Hull* (Beverley, 1991).
M. E. Ingram, *Drypool* (Gloucester, 1959).
Peter Railton, *Hull Schools in Victorian Times* (Cherry Burton, 1995).

Chapter Two
St. Peter's Church, Drypool

St. Peter's Church, Drypool: the medieval church.

It is quite possible that Drypool was a place where Saxon mission priests from a local monasterium, set up a preaching cross before they erected a church. The earliest written record of St. Peter's Church, Drypool, appears in 1266, when Swine Priory was granted the advowson, which gave it the right of recommending a member of the clergy for a vacant benefice, or of making the actual appointment of a minister to fill the vacancy.

However, drawings of the medieval church made before it was taken down in 1822 suggest it may have been erected a century earlier, during the reign of Edward I. Support is given to this possibility by a contemporary record made during the demolition of the early church which states 'fragments of monuments and carved stones as old as the 12th century were found worked into the walls. When taking down one end it was found to be built of cobble stones and mortar.'

The earliest drawing of this church appears in the undated Cottonian Plan, which is preserved in the British Museum. The plan shows a small church, which actually measured 54ft (16.45m) in length, by 20 ft 8 ins (6.3m) in width, together with a graveyard surrounded by a battlemented wall. The round-headed north doorway of five orders appears to date from the 11th or 12th century, while the windows in the north wall of the nave and chancel were of the 14th century. In the south wall of the nave there was a fifteenth-century window of three lights. The nave was broad,

with a minute chancel which has what appears to be a door in the east end. The tower, with a low-pitched gabled roof, is to the south of the nave, at the west end of the south aisle. There was provision for a congregation of about 200 worshippers.

The village, as shown on the plan, appears to have consisted of at least 15 dwellings. One of these is in the process of being built and lacks a roof. All the houses lie to the south of the church, occupying a triangular portion of the Kirkfield, part of which later became the site for the Citadel.

Two pictures also reveal the appearance of the medieval church. The first is a lithograph published in May 1823. The view from the north shows a three-cell church, comprising an aisle-less nave of three bays, with a tiny chancel and squat west tower with hogsback roof. The middle bay of the nave has a Norman recessed doorway of five orders. The windows of the nave are insertions and have a geometric tracery of c.1350, whilst the east window and those of the tower are rather later. The other is an oil painting by Thomas Fairburn Wilson, now in Wilberforce House, High Street, Hull. The painting presents a view from the south and shows a brick porch of 17th-century origin and a three-light Perpendicular window in the nave.

Records show that in the middle of the thirteenth century the church featured in a bitter dispute between the nuns of Swine and the monks of Meaux. The root of the problem was money. The nuns owned Drypool

Grange and the advowson of the church there. However, when the nuns attempted to collect the tithe dues (a tax taken for the support of the church and the clergy) on the Drypool lands belonging to the monks, Papal privilege was pleaded. An enquiry was held and the Archbishop of York found for the nuns of Swine. The monks were fined and put under excommunication until the fine was paid. They appealed to Rome and a Commission was appointed to re-try the case. As a result the nuns declined to plead and, in their absence, were fined 20 marks. When they refused to pay this amount the Prioress was excommunicated. Four times this redoubtable lady and her nuns refused to appear before the Court, and eventually the Archdeacon of the East Riding ordered destraint to be made for the original 20-mark fine, the closure of the nuns' church and chapels, all services to be suspended and the excommunication of two canons and six lay brethren who had appealed to the Sheriff for help in preventing the destraint of cattle for the fine. Even then the ladies remained obstinate, so, driven to extreme measures the Papal Commission awarded Drypool Church with its tithes and profits to the opposite party, i.e. the monks of Meaux. This did not daunt the truculent ladies one bit. A breach was made in the walls of the church and a siege ensued. This action was too much for the Commission. An appeal was made to the civil authorities and this action brought the nuns both to their senses and their knees. A compromise was reached. The nuns withdrew their original claims and compensated the monks by a payment of 200 marks.

In 1297 there was a record of a disturbance taking place in Drypool churchyard. It told of 'certain strangers from the east, who came with a ship to Hulle'. The term 'strangers' generally referred to people who were not of the parish, and in this case, they were most likely sailors from the Baltic or the Levant. Whilst in port, one of the crew fell ill 'the Sunday before Ascension Day'. He asked for his 'Ecclesiastical Rights' i.e. the sacrament of Extreme Unction, which the local priest gave him.

Still hopeful of a recovery, he visited the shrine of St. John at Beverley, 'in search of health'. Unfortunately he died on the return journey and his companions 'as is the custom watched him during the whole night on their ship'. On the feast of St. Augustine, they brought him to Drypool churchyard for burial. The poor man was not to be peacefully interred, however, since the cortège was met by 'a great crowd of the Archbishop's natives' led by John Hayer, John Mynot, Ralph le Porter and William, Clerk of the Archbishop's Manor of Patrington. They seized the corpse and swore on oath that the unfortunate man had died from misadventure. Having immobilised the ship through the removal of the sails, they sequestered it on behalf of the Archbishop and levied a fine of £20. Simon Constable, on behalf of the King's Escheator beyond Trent, investigated the case. The jury, which included William de Grimston of Grimston Garth, Thomas Scolfin and John Lubias, found the Archbishop had exceeded his rights and had trespassed on the liberties of the Earl of Albermarle and in contempt of the King,

since the rights on both sides of the River Hull belonged to the King's Seignory of Holderness.

The church was stated to be in a ruinous condition in 1428, when an indulgence was granted to those contributing towards its repair; it lacked chalices, books and ornaments. Several bequests to the 'church-work' about this time support the view that the indulgence was justifiably sought.

During the Reformation in the 1500s, when Henry VIII ordered the dissolution of the monasteries, which included locally Meaux Abbey and the Priory at Swine, much of the land in Drypool came into the hands of the King. The land was given to Sir Richard Gresham, who was compensated with other land in Holderness when the defences were built on the east side of the river. When the fortifications were complete, the remaining land was let to Thomas Alured, who had come to Hull as Paymaster of the Works and who was described by Thomas Stanhope, the Lieutenant of Hull, as 'The Chief Constable of the Castle' and as being 'very honest and fit to serve in such a place.' The deed referring to the Drypool property, dated 1545, carries the seal of the King. The Privy Council ordered that inventories be made of all church goods in 1551. This was the culmination of the process initiated with the dissolution of the monasteries. The object was to not only suppress 'superstition' but also to redress the economic balance consequent on so much property being in church hands. The list of goods held by the Church of St. Peter at Drypool was quite long. Not only were most of the valuable articles plundered, but its revenues were also confiscated in this Tudor experiment in the re-distribution of wealth.

Since the stipend at Drypool was now low and the parish was held with several others, services at St. Peter's became infrequent and the fabric of the building was neglected, due to lay rectors who did not fulfil their obligations. The church now presented a sorry sight. The old stone altar had gone, replaced with a wooden table, described as having bulbous legs. This could be carried down the body of the church on Sacrament Sundays. A pair of candlesticks and possibly one chalice survived. The altar rails had gone and the Rood (a crucifix, with its supporting figures) had disappeared although the wooden screen separating the nave and the chancel remained until the eighteenth century. In place of the Rood were Queen's Elizabeth's Arms, newly emblazoned. There would have been a few seats in the nave and there may not have been a pulpit since the church was so small. Some of the windows would still glow with medieval glass but the walls had lost their pictures, hidden beneath a coat of whitewash, with here and there a text painted in black letters. It would have presented a strange sight to those who could remember the brightly painted pictures, the figures of the saints and the numerous lights. The Elizabethan church laid great emphasis on 'sound learning'. However, at the beginning of the reign many of the clergy, like those before them, were ignorant and almost illiterate.

When there was no sermon, the congregation had to be content with a homily, the preaching of a long, tedious moralising discourse. Perhaps because of this, quarterly sermons were ordered, and when these were not provided answer had to be made at the Archdeacon's Visitation. This was usually held at some large central church, like Holy Trinity, Hull, or, St. Mary's, Beverley, to where the incumbent and churchwardens were summoned, the former to submit his letters of ordination and the latter to answer for the parish and report on the fabric of the church. In 1597, Drypool was presented 'as it had but two sermons this last year past'.

The earliest entries in the church register date from 1574 and are in fact a rewrite, made in 1598, of the entries made in the original register, when it was ordered that all existing registers should be written into a parchment book. The entries are made in the neat hand of George Cockerill, the Curate of Sculcoates. One entry appears to detail a domestic tragedy. In November 1596, Bartill Rutter was buried, followed two months later by Isabel Rutter, widow. In 1597 'Ann Rutter, a single woman, drowned hirselfe and was buried the 4th daie of Julie'; since she was a suicide, she was interred 'on the north side of the church'. Another entry in 1598 serves to illustrate the dangers of working on the river: 'upon the 4 daie of March, was buried a drowned man cast up on the Drypoll shore, who it was not certainly knowne, but supposed to be Henry Dannison of Hull, a keelman'. A number of entries recall the burial of strangers (people from outside) and the baptisms of children. The parish armour had to be kept in the church, ready for use when needed. It was placed under the care of the Parish Constable. A Muster of Roll dated 1584 details the extent of the parish weapons and militia: 'Common Armour, one corselet, one bow, one sheaf of arrows, one harquebusse, one murrion; and the militia as, 'three pikemen, six billmen, eight calevers, seven archers'. An entry in June 1600 gives the names of sponsors, one of whom was Humphrey Hall, Rector of Patrington, and a notorious huntsman. In 1603 the register records the heavy toll taken by the plague that year. The first burial on 25 July was John Robson. Throughout the warm month of August the number rose to 13, four of whom came from the same family, that of Alexander Medcalfe.

The Reformation brought with it other important changes. During pre-Reformation times, when a church was appropriated to a monastery, as Drypool was to Swine, the tithes which had originally supported the Rector were transferred to the monastery, which employed a vicar to serve the church. With these tithes went the obligation to repair the chancel of the church. At the Dissolution they passed into lay hands, but whilst the Impropriators (the laymen responsible for the fabric of the church) were quite willing to accept the tithes, they often neglected their duty of care, with the result that chancels fell into decay. It was just this situation that caused a charge to be preferred in 1637 against James Watkinson, John Blaides and William Popple, who are described as the Proprietors. It was their responsibility to keep the chancel of St. Peter's in repair and they had failed to do so. They promised 'to make decent seats chauncelwise . . . and to flag or pave the saide chauncell'. It was also noted that there was 'no communion-table and no decent rails before it'.

The first hint of the gathering political storm comes in 1640, when an entry in the register reads: 'a youth that followed the souldiers toward Scotland was buried Julie the 30th.' The soldiers formed a part of King Charles' army sent up to Scotland to take part in the first Bishops' War, which resulted from the King's attempt to impose Bishops on the Scottish Church. The Presbyterians of Scotland refused, signed a covenant to resist and raised an army.

During the next two years the King's increased clashes with Parliament over the financing of his wars lead to the Civil War in 1642. Hull was besieged three times during the next three years as the King tried desperately to capture the town and its important magazine. Hollar's Plan of Hull (1640) shows Drypool as lying completely to the north of the church. Some of the houses are quite close to the castle walls and these would most likely have been destroyed to deny their use to the besiegers. The fortifications were sufficiently strong to repel any attack from the east and there appears to have been very little fighting recorded on the east side of the river, but there was still plenty of excitement for those who were brave enough to stay at home and not seek the protective shelter of the walls of Hull.

Hull Corporation's Bench Book V mentions another problem of the time. On 15 August 1644 it was ordered that: 'A collection shall be made on Sunday next in both churches of this Towne for the reliefe of one Thomas Fisher who was borne at Dripole and has been a Captive in Algier about six yeares and a halfe in miserable slavery as by his letter now shown to this bench appears.'

With the Restoration of the Monarchy in 1660 came a period of relative calm. The Parliamentary Survey had made the recommendation: 'Wee conceive it fit that it (Drypool) be separated from Swine and make a parish of itselfe, being five miles distant from Swine.' It is not known exactly when this recommendation was implemented but the connection with Swine ceased. John Bewe was instituted as vicar at Drypool on 31 July 1662. He was married at St. Peter's Church to Mrs. Ann Pease on 26 August 1663. There was much to do to repair the neglect suffered during the period of the Commonwealth, and at the Archdeacon's Court in 1662 there were three pesentments. The first was 'for not repairing the Chauncel windows.'

The Proprietors were the main offenders. The Churchwardens, Robert Harpham and John Maxey, were directed to: 'set up a font and to provide a sirplice and other things'. In their defence they said they 'had already provided a sirplice and other things but that they had not, as yet, created a font'. Finally, the vicar himself was presented 'for not repairing the vicarage house'. John Bewe died in 1676 and was succeeded at St. Mary's by Samuel Prowde, Rector of Patrington, who married Bewe's widow in 1681. He claimed Drypool in that year but there is no evidence that he was ever incumbent. He died in 1683.

In the 18th century there were two long incumbencies, during most of which time the vicar was non-resident: Edward Robinson (1711-1758) and William Huntington (1759-1783). The latter was presented by Robert Wilberforce, father of the Great Emancipator. Both were local men and it would seem that Robinson came to Drypool straight after ordination in 1711 as he was instituted in that year. Whilst he never relinquished Drypool, he also held at various times Marfleet, Roos, Hilston and Winestead. During the long period of his incumbency there were others who assisted in the parish. In 1743 Archbishop Herring undertook a visitation of his Diocese and Robinson's answers give a passing glimpse of parish life at the time. The number of families in the parish was 23, six of whom were Presbyterians and Independents. They must have gone into Hull for their meetings as there was 'no Licenced or other meeting house of any sort'. Nor was there any 'Charity School or Alms House'. No land had been 'left for the repair of our Church or any pious use'. There was, however, a 'charitable endowment of a farm £15. 15s. 0d. per annum', which was administered by the Vicar, Churchwardens and Overseers and 'no frauds and abuses' that he knew of: 'Services were held once per month, as by law required and I do not find that it were held oftener.' Religious life was by no means dead, however. The Sacrament was administered four times per year, there being about 45 communicants, a good number for 23 families. Robinson, who resided at Hilston, there being 'no parsonage house at Drypool', died in 1758 and was succeeded by William Huntington, who had been at Ferriby and Kirk Ella since 1735.

A Terrier of 1786 describes the meagre furnishings of the church. There was 'a Surplice, a Pulpit Cushion, a Pewter Flagon, a Silver Cup, a Silver Plate, one bell', none of which have survived. The Screen had disappeared after Archdeacon Dering's visit in 1720 and the chief object of interest would have been the three-decker pulpit furnished with its red cushion. Since the church was so small, this would probably have been placed at one side of the nave.

The register continues to record baptisms, marriages and funerals in the parish. The Stamp Act of 1783, which was universally disliked, granted a duty of 3d. on every entry in the Church Register, which remained in force until 1794. Both events are recorded: 'Tax begun Oct. 2nd. 1783' and 'Duty taken off Oct. 1st. 1794'. There is the record, in 1790, of the burial of a centenarian 'Elizabeth Gibson, Widow, aged 101, Pauper', and a sad record of three triplets, Abraham, Isaac and Jacob, who with their mother 'were all buried in the same coffin'.

Drypool had become the Garrison Church, so it is hardly surprising that there are many entries relating to the soldiery. The following is connected with the activities of the Press Gangs, which tried to capture a number of sailors who had just returned from the Greenland fishing grounds. In the course of the attempt a fierce fight ensued, during which two of the gang received injuries from which they died and which are recorded as follows: 'John Burnick, mariner, of His Majesty's Ship 'Nonsuch' killed by a whale lance by a man belonging to the 'Blenheim' a Greenland ship.' Six days later his companion was buried, on 9 August 1798. In 1801, Mr. T. Thorpe, Churchwarden for Southcoates, had drawn attention to the 'ruinous state of the old bell – the wheel and frames being so bad that it had not been rung for several years'. He promised to give a Treble Bell 'if the parish would consent to

having a peel of three bells'. The Vestry agreed and the work, which cost £174. 2s. 4d., was finished the '6th. day of February, 1802 and made the parish echo with merry peels and Triple Bobs the remaining part of the winter'.

Richard Moxon was appointed Curate in 1819. His appointment marked a watershed in the affairs of the church. The population of Drypool had steadily increased during the early part of the nineteenth century. In 1801 it stood at 671, and by 1821 it had trebled itself at 2,207. Such was Moxon's success as a preacher that he filled the old church to overflowing and it became a necessity to rebuild. The old church was closed in 1822 and work on its demolition commenced on Monday, 15 April. The last sermon preached in the old building was by Moxon, on the text, I Peter, 7: 'But the end of all things is at hand.' During the rebuilding services were maintained at the Charterhouse Chapel, where they were held for 60 Sundays.

A petition had been addressed to the Archbishop making the case for the new church. It stated that it was intended to increase the accommodation from 200 to 1,014, of which 724 sittings were to be free, the rest 'to be let to such Parishioners, or others as may choose to take them at a certain rent for the benefit of the Incumbent'. The issuing of 'Briefs', something like appeals for a weekly 'good cause', was used to raise the money to pay for the new church, estimated at £1,900. The Brief was read from the pulpit, and after the service the Churchwardens stood near to the door and exhorted the departing worshippers 'please to remember the Brief'. On their own the parishioners could not hope to raise the total sum in this way, so copies of the Brief were circulated to well disposed Christians. 10,800 copies of the Drypool Brief were issued and 9,386 were returned, yielding £423. 8s. 9d. The expenses and collector's salary accounted for £234. 12s. 6d. the net profit being £188. 16s. 3d., less than half the sum collected. The Church Building Society granted £500 and a subscription list was opened, which included the name of William Wilberforce. In all, £2,170 was contributed to cover the cost of rebuilding'. The Drypool Brief was one of the last to be issued, as the system was open to abuse.

The new church, designed by William Hutchinson, architect and builder, of George Yard, Hull, replaced the old one in 1823. White's Directory for 1823 describes it as follows: 'It is now rebuilding, the windows and the arches of the old structure are carefully preserved, so as to perpetuate the style of the old church.' It consisted of a nave of four bays, with tall pointed windows, filled with tracery and divided by transomes where the galleries came. The chancel was a semi-hexagonal apse. The tower of four stories was at the west end. It had a plain parapet, with vanes and pinnacles at the angles.

Rising as it did from a forest of masts, it had a certain period charm, although the building as such was undistinguished. The whole was covered in 'a product recently perfected by Messrs. Earles, Roman cement.' The interior was described as, 'having a 'neat' appearance'. It was surrounded on three sides by galleries, the fronts of which were painted white, and on the west face were the Royal Arms. Originally, there was a three-decker pulpit in front of the communion table. The pulpit stood in the apse, which, grouped with the reading desk in the middle aisle, gave a view into the galleries, which were supported on slender, clustered columns. The font, beneath the western gallery, was vase-shaped and probably the one placed in the old church after the Restoration. The church was ready in just over a year and opened for worship on Friday evening, 20 June 1823 when the preacher was the vicar, the Reverend W. E. Coldwell.

The furniture from the old church appears to have been transferred to the new one, as three months after the opening the churchwardens were empowered to exchange 'the present Communion Table, it being too small'. Four years later, 'the Lord's Prayer, the Belief and the Commandments' were set up and permission was given 'to beautify the Altar'. It was decided to install an organ in 1834, a committee was formed, and a subscription list opened, to which 95 people contributed. John Ward of York built the organ at a cost of £160. A part of the churchyard was taken by the Dock Company for the construction of Victoria Dock and in 1848 it was agreed to purchase land on Hedon Road for a cemetery. The churchyard was closed in 1855. A sacristy was built at the cemetery in 1852 and in 1877 it was licensed for services under the title of St. Nathaniel, a name changed in 1885 to St. Bartholomew at the wish of the Archbishop of York. It

was demolished in 1929 when the cemetery was closed.

A clock was placed in the church tower in 1846 above the Royal Coat of Arms and three years later James Harrison, its maker, was appointed to attend it 'for the sum of three pounds'. The chancel, was rebuilt in 1867 by D. Watson-Aston. There were galleries on three sides, that on the west displaying the Royal Arms.

In 1865, when there were two Sunday services and celebrations twice a month, the vicar attributed the disparity between the increased population and the modest size of the congregation to the Weslyans and to the influx of artisans who had brought with them 'confined habits of heathenish indifference to religious duties'. There was a distinct break from the past in 1878. The Church of St. Peter became a chapel-of-ease to the newly built Church of St. Andrew in Abbey Street Holderness Road, which then became the parish church of Drypool. The deed transferring the endowments, registers, rights and emoluments is dated 12 December 1878 and so, after 900 years, St. Peter's was bereft of its ancient status. This transfer, in part, reflected the shift in population to Holderness Road as it was developing during the late nineteenth century. The Church of St. Peter was to regain its own parish again in November 1879.

Brown's Guide to Hull (1891) describes the church as follows: 'It is a plain structure, consisting of a long nave, with an apse at the east end and a tower with a clock and bells, at the west end. The tower is in three stages and finishes with a plain parapet and a small pinnacle and vanes. The east window is stained. The interior is neat and comfortable and has galleries on three sides, the organ being in the west gallery. There are 1,000 sittings, one half of which are free. The oldest of the parish registers is very old. A date as early as 1574 may be deciphered but the book is much older . . . During the construction of [Victoria Dock], many bodies were carefully removed to other portions of the churchyard, or to other places, at the request of the friends of the dead.'

The Church of St. Peter was damaged beyond economic repair during the Second World War. Fires caused by incendiary bombs gutted the interior in 1941, leaving only the roofless shell standing. Although it survived the war, it was decided not to rebuild. Under pastoral reorganisation in 1951 the union of the two parishes of St. Peter and St. Andrew was formalised. The tower of St. Peter's was the last part of the church to be demolished, in 1954. The church and churchyard was taken over by Hull Corporation. The site of the

The bomb-damaged 19th-century church (1941).

former church is now a quiet, open garden, overlooked by a statue of St. Peter, the fisherman, who sits pensively, looking across the garden.

The statue of St. Peter is a modern sculpture, which is based on a likeness of Frank Redpath, and was created by Kevin Storch. It was placed in the garden in 1989, on the fiftieth anniversary of World War Two.

On a plinth under the statue is inscribed this poem by Frank Redpath:

> 'Peter, once quicksand man,
> then called A rock;
> three times denied
> The name who gave my name
> The moving ghost filled all
> My shifting, made me firm'.

Sadly, many of the gravestones have now been removed and only a few survivors remain propped up against the western wall, serving as a reminder of the more cosmopolitan life of Drypool and Hull. Those that can still be deciphered, even in part, tell tales of heroism and service, as witness below:

> This stone is erected at the desire and expense of
> his comrades:
> to distinguish the remains and to commemorate
> the virtues and esteem for
> Gunner John Craib
> of the 1st. Battalion Royal Artillery
> who was killed by the falling of a piece of timber
> while exerting himself
> extinguishing an alarming fire in Hull on the
> . . . July . . . Age . . . Years

Another inscription reads:

> In memory of Charles Houghey . . . Master
> Sergeant
> who died on the 27th. September 1849, aged 60
> years
> who served in the Peninsula War
> and fought in the Battle of Salamanca
> and the taking of Badajos

and also:

> In memory of Mrs. Margaret Wright
> Wife of John Wright
> Master Gunner in the Hull Garrison
> who departed this life on the 13th. day of October
> Aged 56 years

and finally:

> To the memory of Richard Edge and John Burgess
> of the Corps. of Royal Artillery, Drypool

The other remaining grave markers cannot be deciphered as over 100 years' weather has taken its toll of the soft sandstone, which has gradually crumbled away, leaving us only able to guess, from the decoration of the headstone, what other tales might have unfolded.

Sources:

Blashill, *East Hull*.
Blashill, *Sutton*.
Christine Gould, *Sculcoates, Ancient and Modern* (Hull, 1991).
Hull City Council, *Beverley Gate, Birthplace of the English Civil War* (Hull, 1990).
Ingram, *Drypool*.
John Markham, *The Centenary Book of Hull* (Beverley, 1997).
Edmund Wrigglesworth, *Brown's Illustrated Guide to Hull* (Hull, 1891).

Chapter Three
A Notable Fortress

In the few years between 1299, when Edward I granted his Royal Charter on all goods brought into the town, and 1321, when the burgesses felt it necessary to petition the king for the improvement of defences for the town, Hull had developed into a port of much greater commercial importance. Until 1321 the means of defence for the town consisted of a large bank and ditch around three sides, which served to mark the extent of the town's privileges and jurisdiction. The bank had been created from the earth thrown up from digging out the ditch and was topped with a wooden palisade. Investigations have revealed that the ditch was probably U-shaped, around 40-feet (12m) wide and 20-feet (6m) deep at its lowest point.

The poor defences, coupled with the town's location, the advantage of which had encouraged maritime trade between Hull and Europe in times of peace and created its prosperity, produced serious weaknesses in times of war. It was, therefore, important for the town, which then occupied an area of around 80 acres, to be adequately defended. In accepting the petition of the burgesses Edward I issued a charter in 1321 authorising 'his beloved burgesses and community of Hull, for the more security of the town, to make sure the same with ditches, and walls of stone and lyme, they to have them and their successor burgesses of the same town forever'. In order to defray the expenses of this edict, a toll was laid for five years.

Work on replacing the earth bank and wooden fence with a brick wall began in 1339, starting along the stretch adjoining the Humber. However, as improvements to the defences were sought, further aid became necessary and therefore grants, or 'murages' (from the Latin word '*murus*' for 'wall') were made for levying further tolls, the last being made in 1406. The

reason given in the grant of the new tolls was as follows: 'The burgesses have begun to enclose the town with walls and a ditch and have expended considerable sums of money in the undertaking, which, if perfected, will add greatly to the security of the whole country and of merchants and others coming to Hull with goods.'

As noted, brick walls were first mentioned in the Bench Book in 1339 as being built along the harbour foreshore and it seems likely that the grants given over the next seventy years were for the rebuilding in brick of the entire circuit and its defences. This was one of the major civil engineering projects of medieval Britain and, given that the length of the building season was strictly determined by the climate (it is equally dangerous for newly laid mortar to be seared by the sun as it is for it to be assailed by frost), it is no surprise that it took the best part of a century to finish.

The walls, when completed, protected the town to the north, west and south but there was no defensive system to the east, the River Hull being considered adequate. The excavation at Beverley Gate has revealed the character of the town walls, which are probably representative of the whole construction.

At that time there was no means of crossing the river except by the North Ferry, which factor, together with the chain drawn across the entrance to the river, was deemed to form a sufficient barrier against attack. *(Fig.3, left)* No other means of defence appears to have been considered necessary until 1377, when Sir Richard de Sutton sold his piece of land on the Drypool side of the river to the mayor of Hull on which to build a tower for the safety and defence of Hull. By the time Henry VIII came to the throne in 1509 Hull was regarded as not only one of the principal ports of the kingdom but also as the best

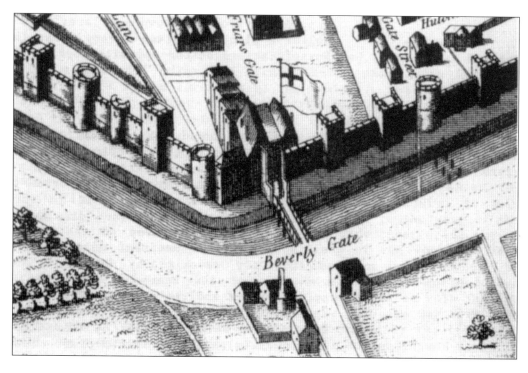

Beverley Gate, 1640.
(Wenceslas Hollar).

Beverley Gate, 1791. (Hargrave).

place strategically to meet any attack from the opposite shores of the North Sea.

The principal feature of Henry's reign was the Reformation and the resulting crises. The Act of Supremacy (1534) made the king the head of the Church of England and this created the means for his suppression of the monasteries, first the smaller ones in 1536, and then the larger in 1539. The rising in Lincolnshire and Yorkshire, known as 'The Pilgrimage of Grace', the nearest approach to a civil war in Henry's reign, was caused by discontent with the religious reforms effected by him and a fear of those to come. There were a reported 40,000 rebels under the leadership of Robert Aske and there were to be important implications for Hull as a result of this ill-fated rising, which locally began on 8 October 1536 with a gathering of rebels at Market Weighton Common. The rebels expressed fears that the King would land artillery at Hull to suppress the revolt and as a consequence, on 13 October, the town became directly implicated in the rebellion when Captain William Stapleton marched a detachment to Hull, then the most formidable fortress in the north of England, held for the King by Sir Ralph Ellerker and Sir John Conyers. The rebels began an ineffective blockade of the town. Men of the hamlets on the banks of the Hull proposed setting fire to the ships in the Haven by floating barrels of burning pitch on the ebb tide, but Stapleton refused to allow them to take this action.

Eventually, on 20 October, a face-saving agreement was reached whereby the rebels were allowed to enter the town without armed struggle. Stapleton immediately garrisoned the town and appointed John Hallam as Governor. Robert Aske met the King, who made various vague promises of pardon for those who had taken part in the rebellion and the revolt fizzled out as the 'pilgrims' dispersed. Sir Robert Constable, one of the leaders, was sent for by the King and, on arrival in London, was committed to the Tower, until 28 June 1537. He was then returned to Hull, and was ordered to be hanged and displayed in chains from Beverley Gate on the next market day, Friday, 6 July 1537, 'as a discouragement to others'.

Henry VIII paid an unexpected three-day visit to Hull, on 10 September 1541, accompanied by his fifth queen, Catherine Howard, and a full retinue of courtiers. He was met by the mayor and sheriff at the 'boarded bridge near Newland', and on arriving in Hull was given the use of the Suffolk Palace (also known as the Manor House) for his stay and received by the Corporation with great enthusiasm and the utmost courtesy, no doubt the fate of Constable, whose skeletal remains still hung from Beverley Gate, being uppermost in the minds of the aldermen. He was so pleased with his reception and the gift of £100 that he presented the town with his sword, which remains in the possession of the City to this day. After his visit the royal party departed for York. He returned to Hull three weeks later, arriving on 30 September, for a five-day visit. Following an inspection of the town's defences, he decided that Hull needed to be made more secure against attack. The King decided that Suffolk Palace was to become a citadel, the town moat was to be scoured, Scots and vagabonds were to be turned out of the city, the ramparts repaired, the gates to be provided with portcullises, and guns of iron, rather than brass, were to be set up. Furthermore, all sluices were to be modified so that the Humber could not be let in to flood the surrounding countryside, and the fresh water dyke was to be diverted to supply the new citadel. He appointed John Rogers as Surveyor of Works for the new defences, and he recommended (in February 1542) that a fourth wall was needed on the Drypool side of the River Hull, with castle and blockhouses and with a moat on the east side of the walls, as the town was vulnerable to an attack from Holderness. The proposed developments on the east bank at Drypool made it imperative to have a better communication link than the old North Ferry so, for the first time, there was to be a bridge provided over the River Hull and a new gate, at the north end of the town. Whilst the new bridge was useful to the townsfolk of Hull and Drypool, it did nothing to improve relations with Beverley, now facing an obstacle to trade, caused by the Hull authorities refusing to lift the trap of the bridge, to allow vessels to pass without lowering their masts. In desperation Beverley petitioned the Privy Council, Hull putting forward in its defence the quite reasonable argument that, whilst Beverley had rights on the 'Old Hull', they did not have similar rights on the existing cut on the east side of the town (i.e. the channel of the River Hull cut by order of Sayer de Sutton in the early 13th century.) The dispute went to arbitration; it was finally resolved by Hull being ordered to 'disclose' the bridge, Beverley, in return, paying £30 in two instalments for the facility.

The King appointed Michael Stanhope as his Lieutenant to command the Garrison. He wrote to the Bench informing members of his decisions and his determination that Hull was to have a 'notable new fortress'. Having taken these momentous decisions in the affairs of Hull, the King and his retinue left Hull through the narrow, low alleyway, arched with bricks (later known as 'Little Lane'), leading from Humber Street, which was then at the water's edge and which was the traditional entry and exit point to and from the town. Stanhope was expected to live in what was now, the King's Manor

House; the rooms were so large, however, that 'he could not furnish even one of them'. He bought a house at the south end of Lowgate instead, setting up the King's guns in front of the doors, pointed at the entrance to the Haven. He employed local men to build the new fortress on the Drypool side of the River Hull.

The foundation stone was laid on 22 February 1542, and by May 1543 Stanhope had spent almost the whole of the £18,000 which the King had provided for the fortress but by the end of the year the work was completed. The scale of the work can be judged by the number of men employed, almost 550 in total, working from 6 am to 6 pm. The bulk were labourers engaged in taking down stone and brick from Meaux and also in such tasks as digging the foundations, digging chalk and unloading ketches. 60 or more were bricklayers, 20 or more were carpenters, 60 were wood-fellers, making scaffolding, 30 were involved in lime-making and 10 were plumbers. Most of the stone was brought in from the ruins of the Abbey at Meaux but some also came from St. Mary's in Lowgate, Hull. Bricks were used in huge quantities and were made at a nearby tilery, utilizing the alluvial clay of the Humber. Brick-making was always associated with the making of tiles (hence the name tilery), and the flat, or plain, roof tiles were known as 'thack tiles' to distinguish them from bricks, which were known as 'wall tiles'. Early brick-yards were very simple and needed little in the way of equipment as the brick-makers needed only a spade and a mould, with a shed for shelter. The clay was dug out in autumn and left for the winter weather to break it down, being turned over at regular intervals. In late spring it was 'trodden' and dug over to obtain the right plasticity and then moulded into bricks, which were left to dry for about a month. They were then made into a clamp with turves and burnt over refuse or coal, or put into simple kilns with an open front.

Henry VIII reputedly spent £23,155. 17s. 5d. on the construction of the castle, the blockhouses, and walls, the North Bridge and in making the canal from Newland, which provided fresh water to the citadel: a relatively small sum of money, when set aside the amount which he had obtained as plunder from the dissolution of religious institutions.

The completed fortifications were very impressive and comprised a principal fort, which became known as Hull Castle, consisting of a rectangular inner keep, measuring 66 feet (20 m) by 50 feet, (15.24 m) with walls 8 feet thick (2.4 m) and which was three storeys high, reached by two separate staircases. It was lit by means of long, narrow windows. A courtyard surrounded the keep, which was 28-feet (8.5 m) wide on two sides and 20-feet wide (6.1 m) on the remaining two. The whole was enclosed by outer walls, 174-feet square (53 m) and 19-feet thick (5.79 m), with an inside corridor on the south side 5-feet wide (1.52 m). It was described as 'an indifferent square building, surrounded by a high wall, the side next to the River Hull and it's opposite, being rounded like the Blockhouses'. The main armament of heavy guns was mounted in, and on top of, the curved bastions. It was built almost opposite Church Lane Staithe and lay about midway between two smaller, yet still massive, two-storey blockhouses. The northern blockhouse lay

Hull Castle. (Hollar, 1640).

very slightly to the south of the new bridge and was so placed as to protect it. The southern one lay on the Humber bank, protecting the Haven. Each of the blockhouses was shaped like a trefoil.

The blockhouses were identical and smaller than the Castle, being two storeys high, *(Fig.7 left,)* shows the south blockhouse) measuring 34 feet (10.3 m) by 27 feet (8.2 m) with 15-feet-thick walls (4.5 m) and an inner courtyard 37-feet square (11.2 m). They were shaped like clubs on a playing card and each lobe formed a bastion. Each bastion held guns at ground floor, the first floor and rooftop level. At floor level the bastion was divided into four compartments, comprising three gun rooms and a chamber for access. The entry passage at the rear of each blockhouse gave access to a rectangular inner court, where spiral stairs rose to the upper level and the roof. A crenellated curtain wall with ramparts 15-feet thick (4.5 m) and 2,500 feet (830 m) in length, connected the blockhouses with the central fort. A moat ran along the length of the wall on the Holderness side, whilst the area of open space between the walls and the riverbank was let out as grazing grounds.

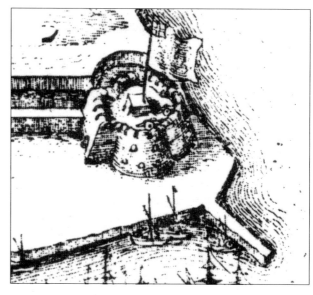

The South Blockhouse. (Hollar, 1640).

The central fort, despite its size, presented a squat appearance and was designed so that ships firing on it from the Humber could do little damage. The castle and blockhouses were intended as gun platforms to return fire and were tremendous fortifications for their time. With the guns at the south end commanding the entrance to the Haven and the guns of the north blockhouse overlooking the only bridge over the River Hull and a complete circuit of walls, interrupted only by the Haven, the town was considered safe from any attack. However, the £1,000 per year received from the Crown proved quite insufficient to maintain such a massive works, so hastily put together and based on marshy ground. Whilst Henry VIII regarded this sum as a nuisance, the officials of his successor, Edward VI, regarded it as a great burden and in 1552, 'in order to rid himself of this charge', granted custody of the castle and the blockhouses to the mayor and burgesses of Hull.

The guns, however, remained the property of the Crown. Some were removed in 1558 for the defence of Bridlington and Flamborough. Thomas Foxley, the Common Officer for the town in 1563, was responsible for the guns, powder, shot and timber and was allowed to graze his horse in the garrison. In the real sense of the word there was no garrison: the fortifications were without soldiers to defend them, except in a dire emergency.

The guns in the south blockhouse were fired from time to time, mainly to hail ships but also on ceremonial occasions, one such occasion being when Mr. Henry Hildyard of Winestead arrived in Hull with his bride and her father, Lord Deyncourt and a salute of three guns was fired from the south blockhouse, an honour bestowed upon them because of the great favour the Hildyard family had shown to Hull.

When, in 1576, the Corporation complained to the Crown, prompted by the fear of invasion from Catholic Europe, about the state of disrepair that the fortifications were falling into, the Privy Council ordered them to be inspected. Sir Henry Gate and Thomas Boynton, with others, were directed to survey the works. They enlisted the aid of Mr. Pelham, from Brocklesby, who had experience of serving in several campaigns in Ireland and in Europe and who was a former Marshall of Berwick. Two months later the Corporation attempted to persuade the Crown to give more financial assistance for their maintenance and the town's representatives were ordered not to give them up (in exchange) for a garrison of soldiers. The report of the Privy Council inspectors was made in April 1577. They found that many repairs were needed, the ditch at the Drypool side was almost completely silted up and the timbers in the central Castle and the blockhouses were too weak to carry guns of any size. The Crown immediately decided to provide 300 trees from the West Riding, each capable of giving good timber 16-inches square (40.64 cm) and 24-feet long (7.3 m), for the repair of the fort, the blockhouses and to create a new jetty to protect the south blockhouse from erosion by the Humber. For the town's share, the Bench ordered 120 spades, 120 shovels and 60 pickaxes for clearing the ditch on the Drypool side and a good store of saltpetre for making gunpowder. The most probable reason for the decay was the hastiness of the construction on marshy ground, rather than any neglect by the Corporation.

The population of Hull continued to grow and the town began to look and smell a little less rural. However, in 1578 the Master Mariners reported to the Bench that a 'ness' was growing on the east, or Drypool side of the Haven, caused by the tipping of refuse. Their opinion was 'that if there were no stables sited near to the river, the risk would be less'. The problem had arisen because much of the rubbish and effluent of the town was dumped straight into the Haven, with the result that in 1579 fines were imposed on anyone who dwelt on the water-side and kept a pig for more than six days within the walls or who had a haystack inside the town.

The mud wall between the North Gate and the Haven, where the ground was not solid enough to bear the weight of a brick wall, was built, or re-built, in 1585, to make the town more defensible against the threat of Spanish invasion. Hull increased its precautions against the threat of a Spanish attack from the Netherlands in 1588. Ten men were placed on watch every night, four with hand-guns in the blockhouse at the south end, which had been newly provided with a chimney, and the remaining men split between the north blockhouse and the Castle. An hourglass was placed in each watch house, so that at each hour a bell would be rung for the changing of the guard. The gates closing off the staithe ends were secured with iron bolts and every night the chain was drawn across the Haven, being removed at dawn.

The Archbishop, as President of the Council of the North, reported in 1596 on the defences of Hull 'which it seems were better than had been thought'. The blockhouses were kept in good repair and watch and ward kept in them when necessary. They were furnished with powder and weapons, though many were old and rusty. Recently, the brass guns had been removed for royal service and iron pieces substituted. However, the Bench wanted more brass guns than before, as the danger of invasion was thought to be greater. They had recently spent £400 on a gun platform at the south blockhouse, considered to be the most vulnerable point of the defences. Every householder was ready with his weapons and 40 or 50 men were on watch every night. Shortly after, the Bench ordered 'that some honest men be placed in the Castle to dwell there', and that the chain across the Haven should be made more effective by being floated on fir logs until it could be replaced with a boom.

The old keeper of the south blockhouse died in 1598 and the Corporation then employed Edward Brown, a mariner, to take his place, at a salary of £13. 6s. 8d. per year. To make sure no enemy vessel entered the Haven, it was his duty 'to search all vessels of strangers', before they were allowed to enter. If they did not anchor in the roadstead when he signalled to them with a flag, he was instructed to fire a great piece, overshooting her and then to keep shooting nearer until she dropped anchor. The offending vessel was to pay for all the shot used. The Castle and blockhouses seem to have quickly fallen into a state of some ruin again, as in 1599 Elizabeth I began a suit against the mayor and burgesses 'on account of they're not being properly upheld according to the tenor of the Grant of King Edward V.' Commissioners of Survey were appointed to examine the works and in the light of their report the suit was not pursued.

After the Reformation, Hull was populated largely by Puritans, people who wanted a simpler, purer form of worship than that offered by the Church of England, which still retained bishops, robes and elaborate services and were not so different from Catholic services. Puritans feared Catholics, not only on religious grounds but also because they were seen as a threat to national sovereignty. Thus the blockhouses were used on several occasions for the imprisonment of Catholics, many arrested as prisoners of conscience, such as Thomas Cletharay, the brother-in-law of the future St. Margaret Clitheroe of York who was held from 1601 to 1603, in which year he died. He was buried in Drypool churchyard 'without the minister and without the order of buriall according to lawe'. The conditions of confinement in the blockhouses were terrible, prisoners were kept in unlit and unheated chambers, with damp floors and a lack of proper toilet facilities.

At that time, apart from what was left of the Charterhouse and the hamlet of Drypool, there were very few buildings outside the walls, and visitors to Hull were said to be impressed by the suddenness of the transition from 'a great flat' to the mainly brick-built, and by now quite thickly populated, town.

The plague arrived in Hull in the early 1600s. In August 1603 the Bench ordered 'that as long as the infection lasted there, no London goods, except soap, oil, or iron were to be brought into town until they had been aired in the Groves for at least twenty-four hours'. Despite many and sensible precautions like these, the plague took its toll, the worst visitation taking place between July and December of 1637, when the registers recorded a total of 763 deaths, of which 626 were from the plague. The Bench now met at the Castle instead of the Guild Hall and the markets were withdrawn to Drypool. Gradually the number of deaths from the plague decreased and the normal commerce of the town resumed.

In 1626, as a response to another threat of Spanish invasion from the Netherlands, the defences of Hull were ordered to be improved and trained bands to be armed and exercised. William Biggins was hired as a full-time gunner, presumably for the proper maintenance of the guns, since by that time there were guns in the Castle and blockhouses that weighed between 23 and 26 hundredweights (1168.5 kg and 1320.8 kg). The Master of Ordnance supplied 300 muskets and suits of body armour and £300 worth of gunpowder from the Tower Armoury in London. In 1628 the Bench asked the king for 20 guns, gun carriages, powder and shot, and in 1630 the Crown promised 12 more. The Bench, for their part, agreed to pay for their shipment in the first convenient vessel and also to buy a ton of shot and a dozen barrels of powder. Guns had greatly increased in size and weight since the Castle and blockhouses were built and it was necessary for the Corporation to repair some of the floors with deal planks. Some of the floors were constructed of plaster laid on timber and the partitions underneath with plaster and hair. All were renewed

when necessary and all floors were screwed up with jacks and under-propped with baulks of timber. In the town there were also arms at the artillery house at the Exchange and these were now removed to the Castle and the blockhouses. These weapons consisted of muskets and calivers (hand-guns). Four of the large guns were directed to the new fort, which was built in 1627 around the south blockhouse and which comprised a rectangular fortification, sited immediately to the east. Fifteen guns were sited on the roof of the south blockhouse and nine below. At the Castle there were nine guns on the roof and twenty below, with some in store, and at the north blockhouse ten on the roof and fourteen below. A substantial new fort was also built in 1627, at the South End on the opposite bank of the river to replace the earlier earthworks. This was armed with 11 guns of various calibres and together with the south blockhouse provided an effective cross-fire over the mouth of the River Hull.

All the quays on the River Hull were on the west bank, and to make better use of the limited space vessels were most often berthed 'stern on', discharging their cargo over the stern of the ship. However, with the tide running, a ship might easily swing and this method of berthing also served to narrow the navigable channel. These factors led to numerous disputes and collisions in the Haven, which had to be resolved by Trinity House, to whom all matters of shipping movement were delegated.

There was a mooring dolphin in the Humber at the mouth of the River Hull maintained by Trinity House and used to assist ships warping in, or out of the Haven. Francis Tennant, a ship's master, rammed it in 1632 with the *Indeavour* of Newcastle and was fined 20 shillings for his carelessness.

In 1636, Charles I tried to impose bishops on the Scottish Church, a measure the Presbyterians of Scotland resisted. The increasing prospect of a war with Scotland drew the attention of the King to the state of the fortifications at Hull and in 1637 he revived the suit against the Corporation first instituted by Elizabeth I. The Corporation once again resisted the suit.

A report to the Bench in January 1638 from Captain William Legge, Master of the King's Armouries, that the Scots were approaching the Borders put the inhabitants of Hull on their guard and they prepared to sustain a siege. In accordance with his royal instructions, the Bench decreed that the gates were to be repaired, large half-moon earthworks were to be constructed outside each of the main gates, the walls were to be made level, drawbridges were to be made and the ditches (moat) of the town were to be cleared. A system of sluices could be opened to allow tidal water to flow through the town ditch, thus cleansing it, and the banks were cleared of reeds and grass by men with scythes and the undergrowth removed. Once satisfied with progress on the repair of the defences, the king dropped his lawsuit against the town. However, the Corporation attempted to share the cost of these works between themselves and the County. The County refused to pay the rate, declaring that they considered the fortifications were for the benefit of the Town and that on that basis they should not have to bear the cost of any repairs.

When the King visited Hull in 1639 to inspect the

arsenal and the town's defences, he was warmly received and entertained. For his benefit, 100 musketeers were paraded under the command of the Mayor, William Popple, and his officers and the town guns fired. During a dinner in his honour, the matter of the fortifications was raised again, this time by the Recorder, who pointed out that the town had been spending more than twice the amount of the annual allowance made by the Crown in maintaining the defences. In September 1640 Sir Thomas Glenham was appointed by the King as the Town Governor with a strong military detachment to assist him. He returned the keys of the town to the Mayor in June 1641.

Charles I believed that he ruled by divine right and did not accept rule by the consent and invitation of Parliament. In the first four years of his reign he called three Parliaments and disagreed with all of them. War and the money to pay for it lay at the root of their disputes, as he expected Parliament to raise the money for his ventures but resented its interference in his running of the country. By 1642 matters had reached breaking point, tempers frayed as Parliament set out their grievances in the Grand Remonstrance and members of the Commons insisted on reforms, with the result that the king attempted to have five Members of Parliament impeached. Conflict became inevitable, and in order to gain control over the huge arsenal in Hull (the largest and best equipped in the country outside London) Charles attempted to impose his nominee as Governor there.

On 15 January 1642, the Earl of Newcastle, appointed to govern in the King's name, and Captain William Legge arrived to secure Hull for the King. Parliament meanwhile nominated Sir John Hotham as Governor of the Town, with the instructions 'that he should not deliver up the town, or the magazine there without the King's authority signified unto him by the Lords and Common House of Parliament' since they too wished to exercise control over the arsenal.

The mayor and aldermen of Hull had the right to select their own governor and at first refused to entertain either nominee but in the end bowed to parliamentary pressure and accepted Sir John Hotham, the Member of Parliament for Beverley and Colonel of the trained bands of the East Riding of Yorkshire. His son, Captain John Hotham, Member of Parliament for Scarborough, arrived in the town soon after, with five companies of the East Yorkshire trained bands, who were billeted on the town. Hull took the side of Parliament mainly because of the poor treatment it felt had received at the hands of the Crown in having to pay higher taxes, particularly the hated 'Ship Money' which the town refused to collect, forced loans, the billeting of troops and the receipt of insufficient help for the maintenance of the Castle and the blockhouses. The King arrived at Doncaster in March 1642 on his way to York, where he was to establish his Court and where he was to prepare his troops for an attack on the Scots. Whilst in Doncaster the King enquired of Sir Thomas Glenham, his former extra-ordinary Governor of Hull, about the taking of the town by cutting off the fresh water supply if he were to find himself shut out. Sir Thomas replied thus: 'In an emergency the inhabitants can do without their supply from the springs. At low tide the water in the Haven is good enough to drink and, furthermore, every man can dig water at his door, they cannot bury a corpse there but the grave first drowns him 'ere it buries him.' In April 1642, with the King and his Court at York, Parliament had to make sure of Hull. The garrison had been reinforced with 1,000 men, the troops were regularly paid and the Master of the Ordnance was directed to send men to service their equipment. Charles mustered his soldiers in the fields outside Hull, fields later occupied by St. John Street, Savile Street and Dock Street. Knowing that there were many Royalist sympathisers in the town, he determined on a course of action whereby he could enter by means of a ruse.

On April 22 1642, he sent his son, Prince James, Duke of York, his nephew, Prince Rupert, Lord Newport and Lord Willoughby, together with an entourage, on a goodwill visit to Hull, where they were entertained and stayed overnight. The following day the King sent word by Sir Lewis Dives, that he intended to join the party. Sir Lewis also presented a letter, which stated that the King wished to dine with the Governor at noon that day. Sir John convened an immediate meeting with the aldermen at the official residence of the town's anti-Royalist M.P. Peregrine Pelham.

Sir John Hotham.

They took the fateful decision to order the gates to be shut at once and ordered soldiers to make sure that the townsfolk remained indoors until sunset. The trained bands lined the walls of Hull with loaded muskets, whilst others guarded the gates with swords drawn, under orders to kill anyone approaching them. Thus it was that at 11.00 am on a rainy St. George's Day, Saturday, 23 April, the King found himself and his retinue on the outside of Beverley Gate, shut out of the town by the Mayor, who was in tears and the Governor, Sir John Hotham, who stood atop the tower above Beverley Gate. Despite the King's alternate shouted demands and threats and pleas for bargains, Hotham maintained his refusal to open the gate, whilst at the same time begging the King's pardon. The Mayor, in tears, was fully in favour of opening them.

At 4.00 pm, after an exhausting and frustrating day the King gave Hotham one hour to change his mind. At 5.00 pm Hotham reiterated his refusal for the King and his party to enter the town. The Royal Heralds announced that this amounted to, 'the most solemn affront which could be put on a king, by sealing the gates against him'. Sir John was accused of high treason by the King and was declared a traitor. Parliament, in reply, called this statement 'a high breach of privilege' and voted the thanks of the House to Sir John.

Thus were sown the seeds of the English Civil War . . .

Having failed to take the town by stealth, several plots were made to seize it for the King. Holderness was largely Royalist and petitioned the King to complain of raids made by the Hull garrison and of the flooding caused by the cutting of the Humber embankments. It was this flooding which prevented the capture of Hull, for so long as Parliament could maintain control of the sea. If the Royalists tried any of the normal stratagems of siege warfare, almost every trench they dug in order to get their artillery in position to destroy the walls was full of water before it could be used. If they tried to advance without the precautions of digging trenches, by making an advance through the floodwaters, they at once came under fire from the walls, without any protection. In response to Hotham's request for reinforcements, Parliament sent 500 men,

commanded by Sir John Meldrum, a Scot and a tough veteran, who was later killed besieging Scarborough. Another 1,500 men arrived a few days later, whilst two warships, *Rainbow* and *Unicorn*, additional to the *Mayflower*, took up their duties patrolling the Humber.

It was determined that Hull would be taken by military onslaught. A Royalist force of 1,000 horse and 3,000 foot soldiers, commanded by the Earl of Lindsey, set out from York on 3 July 1642, planning to take command of the Humber approaches by placing gun batteries at Paull, Hessle and Barton. That same day, Charles moved his Court from York to Beverley, still hoping that Hull might surrender without a siege.

Hotham tried, without success, to destroy the Royalist gun sites but on 10 July Sir Thomas Meetham destroyed some of the windmills outside the walls and a long-range bombardment began. There was heavy gunfire from the nights of the 10th to the 13th. On the 12th, under the cover of the bombardment, a fierce sortie of 500 men, under the command of Sir John Meldrum, destroyed one of the Royalist batteries. A Royalist ship sailed up the Humber and came under fire from the south blockhouse and fort at the South End and was driven off. A week later, the Earl of Warwick, the Parliamentary Commander in Chief of the Navy, was able to report the destruction of all the Royalist forts. When the Royalist headquarters at Anlaby were captured on 27 July, the Earl of Lindsey abandoned the siege. Three weeks later, on 22 August, Charles raised his standard at Nottingham, thus signalling the official opening of the English Civil War.

The people of Hull regarded the Hothams, Sir John and his son, Captain John, with great favour and they were both popular. However, the loyalty of Sir John to Parliament wavered, as extremist Parliamentarians began making demands that savoured of republicanism. He was a man of quick enthusiasm but with an easily changeable mind. Though he had resisted the King, he did not wish to do away with the monarchy altogether. He also felt slighted by Parliament when Ferdinando, Lord Fairfax, was appointed Parliamentary Commander in the North. When Queen Henrietta Maria landed at Bridlington in February 1643 with three ships laden with munitions from Holland, Sir John sent his son to find out what favour he and his family might receive from the King for delivering up Hull to the Royalists. Captain Hotham was admitted to the Queen's presence and had a private interview with the Royalist Earl of Newcastle, during which negotiations were concluded to their mutual satisfaction. Arrested later by the Parliamentarians for desertion, Captain John escaped from Nottingham in June 1643, where he had been detained on the orders of Oliver Cromwell, which was another factor that led to Sir John's disaffection with the Parliamentary cause. However, Parliamentarians in the town became aware

Charles I.

that Sir John was about to change sides, and to prevent this possibility, a group of them, including the Mayor, Robert Raikes, met on 28 June to concert their methods for seizing the town. The following morning, 100 men under the command of Captain Moyer, from the *Hercules*, one of the naval ships stationed in the Humber, took the Castle and blockhouses, without bloodshed. A party of soldiers and townsmen took the walls and gates, together with the magazine (which at that time was probably the largest in England), and arrested Captain John Hotham, on 29 June.

On hearing this news, Sir John himself escaped hurriedly on horseback through the North Gate, with the intention of reaching his fortified house at Scorborough near Leconfield but he was unable to cross the River Hull at Stoneferry and rode on to Beverley, where Sir Matthew Boynton's Parliamentary troops were on parade in the Market Place under the command of Colonel Boynton, his son. Hotham ordered the Colonel (who was his nephew) and his men to follow him to his family home but, forewarned, Boynton arrested him 'as a traitor to the Commonwealth' and returned him to Hull.

Very soon afterwards the *Hercules* sailed for London with both prisoners on board. On 1 January 1645 Captain John was decapitated as a traitor at Tower Hill, Sir John suffered a like penalty the next day, hoping to the last minute for a reprieve. At this time Wressle Castle and Hull were the only places in Yorkshire not held by Royalist forces, forming two pockets of resistance, which limited their freedom of action in the North. In the meantime, following their defeat at Adwalton Moor in June 1643, Ferdinando, Lord Fairfax, and his son, Sir Thomas Fairfax, hastily retreated to Hull, pursued all the way by Royalist forces. Lord Fairfax was appointed by Parliament as Governor, following a petition from the townspeople to Parliament, urging them to appoint him to the position. In the interim they had appointed a committee headed by the mayor, to govern the town and had appealed against the proposed appointment of Sir Matthew Boynton as Governor.

Hull was besieged again on 2 September 1643, but by now there was practically no chance of betrayal from within, and the defensive earthworks outside the walls had been greatly strengthened. A battery of guns was sited just to the south-east of the south blockhouse to provide enfilading fire for the eastern walls and to cover the entrance to the River Hull. The Royalist forces consisted of 16,000 experienced and well equipped men under the command of the Earl of Newcastle, supported by two powerful guns, named 'Gog' and 'Magog'. The troops were based at Beverley, Cottingham and Newland and posed a very real threat to the town. To meet the threat from the north, Lord Fairfax demolished the Charterhouse and had an earthen rampart built on the site. This was countered by the Royalists, who built 'Fort Royal' to its north, but it was sited so far from the town that its firing with stone shot and even with red hot cannon balls, did little damage. 'Fort Royal', under constant fire from the Charterhouse battery, was soon captured. However, an attack by Fairfax on a base established by the Earl of Newcastle at Anlaby was defeated on 9 September. To prevent a counter attack being launched from that direction, Lord Fairfax had the banks of the Humber cut and the sluices opened on 13 September, which flooded an area 'for two miles about the town' and thus ensured that no further approaches to the walls could be made by the Royalists from the west, without their suffering heavy losses. A careless gunner entered the magazine in the north blockhouse on 16 September and, with a lighted match in hand (a slow burning fuse applied to the touch hole of a gun), went to fetch cartridges and set light to some hand grenades, causing an explosion that killed himself and four others, partially destroying the blockhouse. Twelve days later a Royalist magazine at Hull Bank, Cottingham exploded and the Navy ships, *Lion* and *Employment,* destroyed the fort at Paull.

Colonel Oliver Cromwell crossed the Humber with his Lincolnshire Commander, Lord Willoughby of Parham, and expressed themselves so confident in the defensibility of Hull that they withdrew Sir Thomas Fairfax with his twenty troops of horses to Lincolnshire. Meanwhile, there was continuous fighting outside the walls of Hull. The garrison destroyed the gun battery sites at Sculcoates and Derringham Bank but the Royalist forces overran the defences at Hessle Gate, near the west jetty, and also at the Charterhouse, but they came under such intense fire from the walls that they were forced to withdraw.

The heavy rains in late September and the flooding brought about by the October tides made their misery worse. Sir Philip Warwick, who visited the Earl of Newcastle around this time, commented, 'Those without [the walls] seemed likelier to rot, than those inside to starve.' On 11 October the Hull garrison, under the command of Sir Thomas Meldrum, sallied forth at 9 am and in a close-run fight captured all the Royalist positions between Derringham Bank and the Humber. This defeat and news of the Parliamentary victory at Winceby in Lincolnshire caused the Earl of Newcastle to lift the siege on Hull the very same day. This marked the end of the active involvement of the town in the English Civil War. For many years after this event, 11 October was celebrated as a day of thanksgiving in Hull and became the official start date for Hull Fair.

The town had suffered for its stance during the war, both physically and economically. The inhabitants had to endure overcrowding; the enforced billeting of troops without payment, great deprivation and many had died. The merchants of the town lost heavily due to the disruption of trade. The defences had to be kept under repair at a cost to the town of £40 per month and the cost of repairing the north blockhouse, estimated at £2,000, which was damaged in the explosion of the magazine and which also caused damage to the North Bridge had to be paid for.

Sources:
Hugh Calvert, *A History of Hull* (1978).
Edward Gillett and Kenneth A. MacMahon, *A History of Hull* (Hull, 1989).
Audrey Howes and Martin Foreman, *Town and Gun* (Hull, 1999).
Markham, *Hull*.
Beverley Gate.

Chapter Four
A Great Fortification: The Citadel

It seems most unlikely that Charles II, who after his restoration 'reigned nearly absolute', would have forgotten the humiliation of his father at the Beverley Gate, especially as after the Restoration, the townspeople continued to celebrate the lifting of the second Royalist siege. However, he was an astute man and trod carefully in the early years of his reign, not giving way to the excesses that sealed his father's fate and also not upsetting those who had served the Commonwealth, and who thus might not be well disposed to him. He gradually increased his control through taking steps to ensure that corporations in the land were composed of the 'right' people and that towns returned Members of Parliament acceptable to him. The Corporation Act of 1661 laid down that no one was to be a member of a corporation who did not deny the lawfulness of taking arms against the King, and town charters, usually confirmed by each new monarch as a matter of routine, were scrutinised and any anti-Royalist element expelled. Accordingly the charter granted to Hull in 1661 removed two aldermen.

In 1665 England was at war with the Dutch once more (the Second Dutch War 1665-7) and the King considered Hull, as an important east-coast port, to be at risk. Accordingly, the fortifications at Hull were inspected by his brother James, Duke of York, who was received with great favour and expressions of loyalty by the Bench. The Hull Garrison was strengthened with an increase in soldiers during the Third Dutch War (1672-3), most of them billeted on the town, and many other troops passed through on detachment for service abroad. In the years since 1640, however, the structure of the fortifications had been badly neglected and during the first 20 years of the reign of Charles II only essential repairs had been carried out on the defences at Hull, as the money Parliament granted to him for fighting the Dutch Wars was insufficient.

A report of 1673 describes the town's defences, 'It is seated on the mouth of the River Hull where it falleth into the Humber, and is a place of exceeding great strength, being able to bid defiance both to a navy, and a land army, and that by reason of its strong blockhouses, castles, walls, forts, trenches and the inhabitants and soldiers within it being at present a considerable Garrison of His Majesty's, under the command of the Right Honourable John, Lord Belasyse, Lord Lieutenant of this Riding.'

By the 1680s Charles had reached the height of his power and to maintain his authority he made improvements to the defences of his Kingdom a priority, in part by upgrading the coastal fortifications. In order to establish the true state of the fortifications at Hull, the Office of the Board of Ordnance, based at the Tower of London, carried out an enquiry in 1680, primarily to ascertain where the building materials previously allocated for the repair of the defences had disappeared. It became clear that some major items had been misappropriated and the former Governor, Lord Belasyse, and his Deputy, Gilby were identified as the chief culprits and forced to make financial restitution.

It seems the King was not satisfied as the following year he commanded: 'That a strong citadel and blockhouse be built, with a broad ditch cast about all sides but that which faceth the Humber.' The cost of the works was set at £100,000. Major Martin Beckman, the Second Engineer to the Surveyor General, Sir Bernard de Gomme, was appointed to design and supervise the building work for 'the strong citadel and blockhouse', ordered by the King. Beckman surveyed the site in June 1681, making accurate drawings of what existed and in his official report to the King referred to the defences of Hull: 'The fortifications in this place is come most to a total ruin. The moats about the town most grown up; the ramparts are without parapets . . . The stone wall about the town all decayed, cracked and ready to fall down . . . It has not one inch of parapet nor a gun about the walls that can do service, The blockhouses are very much out of repair; the north blockhouse is altogether dismantled, all the lead and wood converted into private uses. The moats about the blockhouses is altogether grown up even with the ground about it, and not a drop of water in it. The King has not one foot of ground beyond this old moat and as it is altogether necessary that the blockhouses be repaired I will say nothing of any new works.'

His plan for the Hull Citadel was drawn up at a period when the form of artillery fortifications was undergoing change. The plan took in 29 acres of additional ground, adjoining the earlier defences, which were purchased by the Crown. Beckman's broad intention was to make an equilateral, triangular fort which incorporated great bastions at each of the three corners (to enable flanking fire to be brought to bear on any attackers who approached the walls) and would feature a wide moat, although his design excluded the old north blockhouse and the line of wall between it and the central castle. One important consideration which dictated the form of the Citadel was the cost. Triangular forts had found favour over a long period because they were relatively cheap to build and also limited the extent of the perimeter to be defended, although a disadvantage was that they only offered limited internal space and were thus considered uneconomic.

In the case of the Hull Citadel, the triangular form was also largely dictated by the two situations, which it was designed to dominate: the confluence of the River Hull and the Humber and, significantly, the town of Hull. Contemporary treatises on fortification advocated placing a citadel next to a potentially hostile town, positioned so as to overlook the principal streets to enable fire to be directed on any rebellious mob. Thus it was certainly no coincidence that his plan for the curtain facing the town formed a long continuous battery with the provision for the mounting of 27 guns, pointed directly at the staithes along the River Hull and the Old Town. The North Bridge and the eastern approaches to the town were also within range of the guns and therefore also exercised control over entry to the town from that direction. Although his design for the Citadel related primarily to the use of artillery as a means of defence, the arrangement of the bastions was partly determined by the limited range of musketry (around 150 yards) in close defence, where an assault had penetrated any outer defences.

Beckman's plans for the new Citadel were approved by the King, and in August 1681 a warrant was issued to the Commissioners who were appointed to both oversee the repairs and the construction of the new fortification at Hull. During 1681 parts of the curtain wall to the north of the south blockhouse and to the north and south of the Castle were cut to allow the passage of workmen, and the curtain wall connecting the north blockhouse with the Castle was removed. The ground condition at the site of the works was extremely difficult, comprising wet, marshy ground which had to support the great weight of the walls, and so considerable ingenuity had to be employed in the design. There were some military advantages in building the fortress on marshy ground by the riverside, in that it could only be attacked at a few points and so required a smaller garrison (which suited the triangular form) and the strength of a marsh fortress increased with every yard of swampy ground that the besiegers had to cross, although in general this advantage could be nullified by summer drought or winter frost. In case of drought at Hull the surrounding land could be flooded by the means of sluices, controlled from the Citadel, allowing the waters of the Humber to flow inland. These are shown on the Woolner plan of 1715.

Work on refurbishing the south blockhouse and digging the moat began before the onset of winter caused a halt in December 1681. Outdoor work commenced in April 1682 and significant progress was reported. A strike by labourers in July 1683 curtailed work for that year and it was June 1684 before new works began, with the building of the casemented entrance to the Main Gate and a start at the south side of the Citadel, at its eastern end. These works formed

a substantial programme of building and comprised a brick sea-wall faced with limestone ashlar at the lowest level, resting on a piled and planked foundation. Given the waterside location of the site, it is thought that the walls most probably rested on footings constructed of a lattice of timber formed in coffers and piled 'with immense piles'. There was little likelihood that the supports would rot as long as the timberwork was embedded in waterlogged ground. Oak and fir actually became harder with long soaking.

The main work of 1685 comprised the completion of the eastern bastions and curtain, the most substantial unsupported earthworks to be raised at the Citadel. A parapet about the Drypool side was ordered to be built in October 1685 to cap these extensive works. The following year saw work commence on the water bastion, the first of the three elements that made up the sea-wall along the south side of the Citadel. The construction of the sea-wall, the south curtain and west water bastion was to take three years of difficult, dangerous work, close to the Humber bank. The most important contractors employed during the building of the Citadel were brothers, Sir Thomas and Mr. John Fitch, builders from London, who had been at Portsmouth, building for Sir Bernard de Gomme, the Principal Engineer of England. They contracted local workers in the main to carry out the great project, including bricklayers, plasterers, masons, carpenters and plumbers. The Commissioners also employed some men directly, mostly to carry out specialist tasks. Other minor tasks were carried out by local jobbing craftsmen, such as painters, coopers, wheelwrights, locksmiths, glaziers and carpenters. In order to maintain the pace of work, labourers were recruited from far and wide and proclamations made in several market towns.

Beckman, who in the early years of construction played an active role and spent much of his time on site, had to write on numerous occasions, through his Clerk of Works, to H.M. Ordnance Department to explain the circumstances of the various delays, which include the non-arrival of building materials and a lack of craftsmen. Local suppliers were used for the majority of the materials used in the construction, including bricks, timber, lead, tools and equipment. 'Country people', i.e. agricultural workers, were employed *en-masse* for the unskilled work, which included the digging of the moat and ditches, wheeling earth in wheel-barrows, spreading and compacting it to form ramparts, or to level the site. They often travelled many miles to their place of work and had to pay board and lodging whilst in Hull.

In constructing the Citadel, Beckman re-worked the Castle and

Charles II.

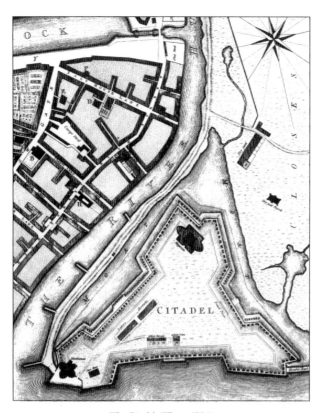

The Citadel. (Thew, 1784).

south blockhouse to form two angles of a massive, roughly triangular fort, including a magazine, three barracks and the Governor's house. The great bastions at the three corners enabled flanking fire to be brought to bear on any attackers. Due to the lack of locally available stone, the major building material used in the construction of the Citadel was brick, made by William Robinson at his brickpits sited to the east of the Citadel site, where clay was readily available, as the ditch was being widened to form the eastern outworks. In 1687, the recently knighted Sir Martin Beckman entered into an agreement with Robinson to supply two million bricks at 11 shillings per thousand for standard bricks and 20 shillings per thousand for best-burned bricks. Most fortification engineers preferred to use bricks, rather than hard stone, since the latter shattered under the impact of a cannon shot, far more easily than did a soft stone or brickwork, in which the ball would drill a small neat hole. In any case, bricks were cheaper to produce, to lay, repair and extend than was stone. Where durable and dense material was required, for example at the scarp and the angles of bastions, Beckman resorted to the use of stone (in this case good quality limestone known as ashlar, thought to have been brought from the Doncaster area). The bricks of the outer walls were laid in Flemish bond at angles of 65 degrees or more and the perpendicular inner wall and buttresses were laid in English bond. The core between the two walls was filled with rubble. An earth rampart, 18.3 m thick at the base, backed the substantial walls to the south and west and utilised the earth removed from the moat.

On the east side the earth ramparts, which were the sole line of defence, were 36.5m thick. A quickset hedge was planted before these ramparts as an additional obstacle for attackers to overcome. To form the ramparts the earthen mass was heaped up in layers between nine inches and one foot deep, each of which was firmly rammed in place before the next was deposited on top. The labourers who performed this task were paid more than those who dug or wheeled the clay into position.

In its profile the rampart usually formed a number of slopes and platforms, which prevented rainwater from standing on top. At the rear a grass slope rose from ground level for between 3m to 4.5m to the wide terreplein, the main artillery fighting platform. The terreplein was terminated along its outer bank by a small bank called the banquette, which served as an infantry firing step. The banquette and terreplein were screened from enemy view and fire by a stout earthen parapet, which sloped gently down to the top of the revetment, or top of the wall.

Gun positions were set at intervals along the terreplein at the top of the rampart, most probably on platforms, firing through embrasures. By 1688 the lower part of the southern side of the Citadel was complete and barracks for 200 soldiers were contracted for, to be built within the Citadel, together with smaller lodging for officers. It is thought that the Town Governor's house was also built within the Citadel around this period.

In November 1689 Beckman left instructions for work on the Citadel to be finished and in 1690 the brick wall completing the upper part of the south sea-wall was constructed. Beckman's original scheme incorporated the provision of a magazine in each bastion. These were casemented magazines (chambers served by a passage and set within the ramparts), which were sited close to the gun positions to allow powder and shot to carried over a short distance to the guns, to permit almost continuous fire. The casements and other underground chambers were usually dug out at the same time as the moat and foundations. The masonry was left to dry over several months and then covered with waterproof cement and several levels of gravel and earth. It was found that five to eight feet of earth, lying on top of an arch three to four feet thick,

Detail of the Citadel wall. (Gent, 1735).

was enough to keep out any mortar bomb. Entrance to the Citadel was gained on the north-east side, via a wooden bridge leading from a designed 'ravelin', or defensive earthwork outside of the Citadel, to the Great Entrance, which was built of brick.

When the Duke of York succeeded his brother, as James II, in February 1685 the work at the Citadel continued, with Martin Beckman supervising the construction. Hull was deemed fit to be 'Fortified as a Citadel' by June 1685, when the Duke of Monmouth, who laid claim to the throne, landed at Lyme Regis with his rebel army. However, despite that assurance, work at the Citadel carried on and was part-funded in 1688 by 'the very rich lading of gold, silver and other treasures salvaged by the *James and Mary* from a treasure ship wrecked on the coast of Hispaniola' (Haiti). Shortly after, in 1689, it was recorded that 'were it finished it would undoubtedly be a very strong fortification', confirming that the Citadel was never completed to Beckman's original design, with the planned outworks on the eastern side never finished due to a curtailment of funds.

The soldiers of the Hull Garrison were divided into a local force of Independent or Unregimented Companies under the direct command of the Governor and Deputy-Governor. The posts of Governor and Deputy were, therefore, most important to the Crown, who always ensured that reliable officers filled the post, to maintain military, as well as political control. Whilst Charles II was on the throne, he so distrusted the town that he refused to put arms in the hands of the inhabitants and there was no militia in Hull as there was in the East Riding. The Independent Companies supplied two of the six companies forming the Garrison. Each company was made up of 50 men, including a captain, lieutenant, ensign, two sergeants, a corporal, and a gentleman-at-arms – the company store keeper, who supplied the companies with ammunition. Additional regular forces brought up the Garrison to its full strength of six companies.

The army increased in size under James II and its impact increased with along with the numbers of soldiers in the town. The King ordered that no soldier be allowed free quarter, and quarters in private houses should only be granted by consent of the householder. The lodging of soldiers had supplemented the income of the poorer people of Hull since 1643 but numbers increased, as many troops were employed as labourers on the Citadel and by 1688 there were between 1,000 and 1,500 billeted on the town, which had a civilian population of around 7,000. Thus during the years when the Garrison increased and the Citadel was being built, overcrowding became a feature of the town as the 'country people' also needed to find private rooms and so soldiers were increasingly billeted on public houses, which by law were required to accommodate them.

Since there was a limit to the numbers of soldiers that could be placed in the public houses of Hull, the military proposed a solution: to redefine other commercial premises as public houses, an idea which did not find favour with the Bench. The *ad hoc* method of allocating housing to soldiers meant that on many occasions the troops left arrears owing to publicans and

householders alike, causing 'a general outcry concerning the great numbers of soldiers in the town'. Relationships between some of the townsfolk and the soldiers of the garrison appear to have been strained for other reasons, particular affront being taken by members of the Bench, as the following tale illustrates. During the services held at Holy Trinity, the officers of the garrison and their wives were prone to taking the seats reserved for the Corporation 'with careless abandon and with complete disregard for the aldermen'. The most junior of officers copied this practice and eventually the practice had to be stopped by order, enforced by the sexton. The soldiers also used the outside western walls of Holy Trinity as a toilet, which also caused friction both with the clergy and the Bench alike.

James II proved an unpopular monarch and particularly so in Hull, as he had been in Hull, as the Duke of York, when his father attempted to gain entry to the town by a ruse, and also as his pro-Catholic policies unfolded, revealed by his removal of the penal laws against his fellow Catholics. After his defeat of the Duke of Monmouth at Sedgemoor he committed terrible atrocities and this, together with his attacks on the constitution, alienated both Parliament and his subjects. In 1687 he appointed Marmaduke Langdale, a Catholic from Holme on Spalding Moor, Governor of Hull and in the same year outrages committed by the troops sent by the King to man the Citadel caused further offence to the townspeople. The King issued a writ in May 1688 demanding the surrender of the recently granted charter, replacing it in September with one that removed all but two of the aldermen and gave the King complete control over the appointment of borough officials. A number of similar acts like this at other places proved to be his undoing. In August 1688 it was rumoured that a large Dutch fleet was about to invade England, under Prince Wilhelm of Orange, the husband of Princess Mary, the heiress to the throne (she was a daughter of James II by his first wife, Anne Hyde). Wilhelm (William) and Mary were both solid Protestants. The invasion plan had been hatched through the invitation of certain nobility and high clergy in England. On receipt of news of the invasion, the King ordered all garrison towns to be strengthened, which included Hull, to prevent a landing in the north. When William of Orange sailed from Holland on 19 October 1688 with a fleet of 655 ships it was anticipated that he would land on the north-east coast, so Langdale prepared for a siege, the chain was hung across the mouth of the River Hull and the sluices were prepared to flood the surrounding countryside. However, Prince William was driven back to port by a violent storm and set out once more on 1 November with an army of 11,000 foot and 4,000 horse, landing on 5 November at Torbay, Devon.

Langdale put in an immediate request for repairs and maintenance to the structure of the Citadel and was granted £5,000 for the work, which was to be overseen by Beckman and carried out by John Fitch. The 'country people' were engaged to clear out the moat and to work with the 'town people' to improve the defences, including the erection of a large half bastion before the North Gate and the Town Bridge.

William III, by Peter Scheemakers, 1734.

Troops of the Duke of Newcastle, the Lord Lieutenant of Yorkshire, were sent to reinforce the garrison, and on 3 December 1688 Langdale secretly prepared to arrest his Protestant deputy, Captain Lionel Copley, and his Protestant officers.

They, however, anticipated his plans and approached the mayor and aldermen, declaring that they were ready to seize Langdale – probably already safe in the knowledge that the nobles and gentry assembled in York had declared their support for William. Late at night, with the help of the magistrates, the townspeople were armed to defend the Protestant faith. Langdale and his Catholic officers were taken without bloodshed. The following morning Captain Copley secured the rest of the Catholics in the garrison. The coup produced a temporary breakdown in law and order in Hull in which some damage was done to Catholics and Royalists. The Bench issued a warning to the lawbreakers and had the Bellman proclaim it in the Town, while Captain Copley summoned his troops by the beating of a drum to warn them about their conduct. He was to remain in his post as Deputy Governor until July 1690, when he was rewarded by being made Governor of Maryland and Virginia.

These events in the 'Glorious Revolution' secured the north for William of Orange and for more than a century, 4 December was celebrated in Hull as 'Town taking day'. The gilded equestrian statue of King William III in the Market Place, by the distinguished sculptor, Peter Scheemakers, erected in 1734, celebrates the association of Hull with the events of the Glorious Revolution. James II found that he had stirred up so much hatred in his subjects, and could not even rely on his army for support, that in December 1688 he went into exile to France and from there resumed his struggle for his throne in Ireland. Once William of Orange and Mary were established as joint monarchs in 1689, the threat from the Dutch disappeared and this further confirms that the work on the Citadel may not have been completed, since, with a Dutch king, the threat from the Dutch had been removed, and consequently the incentive to complete the Citadel.

Sir John Hotham, the grandson of the former and better-known Sir John Hotham, had landed with Prince William at Torbay and was rewarded by being made Governor of the Town, thus following in his grandfather's footsteps. In February 1689, soon after taking office, he made it one of his first priorities to ensure that those in the town who had billeted troops without payment received much of the money owed to them.

Under the Bill of Rights, which set out the liberties won in the Glorious Revolution maintenance of a standing army in peacetime was forbidden and the army became an unpopular institution. Colonel Beverage, the garrison commander, was ordered to march his troops to Scotland in July 1689, and the Citadel fortifications were left in the care of the Town. Men in Hull had to do guard duty with an inadequate stock of 47 muskets, 46 iron caps and 42 swords, previously lodged in the Exchange.

In December 1690, Martin Beckman redefined the role of the Citadel under William and Mary: Now how necessary 'tis that this fortress be finished to keep therein a sufficient magazine for the northern parts of this kingdom, all men of experience cannot but be sensible thereof; and I am well assured that no monarch, prince or state has been nor can be safe in their government without tenable fortifications for their magazines, and security for the respective seaports. The old saying in England, for its objection has been and yet is, that England is an island and the royal fleet is the ramparts; this argument was in reasonable force when the French was inconsiderable at sea and the Dutch alliance beaten out of it; and suppose we may continue in that happiness, yet troubles at home would be uneasy to the government notwithstanding a naval force; but if the seaports were well fortified, all attempts from abroad and at home, would be of no value.' His advice was not followed and the status of the Citadel as a magazine was reduced considerably and proper maintenance of the structure was all but ignored.

Soon after his accession, William III had become embroiled in war, allied with his countrymen, the Dutch, against the French, fighting on the Continent and also against the exiled James II in Ireland. Although the status of Hull as a magazine diminished after 1688, the town faced a renewed influx of soldiers, when the garrison was strengthened against a possible invasion by the French, and additionally many British and foreign troops passed through in transit. Danish troops formed the first contingent of 12,000 foreign troops in transit, arriving in December 1689, in three transports that were packed with horses and men, anchored out in the Hull Roads. Due to sea-sickness, they were unable to march to Chester immediately, as had been planned, and were quartered on the town. They included a contingent of dragoons who were quartered on the inns and taverns of the town, since they could provide stabling facilities. Though they were warned that no excesses would be tolerated, the death of two who did not behave is recorded on a plaque sited on the south side of St. Mary's Church, Beverley.

In 1691 three English regiments sailed from Hull to Moordijck to fight in Holland. The Duke of Newcastle's Regiment continued to provide the regular garrison troops as they had since 1688. Eight companies of the Duke of Bolton's Regiment were quartered in Hull in February 1693 and maintained a presence in Hull until 1696, although its second battalion was at war on the Continent. In reality, the army was supposed to be a voluntary occupation. However, it seems that some men were impressed, as Colonel Bolton's Regiment is said to have forced away 60 or 70 householders from Hull when it sailed for Flanders.

A description of the Citadel in 1695, by Edmond Gibson, noted the accommodation and situation of the defences: 'on the east side of the river, is built a strong Citadel begun in the year 1681, and including the Castle and the South Blockhouse. It has convenient apartments for lodging a good many soldiers, with distinct houses for the officers; has also an engine for making salt water fresh, and is well furnished with ordnance. But yet the strength of the town does not consist so much in its walls or fortifications, as in its situation; for all the country being a perfect level, by cutting the sea banks they can let in the flood and lay it for five miles round under water, which the Governor of the place, at the late revolution had designed to do, if the then Prince of Orange had landed there, as was once thought, for he had caused several flood-gates to be made, and pitched upon certain places about the town and on the banks of the Humber for cutting.'

Invasion by the French seemed possible in 1696 and the garrison was strengthened once more, with troops of Sir John Jacob's Regiment, which was divided between Hull, Berwick and Carlisle, so that the core of the force remained as the Independent Garrison Companies, whilst the contingents of regulars moved from garrison to garrison on a fixed rotation. Great resentment at the quartering of soldiers in large numbers on the town continued to be expressed until the end of hostilities in Europe in 1697, which signalled a phased reduction of the English army and thus allowed the remainder to be spread more evenly between the English garrison towns. In 1700, under pressure from Parliament, expenditure on the army was slashed and the policy of no standing army was upheld. This meant the end of the Independent Companies at Hull and the garrison posts were reduced to Governor, Deputy-Governor, Surgeon, Master Gunner, and six Gunners, at an annual charge of £674. 2s. 6d.

The Mutiny Act of 1703 regulated billeting and stated that 'henceforward, quartering in no private house whatsoever' was to be allowed and at the beginning of the 18th century Hull entered a relatively quiet period and both the Citadel and the Old Town walls, together with their drawbridges, became neglected. Household and building rubbish was piled to a considerable depth against the front of the town walls and the entry gates, a practice which increased during the early years of the eighteenth century. Because planned maintenance was not provided for, the Citadel soon fell into a poor state of repair, stones had fallen out of the sea-wall, the bridge at the main entrance was declared dangerous, 80 of the gun ports had become blocked with earth, the powder room was damp through neglect and the eroded revetments along the River Hull required constant maintenance. Repairs were carried out only as necessary, one of the major expenses being incurred by repairs to the sluice. Despite this, the garrison continued to hold French prisoners of war captured in naval engagements and left there by Navy ships putting in at Hull, and in 1709 expenses were paid for their incarceration. Although the townspeople often complained about the poor state of repair of the medieval walls surrounding the Old Town, they themselves were reluctant to spend any money on their maintenance.

The garrison was placed on a war footing once again during the Jacobite Rising of 1715, when the Scottish supporters of James II raised a rebellion. However, since there was no immediate threat, the emergency evoked only minor repairs to the structure of the Citadel. The Lieutenant-Governor even found it necessary to 'use one of the drawbridges which was taken down from the town' for use at the Citadel.

An interesting comment on the state of disrepair of the Citadel was made by Daniel Defoe, who recorded in 1720: 'King Charles II, on occasion of the frequent Dutch Wars in that reign had once resolved to appoint a station for a squadron of men of war here, with a yard and dock, for building men of war in the Humber; and on this occasion, resolved to make it strong, in proportion to the necessity of those affairs; upon which a large Citadel was marked out on the other side of the river; but it was never finished. The greatest imperfection as to the strength of Hull in case of war is, that lying open to the sea it is liable to bombardment, which can only be prevented by being masters at sea, and whilst we are so there's no need of fortification at all; and so there's an end to that subject.' He had summed up neatly the underlying reason for its neglected state, perhaps unwittingly, since he had viewed the design and setting of the Citadel in the light of contemporary opinion.

The defences of Hull were described in 1733 as follows: 'The Citadel is its best defence, having a double tier of guns, a wide ditch before it, and what is more terrible, a company of Invalids within. This was once accounted the strongest fort in England but now the walls are tumbling down, and the ditches a common lay-stall; why these or others especially northwards are suffered to run to ruin, is the alteration of our proper and natural strength since the Union, which doubtless is the fleet.' The 'East View of Kingston upon Hull',

The Castle converted for use as a magazine. (Gent, 1735).

dated 1735, commissioned by Thomas Gent, shows that the drawbridge to the main gate had been removed at that time and that embrasures had been reduced to hummocks.

Charles Edward Stuart, the grandson of James II, tried to reclaim the throne in July 1745, landing in the western Highlands. After taking Edinburgh, he marched south with his army of Highlanders, causing panic in the north of England. The Bench in Hull decided that the town would be defended and sent a loyal address to George II, which was favourably received. The Mayor and Deputy Governor informed the Duke of Newcastle, as Secretary of State for the Southern Department, (effectively the Prime Minister), of their decision on 24 September, asking for commissions for officers and reporting that the moats could not be filled until they had been cleansed. By early October, Hull's magistrates, merchants and gentlemen had subscribed £1,900 towards the cost of erecting breastworks and batteries and scouring the moats 'which had long been neglected'. It was said that 3,000 people were engaged in the task, including the gentry and merchants of the town, who were there to boost morale. The workers were summoned by the beat of drum every morning, some being paid as labourers, at 1s. a day, whilst others, as volunteers, distinguished themselves with a cockade in their hats. The engineer, Peter Henry Bruce, arrived on 8 October at the invitation of the Bench to lend technical support and he reported, on the following day: 'The moats had been deepened, the ramparts repaired, the embrasures restored and the magazines placed in order. In fact it seemed as though the work had been guided by a skilled engineer. He had nothing to do but to follow in the lines so ably begun, and with the help of all concerned Hull was soon declared to be in a fit state to resist all attack.'

The town's defences were also strengthened by a cargo of arms carried by the frigate, *Success,* which put into Hull en route to Georgia and delivered up its cargo of 20 nine-pound cannon and many smaller guns to the town. A body of gentlemen volunteers provided a force of regimental strength, comprising 12 companies of 60 men apiece, under the Captaincy of Robert Pease, a successful local merchant, and they were armed by 2 December. Regular soldiers were placed in charge of the companies to instruct them in drill, musket drill and to impart a level of discipline. There was a small complement of full-time gunners supported by four artillery companies composed of the Wardens and Brethren of Trinity House, who provided further crews for guns.

Hull also had regular troops billeted on the town once more in November, since they could not all be accommodated in the Citadel. This caused a certain amount of friction between the Mayor and the Deputy Governor, and the goodwill of the Bench was lost. In November 1745, the rebels had seized Carlisle and then marched south, down the western side of the country, reaching Derby. However, they were unable to rally English Jacobites to their cause and retreated intact to Scotland in December. The Board of Ordnance considered further improvements to the defences at the Citadel in December 1745, detailing the need for palisades to be set along the Humber shore, which were to be tipped with iron to prevent the approach of boats. Towards the land they were to be set in a ditch, as storm poles below the parapets, to prevent scaling with ladders; and across the entrance to the Citadel, which had now been moved adjacent to the saluting platform. The report advised planking the edges of the moat, to prevent the moat further washing away the berm, a narrow ledge between the ditch and the base of the parapet, in front of the ramparts. Other works were also detailed and all were reported as being completed in February 1746.

The Bench were by now unwilling to contract for any further expense in the defence of the town and the Governor and Lord Lieutenant were informed that they should see that any new works necessary were paid for. The Citadel continued to house prisoners during the emergency but their presence merely compounded the problems of quartering soldiers in the town. On 7 March a fleet of transport carrying soldiers to Scotland put into Hull, following reports that French warships had been spotted by Scarborough colliers. The soldiers were quartered on Hull, with a large number probably occupying the Citadel barracks until they could continue north. The Jacobite army was defeated and virtually annihilated at Culloden on 28 April 1746 and the emergency was over, allowing the disbandment of the volunteer companies in Hull.

The Bench commissioned a report on the state of the ditches which surrounded the town in 1746, which found that the inner moat (a relic of the medieval defences) was badly silted up, so that the town drains were obstructed, to the point where foul water (sewage) entering into the ditch remained there in a stagnant state for want of a proper outfall into the Humber. 'It has become extremely noisome, putrid and unwholesome to the adjoining inhabitants in particular, and also to the town in general,' noted the report. John Wesley came to Hull in 1752 and noted 'the miserable state of the fortifications, far more ruinous and decayed than those at Newcastle, even before the rebellion. It is well there is no enemy near.'

The Dock Act (1774) vested all the walls, ditches and defences west of the River Hull in the Hull Dock Company and in that year the town walls from Beverley Gate to North Gate were levelled in preparation for the building of the Dock. In 1764, Henry Etherington (who became Mayor in 1767) prepared notes for a speech concerning 'the great detriment to the Inhabitants of the town by the publicke Walls'. The walls in fact, fell within the jurisdiction of the military and were leased out by the officers of the garrison; people had built houses, shops and even pigsties against the walls. In an early plea against urban pollution, Etherington complained that the walls and buildings prevented fresh air from circulating and caused epidemics of infectious disease. He argued that the walls should be levelled and the moats filled in to improve the quality of the air, a task that would not be started for another ten years.

The development of the town docks had an unexpected impact on the Citadel, when the currents of water around the mouth of the River Hull were altered, following the reclamation of the ground on the Humber foreshore in front of the New Dock (Humber Dock). The silt deposit in the Humber was changed and the 'growths' of mud in front of the southern side of the Citadel increased rapidly, to the point where the massive fort became stranded as the shoreline moved out into the Humber. The stone-faced scarp which was to have been defended with obstacles against a sea-borne landing in 1745 could be approached dry-shod 50 years later.

The 18th century saw many changes in the town. The population stood at around 7,500 in 1701, and during the century there was a huge increase, which, together with many other social changes, affected Hull greatly. Increased trade and a growing population meant that most streets in the town were heavily congested and seven major Improvement Acts were obtained, the first in 1755. The Hull mob, which comprised most of the poor, could not have been kept down without the presence of a militia which never consisted of local men who might be sympathetic. The Earl of Euston's Suffolk Militia put down the anti-Catholic riots in 1780, and in 1795 a party of the Surrey Militia were used to disperse the food rioters who were protesting about the rise in the price of flour to a level at which the poor could not afford to buy it.

Their plight was desperate as they faced near famine conditions. More serious riots occurred in April 1796 through the same cause, the Nottingham Militia being called out to the Market Place to disperse the rioters. The food riots by people on the threshold of starvation continued spasmodically during the Napoleonic Wars. The garrison was also often turned out during this period to quell riots in the town caused through the activities of the press gangs, which wore no uniforms and, using great violence, impressed men for service with the Royal Navy. Conditions on board ship were so appalling and the sailors treated so abominably that few men would volunteer for a life at sea. Pay was miserable at 7d. a day for ordinary seamen and 8½d. a day for able seamen. The food, supplied by villainous contractors, was almost inedible. Discipline and punishment were severe, so most sailors were conscripted by the press gangs. In Hull pressed men were removed to *HMS Nonsuch,* the guard ship in the Humber, until there were sufficient in number to fulfil the quota. A quota of Hull men had to be found to serve the navy each year and, although the Bench offered a bounty to volunteers, they were always too few in number, and so in Hull this form of kidnapping, legal only because of long usage, went on year after year, ending finally in 1815. The actions of the press gangs were so likely to rouse the fury of the mob that this formed a further reason for keeping a large garrison in Hull.

The French Revolution in 1789 began the last wars in which the defences of Hull would be involved. In February 1793 the French Republic declared war on Britain and launched a successful invasion of the Low Countries. Hull was under threat once more, and in July 1793 Hull MP, Samuel Thornton, proposed to the Mayor that a frigate or some other armed vessels should protect the town and the Humber.

In 1795 the Bench asked for an independent naval force to be sent to the Humber. By February 1797 the 64-gun *HMS Standard,* and *HMS Lion* and *Director,* were stationed in the estuary. In 1798 the guard ships, *HMS Nonsuch* and *Redoubt,* were on station. They fired warning shots in an attempt to detain the homeward-bound whaler, *Blenheim,* another episode in the long-running fight between Hull sailors and the press gang.

Plans to encircle Hull with new earthwork defences were proposed by General Scott in March 1797, but did not include the strengthening of the Citadel, although they did incorporate the eastern earthworks. They were unanimously endorsed by the Bench, although they pointed out that, as they considered this proposal to be in the national interest, the Government should bear the cost. These plans came to nothing, since the Bench informed General Scott in April that they were unable to raise a sufficient sum to fortify the town.

Major-General Mulgrove proposed new plans for the defence of the region in 1803 which did not rely on fixed defensive positions, since he considered that the attackers would simply avoid them. His plans relied on mobile horse artillery sited at strategic positions and camps of infantry to harry the attackers once they had landed, together with selective flooding of the countryside, which would restrict the lines of advance for the attackers. He proposed siting fixed batteries at Paull to control shipping along the navigable channel of the Humber. His plan also did not call for the Citadel to be strengthened. He reported: 'the Citadel presents its feeble bastions, and useless batteries, which point across but do not enfilade the channel. Under its present circumstances the Citadel is totally useless as a means of defence, should an enemy in flat boats pass fire and land above Hull, the Citadel would become worse than useless; as neither defence nor retreat would remain to the Garrison. The western tenaille from the north to the South Blockhouse, has no guns, nor the means of mounting any; and the whole interior of the Citadel is commanded within musket shot from the houses on the opposite side of Hull river. The north bastion and eastern façade, which point towards the great road from Bilton to Hull town, are so completely masked by the town and church of Drypool, that they could not in any situation see an enemy advancing by that road. The money expended on an estimate to widen the ditch at Hull Citadel; and to prevent an escalade at a point where no escalade would be attempted by any military man of experience and discretion, would be much better applied to secure the advantages which nature has prepared at Paghill. (Paull).' His proposals relied on beacons to provide early warning of attack along the Holderness coastline.

Over the years the Citadel received a number of distinguished visitors. In 1795, Prince William of Gloucester, the nephew of the King, and General Commanding His Majesty's Forces in the Northern District, visited the town and reviewed the Surrey Militia, a troop of the Hanoverian Cavalry and the volunteers. He was the first royal visitor to Hull since 1665 and was received at the Citadel with a Royal Salute of guns and at the *Nonsuch* with another. In 1800, the Russian General Arbeneff visited to carry out an inspection of the huge military force which it was still thought necessary to keep in Hull – the Third West York Militia, the East Sussex Militia and the Sussex Fencible Cavalry. Admiral Trowbridge inspected the Citadel and the shore batteries at Spurn and Paull in 1804.

After Trafalgar (1805), British sea power alone could prevent a full-scale invasion and, despite the Citadel being considered to be an outmoded means of defence in strategic terms, it still had other useful functions it could perform, firstly, as a purely defensive work, secondly, as a major depot and arsenal, to supply the North Sea squadron of the Royal Navy, and, thirdly, as a soldiers' barracks. The provision and improvements needed for these functions prompted an expenditure of much effort and money, which was, in part, necessary to reverse the neglect of the previous century. By 1805 the Castle had been converted to serve as an armoury and the upper rooms in the bastion towers could hold 20,000 stands of infantry arms apiece, and the upper galleries 3,000 stands of cavalry arms. The ground floor rooms included a forge, two workshops and further vacant storerooms. In the same year five gunnery platforms were constructed and others were made between 1805 and 1807. Provision for three traversing guns was also made at the salient angles.

Between 1807 and 1809 the ramparts and parapets were repaired, the moat was drained and a brick-built counterscarp was built to line the outer face. In 1810 it was said that Satan was so much at home in Hull that it now always needed regulars as well as militia to prevent him taking over completely.

When General Vyse was ordered to send a troop of Scots Greys to Huddersfield to suppress the Luddites, they left at 11.00 pm and by 9.00 am the following morning a squadron of cavalry had arrived from Sheffield – their horses must have been almost dead from exhaustion – as it was not thought expedient to leave Hull without military. They were reinforced later the same day with a squadron of the Second Dragoon Guards, who left Huddersfield on a Wednesday, the

Scots Guards returning to Hull on the Thursday. The embrasures on the south front were repaired with stone between 1811 and 1813 and were said to offer a respectable crossfire with the guns of the South End across the River Hull. The storage facilities within the Citadel required improvement and by 1807 a new Great Powder Magazine stood immediately adjacent to the Castle, while Garrison Magazines were lodged in the casements at the former main gate. The new magazines were capable of holding 440 whole barrels, 7,480 half barrels and 1,530 quarter barrels of powder, while the casemented magazine could take 500 whole barrels and 920 half barrels. In 1806 the South Blockhouse was almost completely rebuilt and fitted out as a naval storehouse in which a constant supply of stores was maintained. The store of powder and arms was such that, when the 1807 expedition to Copenhagen was being fitted out, the Citadel could provide arms for 35,000 men and stores for six ships of the line and twelve frigates.

The increase of militia from 1793 forced the government to take an interest in the accommodation of troops. In 1795, the Surrey Militia had complained of the lack of proper quarters in Hull and the expense of providing lodgings. Barracks were urgently required. In 1797 the North Yorkshire Militia, with 757 men, lodged seven companies in the North Blockhouse, which was fitted out to provide makeshift lodgings. A further 2,000 soldiers were also billeted on the innkeepers of Hull. During the Napoleonic wars with France, the Citadel was used as accommodation for troops, between 12,000 and 15,000 guarded the coasts of the East Riding, of whom between 3,000 and 4,000 were stationed in Hull at various times and many were billeted in the town, which by now had grown to a population of 30,000. The War Office decided that a centrally directed programme of barrack building was required and a number of temporary barracks were established in Hull by 1807.

Besides the Citadel, military barracks were established at Lime Street (in buildings at the Greenland Yard rented from Thomas Walton), also near Sculcoates Church, at the end of the old North Ropery (which occupied the line of New George Street formed in 1866), and on the Humber Bank and at a couple of other places. There was a guardhouse at the east end of Waterworks Street. The soldiers' barracks at the Citadel had been built in 1688 to hold 200 men. However, in 1797 the Citadel was reported as having 'enclosed barracks for 400 men' and in 1811 the Citadel could offer accommodation for 'one field officer, three captains, eight subalterns, and 465 men, 292 in double bedsteads'. Shelters for guns, stables for 302 horses and a forage house for the mobile artillery took up much of the internal space and a gravel parade ground was laid out on the central area of the interior, which took up most of the remainder.

Victory at Waterloo (1815) was celebrated by fireworks at Hull, with a military band to play appropriate pieces throughout the display. Following the Napoleonic Wars, the gates of the Citadel stood open. However, it continued to be used by the military, being occupied in varying strengths by the depot battalions of a series of Regiments of Foot, many of the soldiers marrying local women over the ensuing years. The Citadel was also used as a centre for regular army regiments seeking to recruit members of the local militia; the 2nd/82nd Foot, (the Prince of Wales' Volunteer Regiment) and the Royal Artillery held recruiting drives there. For many years the Castle had formed the chief residence of the Governors of Hull, whose office, as well as that of Lieutenant-Governor, ceased about 1840. The office of Fort-Major continued up to the same time. The Town-Major died in 1844 and, as the need for quartering soldiers on the town had diminished, his post was not filled. The Garrison was called out on several occasions to quell riots and the Bench suggested that 'a military zone may be permanently stationed in Hull to be at all times ready to assist the civil power in suppressing riots' but from 1835 the establishment of a civilian police force lifted the duty of maintaining public order from the army.

The number of soldiers in the army contracted dramatically following the Napoleonic Wars and this was reflected at the Citadel, where more accommodation was available than soldiers to fill it, although women and children swelled the paper strength of a depot battalion. Living conditions within the depot were probably better than in most stations, formal gardens were laid out between the southern rampart and the outer ditch, sanitation was improved, earth closets were provided with proper drainage, piped water was supplied in 1845 and long wash-houses were established by 1850. In these latter years the Citadel found itself surrounded by ever-encroaching commercial developments and yet becoming more isolated from the situation it was meant to dominate as the 'growths' of mud in the Humber steadily accumulated in front of the southern aspect.

In December 1846 a review undertaken to determine the defensive value of the Citadel, concluded that the only purpose which it might serve was as a sea battery, and even then it would need the provision of a considerable number of guns of greater calibre than those that existed at the Citadel, together with associated firing platforms. It was noted that the proposed complement of 109 guns should have been sufficient to provide a successful result in an engagement with the heavy ordnance and concentrated mass of fire which ships of war of large classes could bring against it. The disadvantages of the scheme were several tall buildings along High Street providing cover for attackers from the west, whilst, to the east, spoil from the dock excavations closed the view of the defenders. It finally recommended that the forts at South End and Paull be reconstructed, as they would serve the purpose better.

The military presence at the Citadel was gradually wound down after this date, with replacement of regulars by the militia, thus freeing troops for the Crimean War. In January 1855 'the company of artillery, for some time stationed in Hull' left for Woolwich, and thence for the Crimean War. In 1858 the Citadel was transferred from the Board of Ordnance to the care of the Department of Woods and Forests, since the War Department had by then considered that the gun battery at Paull further to the east could control the Humber far more effectively.

The Citadel site was then, apparently, let out for business purposes to various tenants, among them timber merchants who used it as a store for timber, and the soldiers' barracks became the habitation of poor cottagers. However, prior to this date there is one peculiar incident that merits some record. In August 1824 a crowd of 4,000 people had bought tickets giving entry to the Citadel to watch the filling of a balloon with gas and the ascent of W. W. Saddler – one of his last – since he was killed a few weeks later. Many thousands of others in the town and nearby villages saw him go up with one passenger, Mr. Rees Davis, and come down in Preston, a few miles to the east.

In 1859, the 4th Hull Artillery, a newly raised volunteer unit, was given the use of the south blockhouse as their headquarters. The volunteers used the open area of the Citadel for drill and had the use of the 13 guns still mounted there for gun drill on a Saturday morning. A salute fired from the Citadel on the occasion of the wedding of the Prince of Wales on 12 March 1863 is the last recorded use of its armament.

At the beginning of 1859 the Crown offered the Citadel site for sale, describing the buildings (which were to be demolished by the buyer) and foreshore as occupying 60 acres, with a frontage to the Humber of 1,600 feet. In February 1859 the Corporation attempted to buy a part of the site for £105,000, with the intention of turning it into a riverside park and promenade. The startling growth in the population of Hull and the consequent loss of green fields through road building had led many of the town fathers to realise that a public park would be an asset to the town. It was envisaged that the Citadel site could be developed into an 'idyllic spot' where 'tiny children should look out of old embrasures and cricket balls roll where cannon balls were piled of old'. The offer was rejected and the Corporation then considered that, as the military had no further use for the Citadel, it should revert to the town without charge, and a public meeting 'numerously attended by a galaxy of influential local men' was held at the Town Hall in June 1859 in support of a petition to the Government asking for the restoration of the property.

Their plan failed as the Court of Chancery ruled against the claim in 1861, and the Government sold as building materials all the buildings of the castle and Citadel, except the south blockhouse, which passed into the possession of the shipbuilding firm of Martin Samuelson & Co. Instead of being completely demolished, the major parts of the Citadel were simply razed to the ground, leaving behind the foundations, only centimetres below the present surface of the ground. The Citadel lands were drained and planned to be laid out in streets by the Department of Woods and Forests shortly after 1865. Timber stacks covered much of the area once the buildings, walls and ramparts had been taken down and there is evidence to show that the rest of the area was used as a rubbish dump.

The extensively reclaimed foreshore of the Humber in front of the former Citadel was leased to the Hull Dock Company, which constructed a timber quay there. In the later 19th century the area was fully incorporated into the Victoria Dock as it developed and grew in size. Today, all that remains of the once mighty fortifications is the little watchtower which, fittingly, has been re-sited in Victoria Dock Village. Perhaps also surviving is the archway leading from the entrance of the south blockhouse. It was moved to the grounds of Colonel W. Lambert White's house in Hedon where it remained until 1931, when it was once again moved, this time to Hatfield Heath in Essex.

The Thew Plan of Hull 1784 illustrates the layout of the fortifications on the east bank of the River Hull. The triangular shape of the Citadel is shown clearly. The walls and gates protecting the town on the other bank had been neglected and had decayed and crumbled by this time, in spite of occasional repairs. In 1774 an Act of Parliament granted most of these fortifications to the newly formed Hull Dock Company.

The Company acquired the walls, ramparts and ditches on the north and west sides of the town and on the south side as far as Ogle's Tower, and built the first enclosed dock in the country on the site of the north walls.

Sources:
Blashill, *East Hull*.
Gillett and MacMahon, *Hull*.
Howes and Foreman, *Town and Gun*.
Markham, *Hull*.

The mighty Citadel. (Thew, 1784).

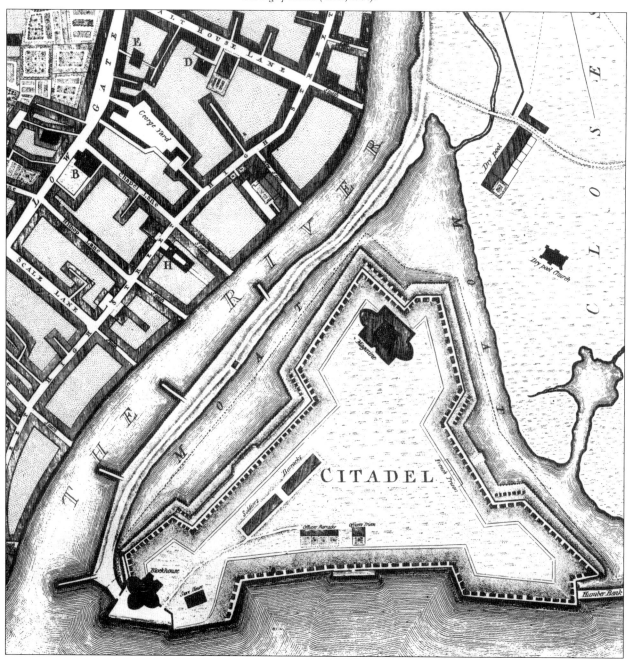

Chapter Five
A Curious Journey: The Watchtower

The watchtower, has had a curious history, having travelled around Hull and having been used by many for purposes unforeseen when it was built. It was originally designed as an overhanging watchtower, or, to use its more correct name, a bartizan, and it formed a part of the Citadel built between 1681 and 1685. Its purpose was to provide shelter for a standing sentinel, who supplemented the role of the sentries pacing the walls along the parapet. The tower was originally sited at the point where the walls met at the junction of the east bank of the River Hull and the Humber Estuary, forming the most advanced work of the western bastion and surmounting the apex of the south and west glacis, or sloping sides, of the fortress.

The Commissioners of Woods and Forests demolished the major part of the Citadel during 1863-4, and the most southerly part, at the junction of the River Hull and the Humber, which included the south blockhouse, was demolished to make way for the South Bridge in late 1863. William Bailey of Hull acquired the site on which the watchtower formerly stood, in 1864, when his company took over the shipyard of Martin Samuelson. Bailey was a partner in the local steamship owners, Bailey and Leetham, and was also a director of the Hull Dock Company. Thankfully, he preserved the watchtower and had it built into the walls of the Humber Iron Works, his newly acquired shipbuilding yard at Sammy's Point.

In 1912 the watch-tower was presented by his family and trustees to Hull Corporation, which decided to place the tower in East Park, opened on 21 June 1887.

The tower was re-sited at the top of an artificially created hill, known as 'Spion Kop', just around the corner from the 'Khyber Pass', a dark, sunless, damp valley located between two artificial hills. A brass plaque stating the history of the watchtower was placed on the wall underneath it. Over the many years the watch-tower was sited in the East Park, it became neglected and steadily deteriorated in condition. It had become a mecca for children and their games, being subjected to many a mock attack. It was also used as a toilet by the desperate and as a wall for graffiti artists.

In 1990 Hull City Council decided to relocate the watchtower from East Park to the newly emerging Victoria Dock Village, where it was proposed to make it a feature at the entrance, where it would act as a reminder of the once mighty Citadel, which stood on the same site. AMARC (Associated Marine and Related Charities), a skills training agency, were given the task of restoring the watchtower and achieved this by completely dismantling it, numbering each of the stone blocks, thoroughly cleaning them, and then painstakingly reconstructing the watchtower, block by block in its new position at the top of a reconstruction of the Citadel wall.

Such a fine job was made of the restoration that it was a finalist in the 1995 British Archeological Awards. Today the watchtower sits overlooking the buildings of Victoria Dock Village, not too far from the spot where it began its military career – over 300 years ago – and its later wanderings around the City of Kingston upon Hull.

Sources:
Fowler, *East Hull*.

The original location of the watchtower. (Buck, 1745).

Chapter Six

Duty Paid! The Coming of the Docks to Hull

In the 16th century the trade of the port received a powerful impetus from a statute of Elizabeth I which directed when and where merchandise should be landed and customs duty paid. This specifically excluded Hull and London from the restrictive clauses, which hampered other harbours. The exceptions were repeated in an Act of 1674, the reason being given, 'that there was no spot of ground which could be spared for the erection of Legal Quays.' As a consequence, for almost the next four centuries, Hull merchants were in a privileged position and free to ply their trade without restraint. It was the expansion in Hull's trade brought about by the Industrial Revolution and the greatly increased amount of shipping using the Haven that forced the pace of change. In the first half of the 18th century the annual tonnage of foreign vessels using the port more than doubled.

However, merchants still conducted their business within the confines of the Old Harbour but they had become so successful in increasing trade that the harbour, wharves and staithes were often blocked and it was said that some ships near the entrance could make a return trip whilst those at the furthest reaches were making their way down the congested river to the estuary. The trade in textiles from Leeds, Wakefield and Halifax was transacted at Hull, lead came from Derbyshire and Nottinghamshire, via Bawtry Wharf, butter was brought down the Ouse and cheeses were

shipped down the Trent from Stafford, Warwick and Cheshire. Hull handled imports of iron, copper, potash, hemp, flax and linen from Scandinavia, Russia and the Baltic; wine linen oil and fruit from the Low Countries and Spain; and tobacco and sugar from the West Indies. Fire on board ship, or in the closely confined and packed warehouses, was a constant and dreaded hazard. Describing Hull in the 1720s, Daniel Defoe noted 'that there was more business done in Hull than in any other town of comparable size in Europe'.

By 1772 the situation had reached crisis point and it had become obvious that something extraordinary had to be done. The reputation of Hull with the Treasury had reached an all-time low, since the lack of a Legal Quay meant that goods could be unloaded without a proper Customs inspection and there was every opportunity for widespread smuggling. The Treasury threatened to make Gainsborough a legal port. Goods destined for Hull would be landed there if nothing were done. So in that year the burgesses of Hull applied to the Treasury for a grant to convert part of the town ditch, from the River Hull to Beverley Gate, into a 'bason for light ships'. The Crown Commissioners wasted no time in seizing their opportunity, with the result that when in 1774 an Act of Parliament established the Hull Dock Company and permitted the building of the new dock (which incidentally would become the first enclosed dock in the country), the

Crowded shipping in the Old Harbour. (Buck, 1745).

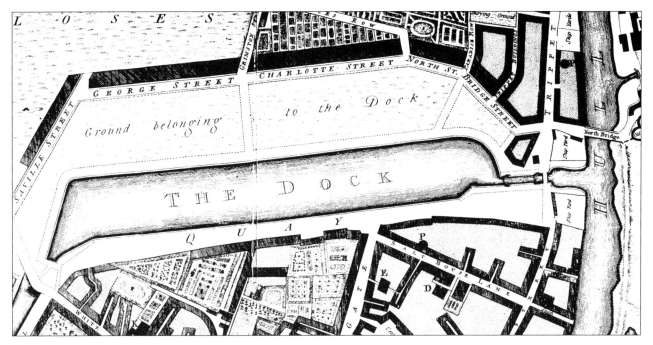

The Dock. (Thew, 1784).

walls and ditch between the North Gate and the Beverley Gate were transferred to the Company, along with £15,000 from the Customs, and 120 shares of £250 each were issued. The issue received good support and was a 'resounding success', paying out massive dividends of 25%. Shares later changed hands at over £1,000 each. The Act also introduced full customs charges to the port 'for the Security and Improvement of the Public Revenue and for the advantage of Commerce'.

The wall, gates and interval towers of the medieval defences were demolished and advertisements were placed for people to cart away the soil from the ramparts, bastions and ditches. Excavation of the dock, using manual labour only, commenced in 1775 and the earth removed from the dock was dumped to the north where George Street now stands. The foundation stone was laid with great ceremony on 19 October 1775 and opened for shipping on 22 September 1778, the Greenland whaler *Manchester* being the first to enter from the lock entrance at the Old Harbour. The water area of the dock covered 10 acres, measuring 1,750 feet (533.5m) in length by 250 feet (76.2m) in width and provided berths for 100 ships. This first dock was named simply 'The Dock'. New roads were laid out providing a link to the north and east of The Dock, including Savile Street, named after Sir George Savile, an original shareholder, George Street, named after King George III, Charlotte Street, named after Queen Charlotte, and North Street, Bridge Street, Dock Street and Quay Street. The old town walls to the south of The Dock remained standing. A contemporary report of the scene at the opening states: 'An immense concourse of people crowded in from all parts of the neighbourhood; so that it may be questioned whether this town has ever been more thronged with people, except on the day of the celebration of the revolution.'

Some of the oldest merchants in the town considered The Dock to be unnecessarily large and the cost (£120,000) a great waste of money. However, they were proved wrong as trade continued to grow, as it was now possible to handle a far greater quantity of goods. Passengers sailed from The Dock to the Continent, while emigrants embarked there for America. Between the years 1788 and 1792 the number of ships using the port rose from 1,058 to 1,522 and Customs' revenue increased from £86,000 in 1783 to £200,000 in 1793. As noted, it paid good dividends to its 120 shareholders out of the dues, which varied from 2d. per ton for coasting vessels travelling as far north as Holy Island or as far south as Yarmouth. For vessels trading with Greenland, Africa and America, the due were set at 1s. 9d. per ton. All foreign vessels were obliged to pay double the dues.

Entering The Dock required skilled seamanship in a crowded waterway, a feat that was made more difficult by the increased size of the vessels in the Haven and the numbers of whalers which wintered in The Dock. An extension to the south from The Dock was one option considered for the second dock in Hull, a solution, which most members of the Dock Company thought, would only cause further congestion. It was clear that a more radical solution was required if Hull was to progress from being simply a port on the River Hull. An Act of 1801 permitted the taking down of the southern defences and in 1802 the Hull Dock Company obtained an Act to construct a second dock from the Hessle Gate to the Myton Gate, which it had been finally agreed would open directly into the Humber. This dock, providing berths for 70 ships, was excavated by the newly invented method of 'bucket-chain dredging', using steam power. The excavated material formed the land to the south of the present Humber Street and new streets were laid out over the spoil, named as Nelson Street and Wellington Street, after the heroes of the day. A grand hotel, the Vittoria Tavern, was built nearby, offering superb panoramic views over the Humber. Hull Corporation and Trinity

House subscribed half the capital for the venture and it was initially known as the New Dock, when it opened on 30 June 1809 at a cost of £230,000, much of the cost being accounted for by the more elaborate entrance which the muddy Humber estuary required.

The opening was attended by great celebration and, as reported at the time, 'Flags were displayed on the steeples of all the churches, and the ships in the roads (ships anchored in the Humber), the Old Dock and the harbour were gaily decorated with colours. At 6.30 am the members of the corporation of the town and Trinity House and the Dock Company assembled at the Dock Office and at 7.15 am set out preceded by flags and a band of music.'

It was realised at the time that a linking dock would enable shipping to enter docks from the Humber, thus removing the need for ships to manoeuvre through the difficult passage in the Haven and powers had also been obtained in 1802 to build a Junction Dock to connect the two docks. Junction Dock opened on 1 June 1829, 18 months after construction commenced and so completed the line of docks connecting the River Hull with the Humber. Appropriately the Trinity House yacht was the first vessel to make the circular tour of the Old Town by water.

The New Dock was renamed Humber Dock, in 1854 and today forms the Hull Marina. Following the opening of the New Dock, The Dock became known as The Old Dock, and was renamed Queen's Dock, in 1854, in honour of the Royal Visit by Queen Victoria in that year when she and Prince Albert sailed through the Hull docks.

Junction Dock was also renamed as Prince's Dock in 1855, in honour of the Prince Consort. This dock now forms the Princes Quay shopping centre. Finally,

Queen's Dock had become redundant by the 1930s, being too far from the Humber and unsuitable for the larger vessels now using the port. It closed in 1931 and was filled in during 1935. The dock was purchased by the Corporation and at the suggestion of Sir Alfred Gelder the space was made into gardens with lawns, paths and fountains. Foundry waste from the National Radiator Company was dumped into the dock by the lorry load and barge loads of silt dredged from the River Hull and the other docks were used to fill in what became Queens' Gardens. The building of the three town docks had finally freed Hull from the corset which the old town walls had imposed on the medieval town.

Excavation of the Railway Dock commenced in 1844 and it opened on 18 July 1846, so becoming the fourth dock to be built in Hull. It was constructed to take advantage of the opening of the Hull to Selby Railway in 1840, which linked with the Selby-Leeds line, further increasing trade through the port. This dock closed in 1968 and now forms a part of the Marina. The 1844 Act, which authorised the Railway Dock, also authorised a fifth dock, principally for dealing with the timber trade. This dock, at first referred to as the 'East Dock', became known as the Victoria Dock, and opened in 1850.

At mid-century, Hull had a population of 85,000 and remained, predominantly, a trading town. Cotton spinning and weaving, introduced to the town in the 1830s, was the only significant addition to the industrial sector, while the decline and eventual demise of whale fishing was the main item of note in the general activity of the port. In 1788 there were 36 whalers based in Hull but fierce competition and a dwindling resource meant that by 1840 Hull's whaling fleet was down to two ships. It was the third quarter of the 19th century that saw the greatest growth in overseas trade in Great Britain and Hull was well placed to take advantage of the increase. Its position on the Humber, 22 miles from the sea, where the deep-water channel approaches the north shore, made it naturally the principal port of the region.

By the 1870s Hull had an extensive dock system and good railway and water connections with the West Riding and North Midlands. Between the early 1870s and the late 1890s the trade of Hull doubled by value. However, as this was a period of decline in prices, the volume of trade must have been far higher. The growth of trade through the port naturally involved a considerable increase in the labour force and in the population of the town. In fact, Hull experienced a population explosion during the 1800s as shown by the comparison of census figures. The 1801

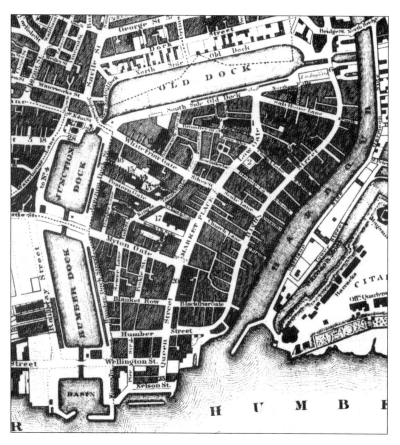

Old, Junction and Humber Docks.
(Goodwill & Lawson, 1869).

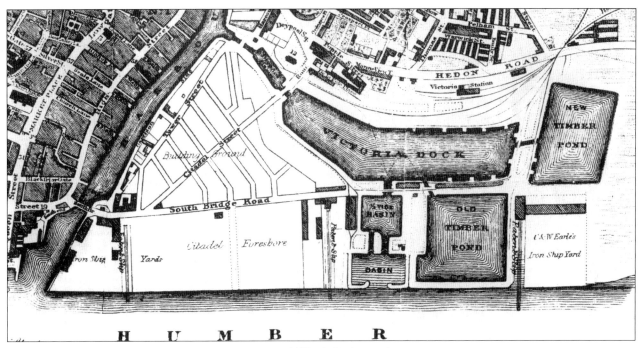

Victoria Dock. (Goodwill & Lawson, 1869).

census recorded a total of 22,161 living in Hull and the 1901 census revealed a population of 240,259 living in the city. Although this figure had been swollen in part by boundary extensions, it was mainly fuelled by the huge increase in inward migration of workers into Hull from the surrounding countryside and from Ireland seeking improved opportunities of employment and better wages. Some of the migrants must have been skilled workers in the engineering and building trades who found work in the shipyards but many other male immigrants would have been labourers who found employment on the railways and the waterfront as builders or dockers. The making of the docks and the railways required men of incredible stamina, toughness and willingness to take risks. By the mid to late 1800s, dockers and allied workers made up a significant proportion of the workforce in Hull.

It is not so easy to categorise dockers. They are usually thought of as an homogenous group of workers with common aims and ideals, shaped by their environment and living conditions, low and irregular pay, casual employment and unskilled work which they, or anyone else with reasonable strength, could do. The general picture painted is of a poor, illiterate, ill-clad army, loading and unloading ships at the docks. This, however, is a much too simplified picture. Dockers, or stevedores to give them their correct name, have always regarded themselves as being in some measure, specialists. And rightly so. The general divisions of skill are, firstly, those working on ships; secondly, those employed on the quayside; and, thirdly, those labouring in warehouses. Even within these three categories there are many sub-divisions, the term 'docker' embracing for instance the following groups, each of which regarded itself as fairly exclusive: raff yard labourers (used as a term for timber carriers), deal porters, coal heavers, coal trimmers, corn porters, and so on. The multiplicity of job titles was motivated, to an extent, by a desire to imply that the holder was of somewhat

higher prestige than that suggested by the general term 'docker', although it is also true to say that all were specialists to some extent.

Life was never easy working on the docks. The work, when it was available, was hard and often dangerous, the hours were long, the working conditions were awful and the pay was poor. Being classed as a casual labourer meant that even finding work on a half-day or daily basis was degrading. From the earliest days and, in fact, until the Second World War dockers had to arrive at the dock before half-past-seven and then had to look for a ship lying at a berth where it was likely that work might be available. Once there, they stood in a group of perhaps three to four hundred men, gathered together at the gangway end, each hoping that they might know the foreman and so secure a job. At about a-quarter-to-eight, the foreman would stand at the top of the gangway and start to make his selection of workers, when the assembled men would seek desperately to gain his attention, or to catch his eye, whilst he shouted out the names of the men he wanted for the job. Those not hired had to walk, run, or cycle to another ship, or even another dock, along the seven miles of waterfront to look for work.

In these circumstances it is not surprising that there were stirrings of discontent, in protest at their conditions, in the early 1870s. The Nine-Hours Movement, which originated on Tyneside as a demand for shorter working hours, quickly caught the imagination of workers in the country at large. Locally, the dockers moved towards a form of trades union to improve their working conditions and on 12 March 1872, the Hull Dockside Labourers met at the Temperance Hall, Mytongate, to consider how to obtain shorter hours and higher wages.

They discussed working practices and drew up a set of rules for work, a copy of which was sent to their employers. Ten days elapsed, during which time no response had been received from the employers' side and it was decided that they would withdraw their labour commencing Monday, 25 March. The strike was so successful that it brought work on the quays almost to a standstill. The employers reacted by hiring seamen to do the work of the dockers at a higher rate of pay, which not unnaturally caused great ill- feeling amongst the strikers. The strike lasted for three weeks and, once over, the strike leaders were unable to get their jobs back. Many agricultural workers from Lincolnshire and elsewhere were said to have come to Hull to do labouring jobs.

The number of workers on the waterside increased from 5,413 in 1871, to 14,032 in 1901, as a direct result of the opening of new docks and the increase in trade during that period. In one of the early examples of collective action on the Hull docks, the raff yard labourers on Victoria Dock went on strike in November 1874, linking their demand for a nine-hour working day with the abolition of payment by the hour. By December, R. Wade, Sons & Co., one of the largest timber firms on the dock, gave the nine-hour day to its raff yard labourers.

The 1889 London Dock Strike, which lasted from August to September of that year and which was led by such famous leaders as Ben Tillett and Tom Mann, won a massive victory in recognising the rights of dockers to organise themselves in unions and is considered to be the birth of the first national docks union. Ben Tillett addressed a mass meeting of dockers in Hull in December 1899, and such was their enthusiasm that 12,000 of them joined his union by September 1890. Hull became a 100% union port – the jewel of the union crown. Sporadic strikes on the docks continued during the late 1800s, the most serious occurring in 1893. The year began with heavy unemployment due to an unprecedented decrease in trade. The Dockers Union, which by this time had gained in strength and had become a force to be reckoned with, suffered a major setback early in 1893 when Thomas Wilson Sons and Company, the largest ship owners in the port, joined the Shipping Federation. This firm of local ship owners had previously shown sympathy toward the aims of the dockworkers in Hull and had improved conditions and offered guidance and support in the past.

The Shipping Federation was an employer organisation formed in 1890 with the aim of fighting the 'strike weapon' through the establishment of a Free Labour Exchange in every port. The Exchange was available to unionist and non-unionist alike for the purposes of registration, which then gave them preference for employment. If sufficient people joined in any port, then the local branch of the national union there was defeated. Where local branches of the union were stronger than the Federation, the Shipping Federation was prepared to import, lodge and feed groups of free labourers who carried out the work of the unionist until the union surrendered its 'closed shop' policy. Hull, the only remaining union stronghold, had resisted the establishment of a permanent Free Labour Exchange until a local branch was opened in March 1893, posing a second and even more serious threat to the union.

Conditions that year were set for a confrontation,

not, it has to be said, at the behest of the union, who were well aware that they had been badly weakened. Thus when a relatively minor dispute occurred in February 1893, involving union dockers working on a coal barge who had refused to pay the arrears on their union dues, it quickly escalated. Wilson's, the employers, refused to deduct the arrears from the men's wages, as they had done on previous occasions. The union responded by refusing to unload coal from three other barges belonging to Wilson's. In retaliation, Wilson's responded by insisting that their foremen and shipping clerks should leave the union. It is generally considered that this dispute, coupled with the tensions caused by the opening of the Free Labour Exchange, laid the foundations for the 1893 Dock Strike.

Initially, the union took a pragmatic view, as they agreed that their members would work alongside 'free' labourers. Despite this action, minor skirmishes took place. It soon became clear that the employers were spoiling for a fight and did not intend to negotiate with the union leaders. Wilson's even used 100 of their clerks to unload goods and brought in labour from Europe. The employers had the emigration sheds rigged up as accommodation for free labourers and on 5 April 400 free labourers arrived in Hull from London and were billeted on the docks for their own safety. Straight away they set to unload some of the ships owned by both Wilson's and Bailey and Leethams. As the men left the *Romeo* for a dinner break, stones were thrown at them and a shot was fired. The men claimed that they dare not return to work in the afternoon due to 'the menacing actions of thousands of dockers'. Tension was such that the Corporation asked the Government for reinforcements to assist the local constabulary. On 6 April they were sent two gunboats, HMS *Hearty* and *Bullfrog,* to patrol the Humber. In addition, 160 Royal Scots from York and 90 Dragoons arrived in the city. The Royal Scots arrived by a special eight-coach train in Paragon Yard, then, 'headed by their screeching bagpipes', left directly for the Artillery Barracks, where they were billeted. The press reported that 'a great crowd had assembled in Anlaby Road' to watch them. The Dragoons arrived two hours later, and the same report in the *Hull Daily Mail* described their arrival and the backing out of the horses from the train on the Paragon platform: 'The platform was shockingly inconvenient and the asphalt made things worse. But the men managed marvellously well and not a single horse fell down . . . Large crowds of dockers assembled in the precincts of the station and hooted loudly as each section of horse passed out of the yard.' Massive police reinforcements were also brought in from Retford, Halifax, Nottingham, Lincolnshire and Huddersfield to join those from Leeds, whilst mounted police came up from London.

A mixture of surprise and outrage greeted this hasty 'preposterous display of force in an "orderly town", where no prosecutions of strikers had been taken for disorderly conduct.' By 14 April, there were about 1,000 free labourers in Hull under strong police and military protection, and both sides in the dispute began to take up extreme positions. On 22 April, five fires occurred, the largest destroying the Citadel Hotel and the timber yards of R. Wade, Sons & Company on the

Victoria Dock. The first fire was discovered in Wade's timber yard in Citadel Street, at about four in the afternoon and was reported by a lad named Slingsby to P.C. Marks at Victoria Dock, who telephoned the Fire Brigade.

The Hull Fire Brigade quickly arrived and, according to press reports, 'commenced their efforts with several steam engines . . . By the time their efforts commenced only one stack of wood was in flames, and a large number of "tars" from H.M. ships *Bullfrog* and *Hearty,* who arrived on the scene almost as soon as the hose was attached to the hydrants, endeavoured to stop the progress of the fire by dislodging huge piles of timber, but the strong wind aided the fire in its devastating course.'

'The Dock Company's and North Eastern Railway Company's fire engines turned up later on, and, although they rendered invaluable help, it was patent to the dullest intellect that the yards of Messrs. Wade, Messrs. Bryson Jameson and Co., Messrs. Newsom and Co. and Messrs. Grice and Hutchinson were doomed to almost entire destruction . . . By six o'clock a vast area of ground was nothing but a blaze. The fire spread towards the buildings on the east side of the Old Harbour, and their position was all along precarious. But, thanks to a large number of voluntary and willing workers, who incessantly poured water on the walls of the warehouses, the flames failed to get them in their cruel grip. Not so fortunate was the Citadel Hotel. The fire crossed Citadel Street and with astonishing rapidity destroyed a large quantity of stock in Messrs. Newsom's yard, not resting satisfied until it had taken the Hotel at the corner in its merciless embrace. The building became a mass of ruins in an incredibly short period of time and it looked as if the offices of the Humber Ironworks and the Fever Hospital would also be levelled. Fortunately these establishments escaped the fate which seemed inevitable.' Thousands of people came to watch, and mounted troops and police, who had to clear them away at times to make room for the firefighters, 'were stoned and hooted' for their efforts. The fire caused several secondary fires in the city and it was reported that the flames could be seen 20 miles away. Arson was immediately suspected, as, when the Fire Brigade arrived, they found that their hosepipes were cut deliberately and that the dockers would not assist in extinguishing the flames, even though offered the fabulous wages of five shillings per hour.

There were two immediate consequences of the fires: the first was the cost, estimated at £50,000 for the main fire alone, and, secondly the campaign mounted by Kier Hardie to have the military and police reinforcements withdrawn was now doomed to failure. The discovery of several pieces of tarry rope and rags saturated in paraffin made the excuse which was offered for the fires seem rather tame, namely, 'that the present summery atmospheric conditions could easily produce fires'.

The Shipping Federation expressed the opinion that the strike could not last a week due to the parlous financial state of the union and the high level of unemployment in the town. However, support for the strike grew. By the second week there were around 15,000 men on strike in Hull from the main waterside unions and the intervention of the State on the side of the employers helped to swell that support, both morally and financially. The employers and the strikers took up even more extreme positions, as the issues at the heart of the dispute had become matters of principle for both parties. It also became clear, following a meeting of the Council of the Shipping Federation at York on 11 April that the employers were not interested in a negotiated settlement to the dispute and wanted a fight to the finish.

Despite having made some concessions to the employers, this position now served to stiffen the resolve of the members of the Dockers Union to carry on with the strike, since it was clear to them and to most other union leaders that a complete surrender would mean the end of trades unions, not only on the docks but on a much wider national scale. Violence during the period of the strike was common, and at its height a Hull gunsmith reported selling 200 revolvers and an untold number of knuckledusters in three weeks. Perhaps the most serious incident occurred on 25 April when George Hopperton, a Shipping Federation official, shot Charles Graham, a dock labourer, in Waterhouse Lane. It appeared that a friend of Hopperton had been struck on the head during a melée and they had run off, only to be chased by the crowd. During the chase, Hopperton had turned and fired his revolver, striking Charles Graham in the thigh. When searched by the police, he was found to be in possession of a knuckleduster and six revolver ball cartridges.

The North Eastern Railway Hull Docks Fire engine.

There were some dockers who benefited as a result of the strike. Work at the ports of Goole and Grimsby increased dramatically to such an extent it was said that the one shilling a week levy paid to the strike fund by the dockers at those ports was a good investment to keep the Hull strike going. Meanwhile, the free labourers in Hull were of such a large number that it was said that there would be no vacancies left for the union men to fill when the dispute was over. A press report from the *Hull Daily Mail* in April 1893 referred to lively scenes on Hedon Road arising from tussles between the free labourers and strikers: 'Some of the free labourers, it appeared, were anxious to leave the dock and explore the town but they had not got far on the road when they were opposed by a number of strikers. The usual conflict followed, but perhaps more jest than earnest was shown in the encounter, and, although some men bore evidence of the scrimmaging, it was not of a serious character. The strikers were not content until the free labourers were escorted back to the dock by the police, a procedure which the unionists seemed to enjoy.'

Gradually, over the next three weeks, the media, which had been hostile to the strikers at first, began to report the strikers' position in more favourable terms and the public of Hull began to press for a swift resolution of the strike, as the true cost of supporting the police reinforcements became clear, especially as even more support had been called for.

In Parliament the Government was constantly harried by a series of questions regarding the Hull Strike, while official figures released for April 1893 for the Port of Hull made it clear just how much trade had suffered as a result of the strike. That served to alienate the businessmen and even the ship owners of Hull against the Shipping Federation, which now found itself becoming increasingly isolated.

The end of the dispute was now in sight. All that was needed was an honest broker who could produce a compromise acceptable to both sides which extricated the dockers from an unwinnable situation without their having to surrender completely. Just such a person arrived in Hull on 10 May in the form of Tom Mann, Treasurer of the Dock, Wharf, Riverside & General Labourers Union, whose President, Ben Tillett, had been instrumental in encouraging the formation of local branches of his union in Hull. Tillett, however, was a fiery character, much liked by the dockers but not a man to negotiate the settlement of this bitter dispute with the employers. Tom Mann therefore spoke to the employers and quickly obtained their agreement that the Free Labour Exchange should not give preference of employment to non-unionists.

He spoke to 10,000 strikers on the Dansom Lane playing fields and obtained their unanimous agreement that they would end the strike if the employers would guarantee that the Labour Exchange would not be used to weaken trades unionism.

On 12 May a group of employers from Hull, including C. H. Wilson, Arthur Wilson and W. Bailey, travelled to London to meet the Chairman and some members of the Executive Council of the Shipping Federation. They reported that the men were willing to return to work providing that an additional clause was inserted in the York Manifesto: 'That neither registration at the British Labour Exchange, nor membership of any union shall in itself carry with it either preference or prejudice with regard to employment.' In other words, no discrimination would be shown by employers against union members.

The Federation already accepted these conditions, which had been proposed earlier. There was a mass meeting of dockers on Sunday, 14 May, at which the men accepted the revised agreement, perhaps not realising immediately that they had lost the closed shop. The two sides to the dispute met at 11.30 am on Thursday, 18 May and the employers produced a nine-point plan, most of which did not find favour with the union negotiators. The meeting was re-convened for an afternoon session at 1.10 pm. As a result of further negotiation, agreement was reached, some of the earlier clauses having been deleted and others amended. The dispute officially ended on Friday, 19 May, but, since it was Whitsuntide weekend, work did not begin until Tuesday, 23 May, exactly seven weeks after it began. On Thursday, 25 May, there were over 2,000 men working on the docks, of whom 900 were free labourers. Several acts of violence broke out, instigated by both sides as a result of the great bitterness felt on both sides. By Monday, 29 May, only about 40 imported free labourers remained on the docks and the police and military reinforcements had left the town. Unemployment in Hull remained high, and so, despite other local difficulties, the men had no stomach for a further fight after such a recent resounding defeat.

The general collapse of morale amongst the waterfront workers led over 2,000 of them to register by 9 June with the Free Labour Bureau, in recognition of the fact that those who did not possess the ticket had little chance of employment as there was still insufficient work. The dominance of free labour in Hull remained until October 1900, when Tillett's Dock, Wharf, Riverside & General Labourers Union had a renaissance, attracting 4,000 new members in Hull, although it was not until 1911 that the union was recognised on Hull docks.

This was how the docks came to Hull, during a century which saw an unprecedented expansion of the workforce through inward migration to Hull, matched by an equally unprecedented increase in the general population, bringing increased trade to the town, improved links with the rest of the United Kingdom, great wealth to those who were able to exploit the conditions and overcrowding, poor housing, poverty and deprivation to those who were not so able. Toward the end of the 19th century the dockworkers in particular had demonstrated how collective action could improve conditions of work, provide increased levels of pay and establish new and safer working practices.

Sources:
Raymond Brown, *Waterfront Organisation in Hull* (Hull, 1990).
History of the Port of Hull. (An unattributed leaflet in the records of Hull Local Studies Library).
Michael Thompson, *Hull Docklands. An Illustrated Guide to the Port of Hull* (Cherry Burton, 1990).

Chapter Seven
Expansion to the East: Victoria Dock

The first steam powered ship to be introduced on the Humber estuary, in October 1814, was the P.S. *Caledonia*. She had been built on the Clyde and was destined to work mainly between Hull and Selby. The advantages of working independently of wind and tide were soon demonstrated, as the following local newspaper report concerning her trials, dated 15 October 1814, confirm: 'The steamboat *Caledonia* lately arrived here and has, during the week, been exhibiting her capabilities on the Humber; it appears that, with both wind and tide against her, her speed is considerable. On Wednesday she left for Gainsborough, and the weather being favourable, reached Burton Stather in an hour and a half. On 14 May 1815 another notice appeared, as follows: The *Caledonia* steam packet, last Thursday, went from Hull up the River Ouse to Naburn, about four miles from York, and returned to Hull the same day, steaming the 122 miles there and back in about 12 hours.' The *Caledonia* marked the beginning of the change from sail to steam power, although, as a precaution, all early steam ships were still rigged with sails. As increased engine power became available, so the size of the paddles were increased to convert the increased power into greater energy. Thus the size of ships greatly increased in the beam, especially when measured across the paddle boxes. These advances were to have a profound and then unforeseen effect on the ship owners, operators and cargo handlers.

By 1838, the size of the steam ships had increased to the point where they were only able to enter the existing town docks with the greatest of difficulty. At that time the town docks comprised Queen's Dock, Junction Dock and Humber Dock, all roughly following the line of the former town moat. These docks all combined narrow entrances with a shallow depth over the sill. There was a proposal in 1829, on paper at least, to create an 'East Dock' on a site to the east of the Citadel but there seemed little urgency to implement the plan. Matters came to a head on 28 April 1838, when a deputation of steamship owners held a crisis meeting with the directors of the Hull Dock Company. The owners put their case forcefully, pointing out the necessity for increased and enlarged accommodation, more especially to suit the larger steamships that were required as a result of both the extension in trade and for the new steamships which were in build. The lofty reply of the directors was 'that the steamship companies should build their vessels to suit the capacity of the docks, instead of soliciting further dock accommodation'.

The owners did not consider this opinion as being in any way satisfactory and commenced agitating more widely for an increase in dock accommodation. The ship owners held many public meetings at which they promoted their case, they wrote many letters to newspapers and sent a deputation to the Board of Trade in London. They pointed out that five steamships trading from Hull, *Victoria, Wilberforce, Seahorse, Queen of Scotland* and *Tiger,* could not be accommodated in the docks, the locks being too narrow for them. Their stated view was: 'that Hull was miserably groaning under the monopoly of a dock company, who will not keep up with the times by making larger docks themselves and obstinately stand in the way of such docks being constructed by others'. A public meeting, presided over by the mayor, was held very early in November 1838, when a very large majority emphasised 'the absolute necessity of enlarging the dock accommodation'. On 9 November the prospectus of a new dock company was issued, capitalised at £180,000, the object being to create a new dock on a suitable site to the east of the Citadel. It was initially known as East Dock but was later styled Victoria Dock, in honour of the visit of the Queen to Hull in 1854. The selected site is said to have been recommended to the dock company by a local merchant, Joseph Sanderson.

Parliamentary Notice of Application for the Bill, given by Thomas Holden on behalf of the Hull Dock Company, referred to 'the apathy of the old Dock Company in refusing to extend their dock system and to provide adequate accommodation needed by the increase in trade'. Victoria Dock would represent the first expansion of the port to the east of the River Hull. John B. Hartley was appointed Consulting Engineer to the Hull Dock Company in 1842, a post he occupied for the next 16 years. He was the son of Jesse Hartley, the renowned engineer and surveyor of the Liverpool Dock Trustees. His great work can still be seen at Albert Dock in Liverpool, where there is a quayside public house named in his honour. By 1843 the proposed dock and tide basins to the east of the Citadel were plotted as cuttings and the Humber foreshore was lined with wood pilings. Over the next three years John B. Hartley planned and designed Victoria Dock and began the work on the excavation of the dock by the firm of Bowers and Murray in September 1845 using steam driven excavators. Excavations for docks and timber ponds were accompanied by extensive reclamation of mud 'growths', whose limits were defined by timber jetties and piles projecting into the Humber. John Beadle, the Chairman of the Hull Dock Company, laid the first stone on 5 November 1846. Stone brought from Sweden was principally used in the construction of the dock.

Victoria Dock was formally opened on Wednesday, 3 July 1850 by Mr. T. Firbank, by then chairman of the Hull Dock Company. The initial entrance to the new dock was via the River Hull, through a 45-foot (13.7 m) wide, 172-foot long, (52.4 m) lock entry at the Old Harbour and via Drypool Basin.

This feature can still be seen immediately to the south of Drypool Bridge on the east bank of the River Hull. The Trinity House Yacht 'crowded with the rising young mariners of the town', was the first to enter the

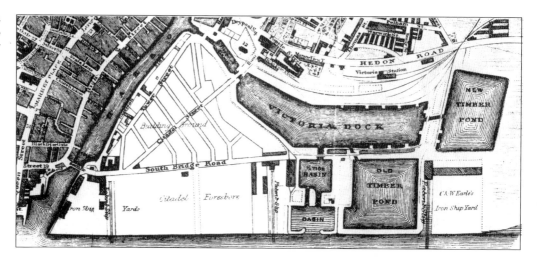

Victoria Dock.
(Goodwill & Lawson,
1869).

new dock, accompanied by the Paddle Steamer *Lion*, the latter having upwards of 1,500 people on board.

The air rang with the cheers of the crowd, who had assembled to witness the spectacle. (The P.S. *Lion* was reputed to be the first ever iron ship to be built in a Hull shipyard, and she was lengthened and converted into a screw vessel in 1854.)

The original area of the dock, with basins, was over 12 acres, and the area was calculated to provide accommodation for 120 square-rigged ships. Over the following three years the dock was given a second entrance, through a southern extension known as the

half-tide basin, having a water area of three acres, which still survives today as a settling pool for fresh water. The second entrance was provided with a 60-foot wide lock, (18.2 m) with a depth over the sill of 27 feet 6 inches. The entry from the half-tide basin into the dock was made through a 50-foot wide (15.2 m) lock entry, over which spanned the Hartley Bridge. The bridge was designed by John B. Hartley and thus bears his name. It has been restored and can be seen close by Sequana Court.

Ironically, around the time that the dock was being developed, the 'Archimedes' screw, or propeller, was

P.S. Lion *(to the right of centre) and* Calder *of Selby.*

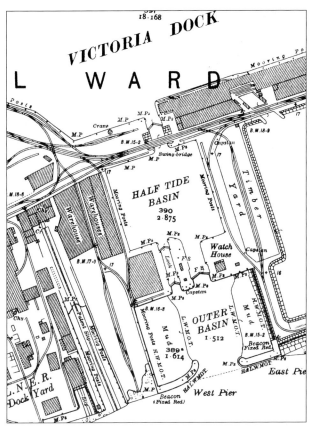

Victoria Dock: the Half Tide Basin and Outer Basin. (Ordnance Survey, 1928).

This area, which had previously formed the moat, was filled and levelled to form an area for timber storage.

The dock incorporated three large timber ponds, two having an area of over 14 acres and the other having an area of just over 11 acres. The ponds served two purposes: one was simply for the storage of large baulks of timber and the other was to make their handling easier. The water level in the timber ponds was regulated by means of a sluice gate from the main dock. As a point of interest, in the 1870s it was thought that one of the Victoria Dock timber ponds could be made deeper and provided with a lock entry to the Humber, in order to accommodate the Hull fleet of fishing smacks. The fleet at that time comprised around 400 vessels of about 60 tons each. It was then based in the Albert Dock and was being subject to much harassment by the operators of larger vessels. However, the plan was thwarted, since all those concerned with fishing, estimated at around 20,000 people in the 1880s, with far more employed ashore than at sea, lived to the west of the River Hull within a few hundred yards of Hessle Road and near to Albert Dock apart from a few of the more prosperous smack owners. This factor above all others was deemed sufficient reason to prevent any move to the eastern side of the river. Eventually St. Andrews Dock was built in 1883, originally for the coal trade but later used for fish.

The York and North Midland Railway Company obtained powers on 30 June 1852 to build a railway line to serve Victoria Dock, since prior to that time goods were moved in, around and off the dock by horse-drawn carts and rullies. The Victoria Dock Line was developed to serve the marshalling yards, which lay to the west of the River Hull and the company realised that goods could be transported more efficiently by the provision of rail access to the new dock. The line was 3.25 miles long, branching out of

perfected as a means of propulsion for ships. Initially, it was considered that screws were too weak to propel a steamship – and there was a risk of their falling off. Loss of the screw was indeed a major hazard. It explains why even the biggest ocean steamships carried auxiliary sail until the 1880s, when the problems were solved. Thus, when this method of propulsion was brought into use, paddle boxes began to disappear, as older ships were converted to the new means of propulsion and newly built ships were designed for it from the outset. The dock was extended again in 1863, this time to the eastern end by a further eight acres, bringing the total water area up to 25 acres. Later the same year the Dock Company obtained possession of the rough ground to the north side of the former Citadel.

Boys playing on the Timber Pond.

the Hull-Selby line near Anlaby Road, running in a semi-circle around the outskirts of Hull at low level and terminating at the Victoria Dock station near to Hedon Road. The line crossed all the main roads leading out of Hull and necessitated the building of six level crossings.

Due to the level nature of the land the line was easy to build and opened to freight traffic on 16 May 1853. The only formidable obstacle was the crossing of the River Hull, and this was achieved by the construction in 1852 of a swing bridge at Wilmington, to the design of engineer Thomas Cabry. The present swing bridge replaced this bridge in 1905. The reason for constructing a swing bridge was that on high tides shipping moved to and from the wharves situated up river of the railway line. By law shipping has always had the right of way over road and rail traffic.

Once the line had opened, a suburban passenger service began on 1 June 1853, one of the earliest in the country outside London. Trains began their journey from Railway Street station and originally, so it would seem, passengers were picked up at stops wherever the line crossed the main roads! Railway stations were later built at Stepney, Sculcoates and Southcoates. At first the services were well patronised but interest soon waned and the number of trains was reduced. Then in October 1854, three months after the York and North Midland Railway became a part of the North Eastern Railway, the passenger service ceased altogether. The Victoria Dock line was destined to have no passenger traffic for the next ten years, although the Victoria Dock railway station had become the passenger terminus of the Hull and Holderness Railway in 1853.

The alignment of the Victoria Dock branch line can still be traced on the ground of modern Hull. It is the level line which led north and east from Paragon station to Botanic, which is where a new station was built (originally called Cemetery Gates), although the track is now lifted. The track then went across Spring Bank/ Park Road, where a crossing keeper's cottage survives, to Stepney, where the Stepney station of 1852-3 by the Hull architect, William Botterill, survives and is now a Grade II listed building. The line was then laid across the Beverley and Barmston drain (the bridge is now demolished) past the Hull and Barnsley Company's Sculcoates Goods Station at Wincolmlee, now another Grade II listed building. The line crossed the Wilmington swing bridge over the River Hull and then ran across Stoneferry Road, south across Dansom Lane, where a pair of crossing-keepers' cottages by William Botterill were demolished recently.

The line of the Mount Pleasant roadway marks the former alignment of track south from Dansom Lane to Holderness Road, where the Southcoates station stood. There was a branch line from here to the Seward Street, Drypool Goods Station, where a signboard remained until quite recently. The line then swung west to enter Victoria Dock. The coming of the railway age meant that goods and people could be transported quickly, easily and relatively cheaply, and the effect on the movement of goods to and from the docks in Hull was profound. Goods traffic was so heavy that trains actually had to queue to get on to the Hull docks.

Each dock office reported daily to the Hull Wagon Control to advise them of the situation regarding the numbers of railway wagons on their docks and reporting on the number of empty wagons, vans and bogie bolsters, how many more would be required for loading and the number of loaded wagons awaiting dispatch.

Trainloads of empty wagons were dispatched daily to Hull from Doncaster, Kings Cross, Nottingham, Whitemoor, Woodford and York. Pilot engines took the loaded wagons to the vast marshalling yards to the west of Hull, where trains were assembled for dispatch to all parts of the British Isles.

Victoria Dock presented many advantages for shippers: it had extensive railway lines and sidings on the dockside and also had extensive quay accommodation, besides numerous sheds for the storage of goods. The dock was equipped with both fixed and moveable steam and hydraulic cranes, one of which could raise a weight of 60 tons. Three coal hoists were available for bunkering ships or for making shipments of coal. It was also close to the North Eastern Railway Drypool Goods Station, from which goods could be rapidly dispatched to their destinations.

Although the timber trade was planned at the outset as the dominant trade at Victoria Dock, it was a trade that had its drawbacks, since it was mainly seasonal. The Baltic ports were completely frozen in during the winter months and thus the trade in timber from that area ceased. As a consequence, the dockworkers were frequently laid off at the hardest time of the year. Because of this, attempts were made to achieve a more even balance of trade and thus the dock became used for the importation of live foreign cattle. An extensive Foreign Cattle Depot was built complete with slaughterhouses and chill rooms. Cattle from North and South American ships were landed at Hull every week. The dock also became used for the importation of seed, nitrates of soda and guano. This latter commodity was widely used as a fertiliser in the years before the Germans invented chemical fertilisers, out of sheer necessity, during the First World War. Guano is the product of the droppings of millions of seabirds over a period of hundreds of years. It was imported into Hull from Peru in such quantity that four large brick-built, slate-roofed warehouses with a total capacity of 40,000 tons were provided to store the product on the dock. The last of these, Warehouse 16, stood opposite the spot where the Sequana Court apartments presently stand on Southbridge Road, i.e. on the site presently occupied by the Surgery. The building was used for the construction of caravans until early 1990, when sadly it was demolished.

Despite the generally successful attempts to achieve a greater diversity of trade, timber remained as the principal commodity shipped through the dock, particularly for the Scandinavian timber trade. In that connection the regular shipping lines between Hull and Finland used the dock, as did the Wilson Line vessels which ran to the Baltic ports. At the peak of the season, in spring and summer, the volume of trade was such that it outgrew the handling and storage facility of any one dock. This explains why, for many years after the opening of Victoria Dock, small sailing vessels continued to berth in Queen's Dock, bringing cargoes of the poorer quality timber from the Baltic ports of Riga and Reval and also from Lithuania. The poorer quality timber was used mainly for box making. However, once bigger steamships began to use Queen's Dock, this trade was eventually driven to Victoria Dock.

Victoria Dock was laid out under tenancy agreements for the storage of sawn wood received by importers and merchants. Rail sidings served all tenancies, and the bulk of the timber was moved to these areas on bogies after discharge from vessels. The bogie system of handling sawn wood from ship to tenancy was unique to the port of Hull, having originated on the North Eastern Railway and is best described as a system of 'moveable quays'.

They proved so successful that a similar type appeared in the 1880s on the Hull and Barnsley Railway's Alexandra Dock. The London and North Eastern Railway, the successor to both of these companies, continued to renew and build the bogies. By the 1950s all were concentrated at Victoria Dock. Each bogie carried a load of about 2½ standards of timber, weighing around seven tons, which was carried on a frame consisting of three cross members, the timber being roped down to hooks fitted on either side of the bogie. The bogie was fitted with small diameter rail wheels which ran on a standard gauge railway track. However, the iron-bound dead buffers were not normal railway standard height or width, so, to assist in moving them around, small dock shunting locomotives were fitted with additional dead buffer beams.

The London and North Eastern Railway later introduced road tractors fitted with steel buffer beams and chain links at either end. Coupled together, the loaded bogies were moved to the stacking grounds, or storage sidings, pending sorting, stacking, or transhipment of the wood to rail or road vehicles for delivery to distant customers.

Many of the well-known local names engaged in the timber trade had estates on the dock. The 1937 edition of Kelly's Directory lists: T. W. Allen & Sons Ltd.; Wm. White Bartle; Beecroft & Whiteman Ltd.; Denny, Mott & Dickson Ltd.; Holdsworth & Midgley Ltd.; Horsley, Smith & Co. Ltd.; A. Laver & Co.; H. Newsum, Sons & Co.; Wm. W. North Ltd.; Sanderson Brothers (Timber Importers) Ltd.; Wood's Timber Co.; and Wright & Co. Horsley, Smith & Company was probably the biggest and best known of the local importers and merchants dealing in timber and their story in the history of the dock is both pioneering and well documented. The firm moved to Victoria Dock from Queen's Dock, renting space from the Hull Dock Company on which they erected what were possibly the first sheds for the storage of timber in Hull. The company began their move to Victoria Dock in 1874, when they acquired an area in one of the timber ponds. By 1881 the whole of their timber stock had been moved to Victoria Dock, leaving only the offices at Queen's Dock. They continued to develop at Victoria Dock over the ensuing years; however, they lost some of their timber storage sheds during the air raids of 1941. The severe damage sustained through enemy action to Victoria Dock in both World Wars is the subject of Chapter 15.

In 1953 the Coronation shed was erected, a huge structure 440 feet (134.1 m) long and 163 feet (49.6 m) wide, made entirely of wood. Named to commemorate the Coronation of Queen Elizabeth II on 2 June 1953, the shed was described as 'an act of faith' at an official lunch held at the Royal Station Hotel on 3 December 1953, to celebrate its inauguration. The year 1967 became a turning point for the company. It had 8.5 acres of land leased at Victoria Dock but in the same year the Docks Board announced proposals for the future development of the Dock, which would deprive the company of all but three acres of their 8.5-acre holding, including the office, the Coronation shed and the canteen. The Docks Board also intimated that they might be closing the Dock in the not too distant future. Despite the offer of other sites, the company had already seen the advantages of an off-dock site and decided to relocate its Baltic Mill to a new 11.5-acre site at Tower House, Marfleet. The remaining timber stocks which belonged to the company were removed from Victoria Dock in December 1969.

Following the Second World War, the docks were geared to the changed demands of peacetime. Before 1947 the docks were often a job of last resort. Competing with the regular dockworkers would be those newly redundant and others who could find no other form of work. A docker interviewed for the Remould Theatre Company in 1992, for the 'Hull City' play, recalled: 'Everybody came on the dock, if you were a forger, you come out of prison, you go on the docks. Ex-boxers, ex-wrestlers, ex-everything, we had them on the docks, they landed on the docks . . . one Monday morning I went on Victoria Dock and the dock was full of ships and they were looking for men. I got a job and we were carrying from the ship onto shore, onto bogies. Every other man on that gang but me had just come out of gaol. I was the only honest man there.'

Unloading timber from the ships was hard work, especially during a hot summer. The deal carriers had to run up and down a swaying, bouncing plank and with amazing balance carry lengths of timber on their shoulders. Despite wearing a leather shoulder 'saddle' to prevent chafing, they would develop blisters, and over a period suffer from a dropped shoulder. It was reckoned that you could always tell a deal carrier because he walked lop-sided. Once they got home a member of their family would have to pick out the inevitable splinters which got stuck in their necks. The work was seasonal and, after a lay-off, the men would rub methylated spirits into their shoulders before returning to work because their skin had gone soft. Quite often they would return home with their work shirt stuck to bare blisters and it would have to be soaked before it could be peeled off their back.

Because the dockers were never issued with safety or working clothes they wore whatever they could lay their hands on, including old suits. Most wore neckerchiefs but they all wore caps to work, as in the hold of a ship it was the only protection available for the head. When they arrived home they would leave their clothes in the back yard – they were never thrown away – and put them on the next morning, even though they might have stunk to high heaven. In spite of the hardships, or perhaps because of them, dockers formed a close community and had a good rapport, usually finding the time for a joke or a good story. Some say there was more entertainment on the docks than you would ever get at a show or from the television.

One funny story which went the rounds concerned pit props arriving from Russia that were covered in snow. On those occasions the dockers had to get into the hold and place wires and slings underneath them, but on one particular occasion they were so badly iced up and dangerous that the dockers called in the union. The official said he was unable to do anything about it as it was Russian snow and not English. The humour and comradeship made a hard job easier and, perhaps not surprisingly, most were glad to get back to work after a holiday.

During the 1950s and 60s pit props in their hundreds of thousands were imported through Victoria Dock for the coal mining industry and hundreds of stacks could be seen stored on the dock estate awaiting transfer by rail wagons to the coal mines of West Yorkshire. There were frequent fires, especially in summer, and some spectacular blazes resulted. By return came thousands of tons of coal for export. The coal-carrying rail wagons were picked up individually by the coal hoist at the eastern end of the dock and were then emptied into the waiting ship alongside

In 1958, Hull was the largest softwood importing port in the UK. There were over 80 firms involved in the import of timber and saw milling, the market for timber expanded by the post-war building boom. Many of those firms had storage sheds and offices on Victoria Dock. Ships from the Soviet Union were by then, common callers to the dock during the summer 'soft-wood season'. In 1964 the entrance to Victoria Dock from the River Hull was closed, the area between the lock gates being in-filled with concrete and a permanent roadway placed over it linking Tower Street with St. Peter's Street.

The eventual decline of the Dock was due to many factors, including the containerisation and packaging of cargo, the importation of prepared timber, the introduction of Ro-Ro ships, together with improved mechanical handling systems on the ships and on land, and the drastic reduction of rail-freight following the recommendations of the Beeching Report. Other significant factors were the increasing number of labour disputes, the restrictive practices of the Dock Labour Scheme, and what employers saw as excessive labour costs which caused shippers to look at smaller non-registered ports for their business. The Dock was closed to commercial traffic on 1 February 1970 and was filled in during 1971.

The area which had been Victoria Dock stood largely unused for many years, the main water area was filled in with building and household waste and, except for a few small enterprises which carried on business, mainly around the half-tide basin, the area was left derelict.

Albert Draper, a well-known local scrap merchant, used the slipway for a number of years, breaking up, amongst other things, many vessels of the Hull distant-water trawler fleet, at least one of the Humber Ferries and even one of H.M. submarines. The vessels due to be scrapped were floated from the Humber on to a cradle at the open end of the slipway. This was timed to happen when the state of the tide was just right, as a falling tide ensured that the vessel dropped securely to the cradle bed. The cradle was fitted with rail-type wheels which ran on a track fixed to the slipway bed. This arrangement allowed the vessel to be hauled up the slipway by means of a winch.

The red-brick Engine House at the northern end of the slipway pool formerly housed the engine and winch, used to pull vessels from the Humber, is all that remains as a reminder of this activity. The actual engine and winch can now be seen in a glass case on the east side of Hull Marina. The half-tide basin also continued to perform a useful function for several years after the closure of the dock. The lads of Trinity House School (there were no lasses then!) practised lifeboat drill in the basin and could often be seen rowing vigorously around, urged on by the prompting of their instructor. The half-tide basin now performs the more mundane function of a ground water balancing system for the village.

Hull City Council acquired the 150-acre site of the former dock from Associated British Ports in 1987 and formed the Victoria Dock Company in partnership with Bellway (Urban Renewals) Ltd. to oversee the re-development of the dock into housing. Hull City Council is the minority partner owning 40% of the company's equity, Bellway holding the remaining 60%. It was the intention of the new company to transform the area of the former dock into a community with over 1,200 dwellings at a projected cost then of over £343 million. Work began on the project on 11 May 1988 and was anticipated to be finished by summer 2000.

Sources:
Gillett and MacMahon, *Hull*.
History of the Port of Hull.
Christopher Ketchell, *Notes on Victoria Dock* (Local History Unit, Hull College).
Thompson, *Hull Docklands*.
Michael Thompson, *The Railways of Hull and the East Riding* (Cherry Burton, 1992).

Chapter Eight
Shipbuilders to the World: Charles and William Joel Earle

The two Earle brothers, Charles and William Joel, began in business as engineers, millwrights and general smiths, establishing themselves in 1845 at the west end of Junction Dock in premises formerly occupied by James Livingston, known as the Junction Foundry, off Waterhouse Lane in Hull. They were the sons of Thomas Earle, who, together with his brother, George, founded the Earles Cement Company in Hull, which later became part of the Blue Circle Group.

Some time in late 1851 Charles and William expanded their business by renting out an area of land at the eastern end of the newly opened Victoria Dock, which they laid out as a shipyard. The first vessel built at the new shipyard by C. & W. Earle was named the *Minister Thorbeck*, of 100 tons, built for the Zwolle Steam Navigation Company and launched on 15 March 1853. A screw-driven ship, she was 130 feet (39.6 m) long and fitted with a 60-horse power engine. This vessel sailed out of the Humber for Holland for the next 20 years before being transferred to London.

During their first ten years at the shipyard, vessels had to be launched directly into Victoria Dock, since the yard did not have access to the Humber and this placed a limitation on the size of vessel that could be constructed.

Launches into the dock were not without incident. On 13 July 1854 a tragedy occurred when the iron-hulled sailing ship, *Dowthorpe*, built for Stuart

and Company, was launched. On the morning of the launch a huge crowd had forced their way through the dock gates and then assembled at the dockside to witness the event. An estimated 300 crossed the gangplank and boarded the *Dowthorpe* packing her decks, many perching precariously on top of the deckhouses.

Surprisingly the launch was allowed to go ahead as planned at 11.00 am Miss Baird christened the vessel, which entered the water with a terrific force, just missing the dolphin in the middle of the dock. A cry then went up, 'Sally her' and the unofficial passengers ran backwards and forwards across the deck, causing her to rock from side to side. Suddenly, one of the restraining ropes broke and the unballasted ship quickly keeled over, throwing scores of people into the dock. Four people were drowned, two of them shipyard workers. Despite this inauspicious start the ship made a successful trading voyage to Bombay and returned to Earle's two years later for lengthening. The *Howden*,

Minister Thorbeck.

Dowthorpe.

the *Hawk* and the *Alert* followed the *Dowthorpe* into the dock. Engines and fittings for these craft were carted across the town from the Junction Foundry and the boilers, after being plugged, were lowered into the dock, where they floated until ready to be hoisted into position.

The whaler *Diana*, built as yard number 20 and launched into Victoria Dock in 1857, forms the centrepiece of what is one of the most evocative paintings ever to depict the tough and dangerous life of the Hull men engaged in whale hunting. Painted by Richard Dodd Widdas (1826-1885), an accomplished local marine artist, it depicts the *Diana* trapped in pack ice whilst on a whaling trip in the Arctic, in the winter of 1866, during the course of which her captain and almost a quarter of her crew died. Seen by the cold light of the moon, the crew have temporarily abandoned ship and the bulky figure of the ship's Surgeon, Charles Edward Smith, and his Scotch terrier, Gyp, appear in the foreground. Surgeon Smith kept a journal of the voyage recording the harrowing events, and the painting, which was completed shortly after the return of the *Diana* to Hull, is most likely based on the sketches and descriptions given to the artist by him.

It was around this time that Martin Samuelson had opened his shipyard at the western end of Victoria Dock. He proceeded to turn ships out at a prodigious rate from Sammy's Point, which had the advantage of permitting launches directly into the Humber. In 1863, no doubt inspired by his apparent success, the Earle brothers purchased 47 acres of land along the Humber bank for £23,838. 9s. 0d. This was an important advance since the new acquisition now allowed their ships to be launched directly into the Humber and also removed the restriction on the size of vessels, which the Victoria Dock location imposed.

The last vessel to be launched into the dock in 1862, was yard number 72, the *Dido* of 1409 tons, for Thomas Wilson and Son. Between 1853 and 1871 one third of their output was ordered by Wilson's, who at the turn of the century would claim to be the largest privately owned steamship company in the world. Yard number 73, the *Cecile,* launched in April 1863, marked the first launch directly into the Humber. This date also marked the period when Martin Samuelson was beginning to run into financial difficulties through his lack of working capital. The Earle's yard operated successfully for the next seven years, launching an average of almost seven ships per year, when on 17 August 1870 Charles Earle died suddenly outside his house in Charlotte Street. He was interred at the Hull General Cemetery,

Spring Bank. His brother William was in poor health at this time and so negotiations were opened for the formation of a joint stock company, the inauguration of which was marked by the launch of the *S.S. Oxfordshire* on 12 October 1871. Sadly, William Joel Earle had died at his home in Hessle on the previous day, aged 49. The two brothers had made an important and lasting contribution to the history of shipbuilding in Hull.

Sir Edward James Reed had been selected to be the Chairman and Managing Director of the new company, Earle's Shipbuilding and Engineering Co. He was a naval architect of great renown with an international reputation, who had only recently resigned his post as naval architect and chief constructor to the Admiralty. His brief association with Earles, from 1871 to 1875, put the company on the world stage. Earle's were asked to build a steam yacht for the Grand Duke Alexander Alexandrovitch of Russia. Reed personally designed the yacht, which was ready for launching on Saturday, 5 July 1873 as yard number 189. The Grand Duke came to Hull from London on 4 July to witness the launch, arriving at Paragon Station to be welcomed by Sir William Wright, chairman of the Dock Company, Sir Edward Reed and the civic heads of Hull. He was taken from the station to the shipyard, where he made a selection of items for the internal fittings of the yacht. The next day, at about 2.00 pm, the launch took place to the strains of the Russian National Anthem. Miss Cissy Reed, the daughter of the Chairman, named the 160-ton vessel *Slavyanka*. Later, in August of that year, the yacht was used by His Royal Highness during Cowes week at the Isle of Wight, where he was the guest of the Prince and Princess of Wales. The yacht proved to be too small for the number of guests the Grand Duke had invited on board, so as a result Sir Edward was invited to the Isle of Wight where he met him at Queen Victoria's Osborne House and received instructions to build a much larger vessel.

The 800 ton *Czarevna* was launched by Miss Reed on 1 September 1874. The three-masted, schooner-rigged vessel raised steam shortly after entering the water. The saloons were of polished oak, walnut and rosewood, upholstered in velvet and deck houses of polished teak. Davits, stanchions and anchor were of galvanised iron and she was rigged with galvanised rope.

Czarevna, built for the Grand Duke Alexander Alexandrovitch of Russia.

An engine of 130 horse-power by Penn of Greenwich turned a propeller of 11-feet 6-inch diameter, to achieve an average speed of 9-10 knots. Four guns were also carried. Captain Raguly, who was to captain the new yacht, must have been immensely proud of his new command. During trials at the mouth of the Humber a maximum speed of 14 knots was achieved and, after satisfactory completion of the trials, the yacht left for St. Petersburg at the end of that week.

The Khedive of Egypt ordered an iron-hulled paddle-steamer of shallow draught for use on the Nile. Reed designed a ship of 242 tons, described as having great elegance and powered by a pair of engines developing 625 hp which gave an estimated speed of 18 knots. Built as yard number 198, it was named by Cissy Reed and launched into the Humber as the *Bosphorus* in 1875.

The yard constructed the mundane in addition to the magnificent, launching barges and tugs at regular intervals. Perhaps the most remarkable, ingenious and arguably the most unusual vessel ever to have been launched into the Humber was the *Bessemer* designed by Reed for the London, Chatham and Dover Railway Company. This vessel incorporated Sir Henry Bessemer's 'Swinging Saloon'. He experienced a particularly rough crossing on the Channel which gave him a serious attack of seasickness, and so he determined to find a method of overcoming the violent motion of a ship in heavy seas. His idea was revolutionary and probably a hundred years before its time!

He designed a system for a passenger saloon, which was intended to cancel out the movement of a ship. The 75-feet-long by 35-feet-wide saloon, which was 20 feet high, was hung on pivots. An arrangement of hydraulic rams was installed, one at each end and two close together in the middle, all of which extended to a little below the mid-height of the saloon but above the centre of gravity. So, in effect, the saloon was not freely suspended as the name implied. Hydraulic engines pumped water to each of the supports, controlled by a large gyroscope situated between the two middle jacks. The massive force of the very heavy disc spinning in the horizontal plane created a highly stable system which moved the valves of his hydraulic system to keep the swinging saloon as persistently horizontal as the gyroscope itself.

This arrangement was intended to cancel out the motion imparted by the rolling of the ship or the effects of wind on the upper works of the saloon. Ideally, the system would work automatically, but if this failed, as it frequently did, there was a console at which an engineer sat. By carefully manipulating a collection of levers he could adjust the trim in such a way that the motion was kept to a minimum. This was an ambitious proposition, since the actions of one man had to be relied on to adjust the level of the swinging superstructure which was being subject to different stresses every second; it was thought that, with experience, he would be able to anticipate the motion of the vessel. However, the *Bessemer* did not see sufficient active service for anyone to become proficient.

The saloon itself was installed amidships, occupying a 90-foot space in the middle of a breastwork 254 feet long and 8 feet high, on a hull with an overall length of 350 feet and 40 feet wide at the maximum. Each end of the double-ended vessel, for a distance of almost 50 feet, had a surprisingly low freeboard of only 4 feet. In rough seas the water would wash over, but this was not so important, since there was little need for anyone to be there, except when leaving or entering port. The middle section had a further eight-feet-high breastwork erected all along its 254-feet length, and this breastwork supported a deck with smoking rooms, refreshment bars and cabins for families. Entrance ports on the outer part of the paddle boxes led to the swinging saloon by two broad staircases meeting at a common landing, from which ran a flexible passage.

The interior was fitted out in a style which was regarded as the epitome of luxury. At the head of the stairs, there was an entrance hall and a cloakroom, rather like that of a theatre. There were bars, retiring rooms for gentlemen, a smoking room, described as being worthy of a West End club, an enclosed promenade deck, nine private cabins (with sofas stuffed with feathers and finished in maroon Morocco leather, and with fixed mahogany trays for bottles and glasses at either end) and two state cabins for Very Important Persons. A dozen spiral columns supported the roof. In the recesses formed by them, there were comfortable sofas covered with Russian leather. There were other sofas in the centre of the room, and the carpet was a crimson velvet affair of arabesque design. At the far end, as if to match the facilities for gentlemen at the entrance, there were retiring rooms for ladies – where they could withdraw from the public gaze, 'hidden demurely by

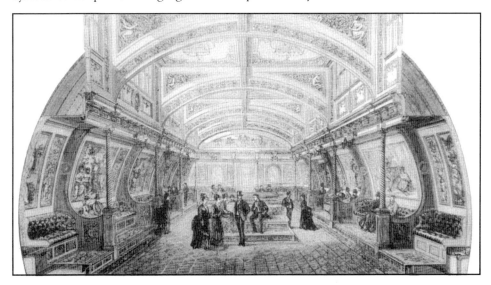

The saloon of the P.S. Bessemer.

silk curtains to match the carpeting'. The crew accommodation was also of a very high standard as was the second-class accommodation, which was independent of the saloon.

The *Bessemer* was fitted with four paddles, two in tandem at each side, though the stern paddles turned faster than the 32 revolutions per minute of the forward paddles since they were taking the wash of the leading paddles. The engines were expected to develop 5,000 horse power and to give the ship a speed of 20 miles per hour. There were many innovations, which then were modern: all orders from the bridge were conveyed to the engineer by telegraph and the levers were so concentrated that a man could work all the engines by himself if necessary. There was efficient ventilation, an adequate kitchen, a derrick to handle passengers' luggage and a compartmented hold to avoid the tossing about of the luggage on the voyage, which was then a considerable nuisance to cross-Channel travellers. Four life-boats and two patented rafts were carried. This unique vessel, which at 1,886 tons gross was about three times the size of a conventional cross-Channel steamer, was launched into the Humber on 24 September 1874 by Mrs. Bessie Wright, granddaughter of Sir Henry Bessemer, with the shipyard, riverside and neighbouring piers crowded with hundreds of spectators. Due to industrial disputes, completion of the fitting-out was delayed, and it was not until March 1875 that she left for London, attracting thousands of visitors to the Millwall Docks. On the journey south her two pairs of engines had driven the four paddle wheels (two on either side) of 27 feet 10 inches diameter at a rate of about 32 r.p.m. to maintain a speed of 14-16 knots, despite a heavy cross-sea.

On 10 April the *Bessemer* made a trial trip from Dover under the command of Captain Pittock, with Lord Alfred Padget, Admiral Spencer Robinson (a director of Earle's), Sir Sidney Waterlow, deputy chairman of the railway company, and Captain Davies, chairman of the Bessemer Steamboat Company, all on board. The great size of the ferry made access to Granville Dock extremely difficult and so, to prevent a great waste of time in manoeuvring, it was decided to leave her off the Admiralty Pier on the outer harbour when services began.

A special day trip to Paris was announced for 3 May 1875, and when she arrived off Calais after the one and a half hour trip from Dover the captain ordered the engine room to reduce speed. The way went off her and, caught by the tide, she failed to answer to the helm and so demolished about 50-60 yards (45.7-54.85 m) of the eastern pier, though without serious damage to herself. A week later she collided with Dover Pier and the decision was made not to persevere with this unique vessel, which was withdrawn from service and scrapped. The Bessemer Company went into liquidation owing Earle's £17,000, quite apart from the losses accruing from a shareholding in this ill-fated venture. Further losses of £40,000 were incurred on vessels built for the North German Lloyd Line, which threw the yard into financial disarray, forcing the sale of a parcel of land to the Dock Company to raise some cash. The hard realisation had to be faced that too many contracts had been accepted without provision being made for the soaring costs of labour and materials.

Sir Edward Reed resigned as Chairman at the end of May 1875 in order that he could concentrate on his parliamentary career, having been elected that year as the Member for Pembroke. His fellow director, John Brown, founder of the large Sheffield steel company which bore his name, succeeded him. He was the first person to employ the Bessemer process for steel production and to manufacture rolled steel plate to armour iron ships. He was a particularly useful man to have serving on the board of the company during Earle's first venture into the building of warships, and his expertise would remain in demand for the next two decades.

Another key figure in this next phase of the company's history was A. E. Seaton. Born in Padstow in Cornwall in 1848, he joined Earle's as a marine engineer designer, was appointed Chief Draughtsman in 1874, Engineering Manager in 1879 and General Manager in 1884, finally being elected to the Board two years later. He became a lecturer in Marine Engineering at the Royal Naval College at a later period in his life.

Regular orders from the Wilson Line proved to be an important mainstay during the next decade, as the

The Bessemer *collided with the pier at Calais, 3 May, 1875.*

company found it difficult to compete on price with the North East shipbuilders. Foreign orders slumped compared with those obtained during Reed's time as chairman. This loss was, however, compensated for to some extent by the increase in orders from British firms, and a number of contracts were signed with the Admiralty between 1880 and 1890.

The development of the triple expansion steam engine proved to be an important feature of the company's progress at this period under the direction of A. E. Seaton. Earle's was one of the first companies to produce this type of engine on a commercial scale. The triple expansion steam engine revolutionised shipping by allowing vessels to keep to a reliable schedule of arrivals and departures. The *Draco,* a liner built for the Wilson Line, launched in 1882, was powered by this powerful and economical new engine. Fed by a boiler of 100 p.s.i., she achieved a saving on fuel of nearly one quarter when compared with her predecessors, using more primitive forms of compound engines.

In 1880 the yard had built its first steel-hulled vessel, the 4,000-ton giant *Assyrian Monarch* for the Royal Exchange Shipping Company of London, and in 1882, they launched the first-ever purpose-built steam trawler, named the *Zodiac* for the newly formed Grimsby Steam Trawling Company. Overall the trawler was 98 feet (29.9 m) long, 20 feet (6 m) wide, with a hold depth of 10 feet 6 inches (3.25 m).

Earle's were placed on the list of Government Approved yards as a result of the technical advances the company had made and their ability to fulfil orders to time. As a consequence they were given the order for the belted cruiser *Narcissus* in 1885. The cruiser at 300 feet (91.45 m) long, with 10 guns, had a displacement of 5,000 tons. She was launched on 15 December 1886.

A five-year rapid expansion plan to provide the Royal Navy with modern warships was proposed by Lord George Hamilton in 1889 at a proposed cost of £21.5 million and was accepted by Parliament. Earle's were immediate beneficiaries of the plan, receiving orders for the first-class cruisers *Endymion* and *St. George*. The former was launched on 22 June 1891 by Lady Salisbury. H.M.S. *Endymion* was a twin-screwed vessel of 7,350 tons displacement, designed to reach a maximum speed of 20 knots at full power from two independent sets of triple expansion engines and five

boilers at a pressure of 155 p.s.i. The double bottom was divided into 27 watertight compartments and the machinery spaces were protected by glacis Armour 6 inches (15.25 cm) thick with a protective deck over the greater proportion of the vessel, up to 5 inches (12.7 cm) thick, though most of it being half that depth, diminishing to 2 inches (5.08 cm) at either end. The conning tower had 12 inches (30.5 cm) compound armour and armoured communication tubes. Ready-use magazines lay between the protective and main decks for supplying the casement guns and the 6-inch (15.52 cm) guns mounted on the upper deck.

Triumphal arches were built in preparation for the launch. The North Eastern Railway built one in Paragon Street and the Corporation built two, one in Whitefriargate and one in Witham. Earle's themselves built a huge arch across outside their yard in Hedon Road, consisting of two castellated towers, between which had been placed four large model steamers, two merchant vessels, the other two being naval vessels, with the motto written beneath them:

'WHO COMMANDS THE SHIPS
COMMANDS THE SEAS,
WHO COMMANDS THE SEAS
COMMANDS THE WORLD'

After the launch a banquet was held in the Dock Offices to celebrate the yard's magnificent achievement in completing the vessel, receiving the order in 1889 and launching in 1891. Serious delays, however, caused by industrial action and liaison problems with the government inspectorate, meant that the fitting out was not complete until May 1893.

The sister ship, *H.M.S. St. George,* was launched on 23 June 1892 by Lady Hamilton, in the presence of her husband, together with Vice Admiral Sir F. W. Richards, Rear Admiral King, Captain Gamble, the company directors, local politicians and ship owners. Excursion trains brought large numbers of visitors to see the great event and an estimated 15,000 people crammed into the yard, including 200 special guests who occupied the two stands erected around the bows of the ship. Lady Hamilton cut the tape with a pair of golden scissors, thus releasing a bottle of wine which refused to break until she seized it up and hurled it against the ship's side to great applause. The *St. George* slowly entered the water and was then towed to Alexandra Dock for the boilers and engines to be fitted.

H.M.S. Narcissus,
launched 15 December, 1886.

Strikes seriously delayed her completion and she left Hull for Portsmouth in December 1893, four years after the original order had been placed. Additional problems had also been experienced because of the lack of detail in the plans supplied by the Admiralty. Earle's made a claim to the Government to compensate for the financial losses which resulted from arguments over the specifications. On the plus side many lessons were learned from the construction of such a large and complicated vessel, which led to new advances in shipyard technique. Despite the many problems, other orders were received from the Admiralty and duly accepted.

Whilst the two cruisers were under construction, two new patent slips were completed in the spring of 1892. They were situated close by the engine works and a railway line led from them straight to the engine shops. Propellers, shafts and other components could be transported quickly and cheaply, keeping down the cost of ship repairs. Each slip was 340 feet (103.6 m) long, with a cradle of 120 feet (36.6 m) capable of being extended to 140 feet (42.7 m) overall. The cradle allowed a vessel of 400 tons deadweight to be hauled out of the water to allow the bottom to be examined and repainted ready for the next tide. This new development brought the total number of patent slips in the company's hands to six, four in the main yard, one adjacent (from the old yard) and one at New Holland.

The yard continued to receive orders for fishing vessels from the Grimsby trawler owners and important national and overseas naval contracts were awarded to the yard during the late 1800s, including a warship for the Republic of Haiti and two third-class cruisers for the Royal Navy. However, the yard continued to be be-devilled by labour problems and the company's Annual Report of 1899 pointed out that for 53 weeks of a three-year period, the engineering department was totally paralysed. Not, it should be added, that this was this problem peculiar to Earle's; it was simply the local expression of a nationwide militancy shown by shipyard engineers.

In June 1900 the directors were forced to put the company in voluntary liquidation as a result of the depressed state of the market and a chronic lack of working capital. The following year the company was purchased by Charles Henry Wilson for £170,000. He formed a private limited company with a capital fund of £150,000, bearing the same name as its predecessor. Almost half the output from the yard in the years leading up to the First World War was for the Wilson Line of which Charles Henry Wilson (later Lord Nunburnholme) was a principal shareholder.

As a result, the shipyard was cushioned from the worst effects of the lean years between 1906-1908. The first vessel launched under the new management was the *Swift* in 1902 for the Hull and Netherlands Steamship Company, followed by the *Sappho* for the Wilson Line. This latter vessel also had a dramatic and tragic encounter with the Arctic ice. On 28 November 1915 the *Sappho* left the Russian port of Archangel, bound for Hull with a cargo of pit props. The crew were no doubt looking forward to being home in time for Christmas with their families. However, the ship became stuck in ice, and, despite efforts to break free by continuously dropping the anchor, no progress was made. By Christmas Eve only one week's rations remained and the *Sappho* was still stuck firmly in an icy embrace, by then nine-feet thick. Captain Martin decided that, as the weather was clear, he and the crew, which had by then grown impatient, should abandon ship to walk the 18 miles to the lighthouse at Cross Island. The crew set off, wearing only ordinary sea clothes and their sailors' boots covered by strips of blanket, with the few provisions in packs.

Of the 19 who set out, only three reached land, on 27 December. They followed telegraph poles until they met a Laplander with a sleigh who took them to the village of Sosnovetz, where they were fed and warmed. They returned to Hull on 26 February 1916, but no trace was ever found of the other crew members. The *Sappho* was found in January 1916, about half-way between the islands of Danilof and Morshovetz, roughly ten miles off the mainland, by the icebreaker *Sadko*. The icebreaker could not get near her but sent a search party to board her. It was May 1916 when *Sappho* was next sighted drifting in the White Sea, 30 miles north of Cape Kanin, by the Hammerfest sealer *Alfred Edward*. The sealer took her in tow, intending to reach the nearest harbour. Attempts were made to keep her afloat, using pumps and buckets to reduce the amount of water which had accumulated in the fore hold and engine room. However, a heavy north-west swell which commenced late on 16 May, two days after her discovery, swamped the cargo in the fore hold, causing the *Sappho* to founder, ending another of the many tragic episodes in the maritime history of Hull.

Other vessels continued to be delivered from the yard, including a new lifeboat for the Spurn station in 1903. A product of the boat shed, the vessel had two masts and ten oars and was built at a cost of £700. The Wilson Line launched some of the most luxurious liners that ever sailed from Earle's shipyard and some of the most technically advanced in Edwardian times. An example was the S.S. *Aaro*, launched in 1909 and described as a 'floating hotel', the first ship on the Humber to be equipped with wireless. It steamed at 15 knots and could carry 120 first-class and 60 second-class passengers (who were housed quite lavishly above the engine room). Third-class accommodation was available for 100 in cabins, each of which had four or six berths, at the stern of the ship. She had a spacious first-class dining room panelled in fumed oak which could take more than 100 passengers at each sitting and an equally magnificent lounge panelled in mahogany and fitted with windows of bevelled glass.

The *R.M.S. Eskimo,* a steel vessel of 3,326 tons, completed the following, was considered to be even more magnificent, proving a firm favourite on summer cruises to Norway. The promenade deck had thick plate glass at the fore end, which meant that passengers could sit there in rain or a head wind and observe what was happening from a sheltered position.

Lounge chairs, garden seats and a wireless telegraph office were also situated in this part of the ship. She was converted to a merchant cruiser during the First World War and was captured by the Germans in 1916. The *Eskimo* was returned after the hostilities but was never restored to her former glory and was sold to French owners in 1921 and then was broken up eight years later.

July 1911 saw the trial voyage of the *Bayardo,* which became known as 'The Queen of the Fleet'. Returning from Gothenburg on her thirteenth voyage, almost a year to the day from when she entered service, the 330-feet (100.6 m) long Wilson liner grounded on the Middle Sand, off Alexandra Dock, in thick fog. The passengers were taken off safely, and subsequently many of the fittings were removed, but the vessel broke its back and finally, being declared a hazard to shipping, was demolished by explosive charges.

Thomas Wilson & Sons lost much vital tonnage during the First World War and that, coupled with the troubles in Russia, forced its sale in 1917 to Sir John Ellerman, who originally came from Hull. Earle's however, remained in the hands of the Wilson family, though, following the Great Depression of the 1920s, the company suffered badly and slid inexorably towards final closure. The yard was bought by National Shipbuilding Securities Ltd. in 1932 with the proviso that shipbuilding could not be carried out on the site for the next forty years. The T.S.S. *Sir Richard Greville* of 335 tons, yard number 682, was launched in 1931, the last vessel built at Earle's in a period of activity spanning almost 80 years. Output included 17 warships for the Royal Navy, 148 steamers for the Wilson Line and 284 sets of machinery.

All the tools, machinery and fittings were sold in 1932-33, including one of the great landmarks of the Humber bank, the giant Earle's crane, which was sent to the Far East. It survived the Japanese attack on Kowloon during World War II and remained in use there until the 1950s. The dissolution of this great iron and steel shipbuilding company and the sale of its equipment marked the end of large-scale shipbuilding in Hull.

Sources:
Arthur G. Credland, *Earles of Hull* (Hull, 1982).
Arthur G. Credland, *Maritime Painting in Hull Through Three Centuries* (Hull and Cherry Burton, 1993).
Arthur G. Credland, *The Wilson Line of Hull* (Stroud, 1994).
National Maritime Museum, *The Ship* (1980).

This evocative photograph, entitled 'The Last Man', was taken by Harry Cartlidge in 1933, just before the jib crane at Earles was dismantled and sent to Kowloon.

The S.S. Bayardo aground on the Middes Sand off Alexandra Dock, 1912.

Chapter Nine

To the Brighton of the East: Victoria Dock Railway Station

Although it did not operate for very long, Victoria Dock did have its own passenger Railway Station, sited on Hedon Road, almost opposite Emily Street, and shown on the detail from the Goodwill and Lawson plan of Hull, dated 1869. It was the Hull terminus of the Hull and Holderness Railway Company, which operated a single line between Hull and Withernsea, from 1854 until 1864, when trains were diverted to run into Hull's Paragon Station.

The mid to late 19th century were the boom years in the development of rail travel. The Duke of Wellington opened the 31 miles of the Manchester to Liverpool Line on 15 September 1830 and contrary to expectations, proved to be highly successful for both goods and passengers. They deserted both canal and road travel (by stagecoach and cart) for the speed and cheapness of the railway. This success story encouraged and inspired lines to be considered and built elsewhere. Railway companies mushroomed; over 250,000 navvies were employed in building railways at their peak in 1847. The equipment they used was basic, comprising of picks, shovels and wheelbarrows but their achievement was astonishing, within fifteen years many of the major rail links were in place.

Locally, the pace was no less exhilarating, with proposals for the railway in Hull which was considered both as an outlet port for the developing European market and as a port for the importation of the raw materials required by the distant manufacturers. It was, therefore, almost inevitable that the first proposals for the railways concerned linking Hull with the industrial west of the region. The Leeds to Selby line opened in 1834 and the Hull to Selby line opened 1 July 1840. It did not take too long, however, for the benefits of linking Hull to the coast to be realised and the first line, to Bridlington, was opened 2 October 1846, the resort became such an attraction that, by the Edwardian period, it was known as 'Hull by the sea'.

An even more ambitious plan, based on the success of the Bridlington venture, involved connecting Hull to the coast by as many of the villages in south Holderness as was possible. This prospect formed the vision of Anthony Bannister, a prominent figure in mid-Victorian Hull. He was born in 1817 and became

apprenticed to John Beadle, a merchant ship-owner, rising to become the manager of the Humber Union Steam Shipping Company before striking out and forming his own business. He became a successful fish merchant, ship-owner and coal exporter, based in Humber Street, with many other commercial interests in the rapidly expanding town of Hull. In 1845 Bannister became a town councillor for the North Myton Ward and was elected alderman in 1855. He served as sheriff in 1849 and 1850 before becoming mayor for the first time in 1851, at the age of 34. He became the mayor for a second time in 1855.

There was little in the life of Hull that Bannister did not touch in some way or another. He was also a Justice of the Peace and acted as an arbitrator in a dispute between the owners of fishing vessels and seamen in 1852, earning the gratitude of the United Fishermen's Society, which presented him with a snuff box, for 'services rendered to their body'. He was also one of the instigators in inviting the Queen and Prince Albert to visit Hull and, when they accepted, was made Chairman of the Programme Committee. In 1859, when it was thought likely that war with France would break out, Captain Bannister formed one of the Hull companies of the East Yorkshire Rifle Volunteers, eventually attaining the rank of major. He established the Hull Men's Working Club in 1864 and built a new theatre in Humber Street the same year. It was said of him that his energy and drive, as well as his penchant for colourful language, 'culled from the coal yard and the fishing smack' and delivered in a broad Yorkshire accent, were greatly admired by his contemporaries. His portrait appears to have been painted at the time of his first becoming the Mayor of Hull.

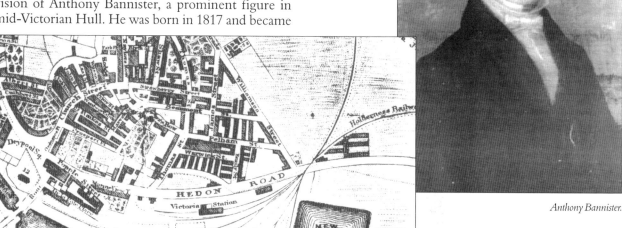

Anthony Bannister.

Victoria Station. (Goodwill & Lawson, 1869).

He was a complex individual, said to be capable of much good but not a man to be crossed, as the following tale will reveal. About the time Bannister was mayor, a certain Henry Storrer owed him £60. Bannister sued him for debt and obtained a verdict in his favour. The debtor could not pay and suffered imprisonment until he could meet the debt. It was paid very soon after but Bannister refused to sign a discharge or any document certifying that the debt was no longer owed. Henry Storrer, therefore, remained in the abominable Hull Gaol, not, as might be supposed, for a few weeks or months but for six years. Some well-disposed lawyers took an interest in his case, which, as Storrer v Bannister, was heard in the Queen's Bench, in 1858. Bannister was ordered to pay his victim, whose family and health had suffered considerably, £225 damages. This, then, was the man who realised that railways could be the source of further fame and fortune. He had done much preparatory work when he outlined the possibilities for the Hull and Holderness Railway Company and issued a prospectus at a meeting convened at the railway offices in Paragon Street in August 1852, at the time of his first mayorality.

Not only was there potential for developing the chosen coastal terminus (which had not then been selected) as a seaside resort, both for the benefit of industrial Hull and the East and West Ridings; but also there were also greater financial advantages in prospect, through the carriage of goods, cattle, grain and produce to and from the wealthy agricultural area of Holderness. The growth of Sunk Island by the middle of the 19th century had caused Patrington Haven to rapidly silt up, so much so that the vigorous trade in grain, lime and coal with the West Riding, by keel and ship, had declined considerably. A railway serving Patrington could revive this trade, allowing farmers to send cattle, grain and produce quickly to the best markets and to obtain coal, lime and manure at a more reasonable cost. Moreover, the countryside of Holderness was level, which meant that building costs would not be expensive, and landowners along the route were only too willing to sell to the Company at a reasonable rate. The Bill initiated by the Board of Directors received Royal Assent on 8 July 1853 and the raising of £153,000 by share issue and loan was authorised. Many of the subscribers to the share issue held business interests in Holderness but support also came from Hull merchants and bankers. Work began on the line almost immediately. The main contractors were Messrs. Jackson, Bean and Gow and the engineer was Thomas Cabry. The three contractors agreed to build the line, with the exception of stations and gate-house, for the sum of £67,000, or £3,390 per mile, with a promised completion date of 1 May 1854.

The Holderness coast between Easington and Tunstall was surveyed for an appropriate coastal terminal. Withernsea was eventually selected because it had a good sandy beach with easy access, since there were no cliffs, and it was reasonably sheltered from the North. The 1851 census return revealed that the town had a population of 109 people living there. Some three years later a contemporary description said, 'It consisted of a handful of houses with a single shop and a very apocryphal [unsubstantiated] public.'

Withernsea, however, was to be transformed into a resort for the visitor, the vocation of landlady was to be encouraged and a scheme for an imposing and dignified Station Hotel was to be the keystone of the project. It was almost immediately re-named the Queen's Hotel to commemorate the visit by Queen Victoria to Hull in 1854, an occasion when Bannister had presented the Loyal Address. The hotel was to be a mere part of an ambitious scheme of boulevards, promenades, crescents, tree-lined avenues and assembly rooms, designed to attract a distinguished, refined and genteel clientele.

Cuthbert Brodrick, a Hull man, who was engaged as the company's architect, was later to find fame as the designer of Leeds Town Hall and the Grand Hotel, Scarborough. By early 1854 his design for the station was well advanced as were his plans for the hotel: a luxurious building of 40 bedrooms standing in its own grounds with well-laid-out gardens and a clear uninterrupted view of the German Ocean (as the North Sea was then known, until 1914). This elegant hotel, which opened on 12 April 1855, cost £10,530 to build but is now demolished.

Although there was much local support for the railway, there were also some difficulties, notably at Hedon, the largest township between Hull and Withernsea, where the Corporation refused to relinquish its rights to tolls. The line, therefore, had to be altered in order that Hedon railway station should be as close to the town as possible but also be sited outside the parish boundary; this was accomplished through a land purchase. The tolls imposed by Hedon would have seriously affected the profitability of another business opportunity that Bannister had identified, which was to supply the numerous gasworks in Hedon and Holderness with coal, the raw material used to produce gas for lighting premises and the streets. Although there were two tracks through the station, there was only one platform, on the south side of the line. The remainder of the route was rural and a number of stations were remote. Ryehill and Burstwick station was midway between the two villages, about a quarter mile from each, Keyingham was a half mile from the centre, Ottringham station was a mile to the north of the village and Patrington some way to the west of the village but on a main road. The building of the railway proceeded rapidly and was completed in less than one year, thanks to the level terrain, the lack of civil engineering problems and the fact that ballast for the track was available locally, from Kelsey Hill, near Burstwick.

The company had decided to share the use of the Victoria Dock Railway Station as its Hull terminus. This brick-built, slate-roofed, station was the existing terminus for the Victoria Dock Railway, an unproductive line, one of the first suburban passenger services in the country, operated by the York and North Midland Railway, which ringed Hull with a three-and-one-quarter-mile sweep of track from Victoria Dock to Manor House Street. By crossing the main radial roads of Hull on the level the Victoria Dock Line sowed the seeds for later urban traffic problems. When the service was withdrawn in October 1854, the Hull and Holderness Railway became the sole user from 1

November 1854, with G. H. Dippie as the Station Master.

The line was completed in March 1854 after a mere 11 months in the making and, following inspection by Captain Taylor, the Inspector of Railways, it was formally opened on 26 June 1854 and to the public the following day. At 11.20 am the first of two trains left Hull Paragon Station 20 minutes late, and proceeded to the Victoria Dock Station. Over 500 invitations had been sent out by the secretary to the company, George Locking, for this initial journey to Withernsea. In celebration the long train was brightly decorated, and in scrollwork carried the words 'Success to the Hull and Holderness Railway'. The departure of the second train was delayed as the Mayor of Hull, Henry Cooper, was detained on business. Great celebrations took place at stops along the line. At Hedon the Church bells rang out as if in welcome and one traveller recorded the scene thus: 'As we approached, the bells were ringing a merry peal; the whole population of the ancient borough seemed to be mustered about the station, and a miniature park of small artillery greeted the strangers with its diminutive thunder. High across the line, from one side of the station to the other, stretched an arch of evergreens, while flags and banners flaunted at every available spot. Here we stopped for a few minutes and then, amid the cheers of the crowd, moved on again.' At Withernsea a crowd from the town and surrounding villages had gathered to welcome the trains and a lunch was provided for the 500 guests in a huge marquee, which, due to strong winds, partly collapsed during the meal. The distinguished company soon re-arranged themselves and settled down to hear the speeches and toasts. Anthony Bannister, as Chairman, was seated between the Rt. Hon. Lord Londesborough and the Hon. Arthur Duncombe M.P. Thirteen toasts were proposed and replied to in an atmosphere of optimism and confidence in the new venture. The celebration ended at 4.00 pm and, after the guests had taken a stroll along the sea front, the whole assembly entrained for the return journey. The trains left Withernsea at 4.50 pm., making a leisurely return to Hull, arriving safely a little before 7.00 pm.

The novelty of the service attracted 63,764 passengers within the first four months including, in September 1854, a temperance excursion of 2,000 people. Receipts from passengers during the summer months were four times those from goods receipts, but this early success could not be sustained. Today, it is difficult for us to imagine the almost impossible living conditions in the mid-19th century, when residents lived with the smoke, dirt, stench, squalor and incredible overcrowding that existed in the courts and alleys of Hull and other industrial towns. People were born and died there without ever seeing the green countryside, let alone the sea. But presented to them now, no more than one hour's journey away, was a paradise of fresh air, sea, clean sandy beaches and space to run free. Small wonder that people went in their thousands.

Initially, though, only merchants, traders and skilled artisans could afford the fare and it was they who were the early citizens of the new town. They came first for the day, then with their families for the weekend, they gradually extended their visits until they either rented, or had built, their summer seaside homes. Why not? Travel was reasonably cheap and the journey short. It was only a small step to transfer their homes to Withernsea and the commuter age was begun. In 1892 Withernsea residents included such prominent members of the Hull community as Edward Robins, the mayor, Richard Pickering, editor of the *Hull News*, and Alfred Strong, chief clerk of the North Eastern Railway. By 1901 the population of Withernsea had increased to 1,426, rose in the next ten years to 2,384 and in the following ten years to 4,701. In the summer season finding holiday accommodation was not difficult: it would seem almost everyone 'took in visitors', not boarding house keepers but ordinary housewives who took in boarders at reasonable rates. A few genuine boarding houses sprang up, 75 in 1873 and 116 by 1890, but most visitors preferred to stay with private families.

The railway company offered exceptionally cheap day return tickets and the poorer people could now afford the occasional trip to the seaside. It was then that thousands of day trippers began to pour into Withernsea. The railway company ran special excursions at weekends and holidays to cater for this ever-increasing demand and by 1914 there were 12 or 13 trains running daily between Hull and Withernsea. Bathing machines were set up on the beach by the railway company, which also offered special facilities for anyone building at Withernsea. The railway company did not build but preferred to sell at a profit the land they had purchased to others who were willing to risk their money. The reality of the situation was that the stockholders had lost their nerve and their grandiose schemes were quietly abandoned. After their first rush occasioned by curiosity, the rich and distinguished failed to return, for they wanted more from a resort than a sandy cove and an hotel and thus it soon became

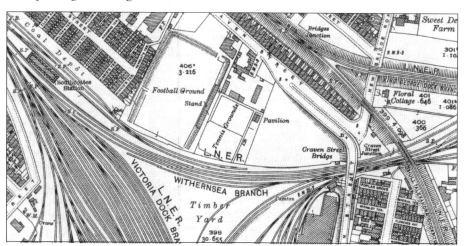

The Craven Street Link. (Ordnance Survey, 1928).

evident, that the hotel would be a white elephant, as it was already running at a loss.

The Reckitt family eventually purchased the hotel, in 1901, anxious to provide a convalescent home where the poor people of Hull could recuperate after serious illness. Consumption was rampant in Hull and the medical profession of the day concluded that the only cure was fresh air and rest. The 'pure life-giving air' of Withernsea was recommended, and so it was, in 1902, that the Reckitt family presented the Queen's Hotel to the Hull Royal Infirmary. It was renamed the Withernsea Convalescent Home and was opened as such in 1903 by Lord Herries and successfully continued to provide care for many decades.

There were several reasons why the line was never to be a financial success. Another major cause was its being a single line track, with passing loops only at stations, and therefore only one train at a time was allowed on the main line. At Withernsea Railway Station locomotives were revolved on a turntable for the return journey to Hull. A further loss-making factor was due to the company seeking to prove its independence by using its own coaches and locomotives, a practice for a small concern that was neither efficient nor economically viable. In the boardroom the forceful and sometimes arrogant Anthony Bannister made enemies and in 1855 an attempt was made to remove him from office. He managed to fight off the challenge and remained in control. However, he and his co-directors were only interested in making a profit from the venture, and, when it became clear that prospects for that outcome were unlikely, since the revenue from all receipts was insufficient to make the line viable, the line was leased to the North Eastern Railway on 1 January 1860, only six years after its inception.

By 1862, the financial crisis was such that the company was dissolved through an Act of Parliament, and the Hull-Withernsea line was taken over by the North Eastern Railway. It decided, in 1863, to make Hull Paragon Station the terminus, as the Victoria Dock terminus had proved to be very inconvenient in operation and closed on 1 June 1864. The diversion to Paragon Station was achieved by laying a double track, a half mile in length, between Craven Street and Southcoates station. It had been hoped to bring the new junction into operation from 1 July, 1863. However, the Board of Trade inspector found that the signalling system was incomplete and refused permission, so that services actually commenced from Paragon Station on 1 June 1864, by-passing the Victoria Dock station. The North Eastern Railway developed the line and introduced a second track in the early 1900s in an attempt to make it a more viable proposition but the sections between Hedon and Ryehill, and Ottringham and Winestead remained single. Winestead station closed to passenger traffic in 1904 but remained open to freight until 1956. In other efforts to economise, station staff were reduced in number but the line still continued to run at a loss. Despite the control of the railway passing out of his hands, Bannister maintained his faith in the potential of Withernsea as a high-class seaside resort and launched a fresh initiative in 1870 with the formation of the

Withernsea Pier, Promenade, Gas and General Improvement Company Ltd. of which he became Chairman. Once again land was purchased with the object of laying out avenues and housing estates. Five groins were built in 1871 to protect the beach and by 1873 part of the north promenade was finished. The long-awaited pier was completed in 1877. Following the death of Bannister in 1878, a local man, James Young, succeeded him as Chairman but unfortunately, as with the independent railway, the company ran out of money and went into liquidation in 1881.

Fittingly, given his love of the town, Anthony Bannister, shown, in the uniform of the Hull Company of the East Yorkshire Rifle Volunteers, spent the last full day of his life in Withernsea. He had lived at High Paull House during the 1850s until he sold it to the military in 1861 and he then moved to Kingston Lodge at Hessle. In July 1861, he developed a cold as a result of taking part in a regatta at Withernsea and spent the day in the town recovering. Declaring himself to be 'about all right', he made the journey home during the evening by train, first to Hull and then to Hessle, where he died at his home that same night, on July 18 1878, at the relatively young age of 61, without having achieved his ambition for a 'Brighton of the North'. His place in history through bringing the railway to Withernsea is commemorated by Bannister Street in Withernsea, which is named in his honour, as is the recently developed Bannister Street, off Williamson Street in Hull, not too far from the site of the former Victoria Dock Railway station.

The last major change on the Hull-Withernsea line was the introduction of diesel multiple-unit trains from 7 January 1957, which, as they could be driven from either end, made the turntable at Withernsea redundant. The Hull-Withernsea railway line, despite vigorous objections, closed to passenger services in 1964, as a result of the Beeching Report. It was noted that the annual operating cost of the line was £78,000, whilst the estimated annual income was only £37,000 and it was reported that the line was therefore uneconomic to operate. The last passenger train to use the line was the 6.25 pm to Withernsea, which ran on Saturday, 17 October 1964. On the return run to Hull, the buffers of the train were adorned with wreaths as the communities along the line mourned the loss of their rail service. Some goods traffic continued to use the line on a regular basis, until 3 May, 1965. The last goods service, from Hedon to Hull, stopped on 3 June 1968.

The Victoria Dock Railway Station building outlived the line which it had served so briefly, from 1854 until 1864, and it survived until 1984, when it was finally demolished during the creation of the Citadel Trading Estate.

Sources:
Martin Craven, *The Hull to Withernsea Railway 1854-1964* (Beverley, 1997).
K. A. MacMahon, *The Beginnings of the East Yorkshire Railways* (East Yorkshire Local History Series No. 3, 1953).
P. G. Mason, *Lost Railways of East Yorkshire* (Driffield, 1990).
Peter Price, *Lost Railways of Holderness* (Cherry Burton, 1989).
Thompson, *Railways*.
John Whitehead, *Withernsea* (Beverley, 1988).
Flashbacks (Hull Daily Mail).

Chapter Ten
Sammy's Point: Martin Samuelson

Sammy's Point is formed by the 12-acre corner of land on the east bank of the River Hull, at the point where it meets the Humber Estuary. Until the mid 1990s it was occupied by the huge engineering sheds which housed the workshops, light, buoy repair depot and offices of Associated British Ports.

The nickname of Sammy's Point is derived from, and is a discreet reference to, an earlier occupant of the site, Martin Samuelson, a local shipbuilder who set up a shipyard there in 1857. Born in Hamburg in 1825, he worked as a railway engineer before moving to Hull in 1849, taking over an iron foundry in Scott Street. The business grew, and, in the style of a typical Victorian entrepreneur, ever alive to new ventures, he expanded into iron shipbuilding in 1853, forming the Groves Iron Shipyard at the Lime Street dry docks, with his first vessel, the *Irwell*, launched from there the following year.

Pressure arising from the lack of space at Lime Street forced a move to open the new shipyard in 1857, near the mouth of the River Hull, on land, formerly occupied, in part, by the Citadel. Here modern machinery was installed and, with the other advantages of the huge site, which had access to both the River Hull and the Humber, it became one of the finest shipbuilding yards in the country. Initially, his occupation of Sammy's Point was very successful, one of his earliest commissions in 1858 being the installation of an 80-horsepower steam condensing engine into the American built *Chase* of 558 tons, which was bought by Brown, Atkinson and Co. for the whaling trade, after they had seen the success of the similar conversion carried out by Earle's shipyard on the *Diana* the previous year.

As further examples of his early success, the yard was commissioned to build two large iron-paddle steam ships in 1859 for the short-lived Atlantic Royal Mail Steam Navigation Company, known as the Galway Line, which was formed in 1859 under contract with the British Post Office. The company was formed for the transport of H.M. mails to Boston and New York,

via Galway and St. John's, Newfoundland, and a total of four new paddle steamers were ordered for the service. The two built by Martin Samuelson and Company were the *Anglia* and *Columbia* of 800 nominal horsepower. They had three decks, fitted fore and aft for a total of over 400 passengers, and their immense strength and their build and form, ensured that they became fine sea boats.

Towards the end of 1859, around 40 ships had been built at the yard. It was said that 'The River Hull bristled with iron ships in various stages of completion', and the weekly wage bill rose to a staggering £1,200 per week.

Samuelson was described in a contemporary report in the *Hull Free Press* as 'having dark eyes and black bushy whiskers; white hat, blue coat and light trousers; who bowled along like an express train, in whose expression there was more of energy than of dignity'. A real bundle of energy, in fact, it was said that he seemed to exist without sleep and he was a familiar figure dashing along the streets of Hull: 'At one hour he is in the building yards in Groves, a few minutes later and he is inspecting the docking of a ship, half an hour more and he has visited both the boiler works in Church Street and the engine works in Scott Street.' He was a man of his word who had no time for those who tried to thwart his honourable intentions. On one occasion he had contracted to have ships completed on a given day and, as the work was behind schedule, he made an agreement with his workforce that anyone who left without permission or notice should forfeit a fixed sum. The joiners at the yard went on strike, but, rather than be blackmailed into increasing wages, he called their bluff by enforcing the penalty and bringing in outside labour.

One of the high points of his career occurred on one extraordinary day, 31 October, 1863, when four vessels were launched. The former Lord Goderich, who was unseated for corruption after his election as a Member of Parliament for Hull in 1852, had returned in triumph to the town, with two inherited titles as Earl de Grey and Ripon, both to witness the launches and for his installation as Lord High Steward. A contemporary news report in the *Illustrated London News* stated: 'The preparations for the launch were completed shortly before seven in the morning and soon after that hour the Earl de Grey and Ripon; James Clay Esq. M.P.; and Joseph Somes Esq. M.P., together with the Mayor and several members of the Corporation as well as the leading merchants of the town entered the yard. Shortly after a signal-gun was fired from Her Majesty's Ship *Cornwallis* and the sailing ship *Countess of Ripon* and her sister ship *Lightning*, two fine East-Indiamen, both of 1206 tons, were released from their bondage to find a haven in the waters. The steamer *Earl de Grey and Ripon*, of 723 tons, which had been built for a London firm, and a small steam tug *Solferino*, of 247 tons, built for the French Government, were then knocked off their slips.

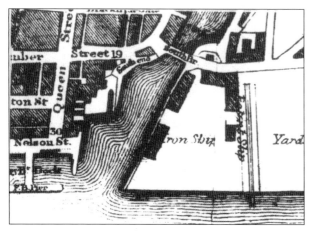

Sammy's Point. (Goodwill & Lawson, 1869).

'Thousands of spectators had also assembled along the riverbank to watch the spectacular launch of the four ships. After the launch, his Lordship and about 200 invited guests sat down to a superb champagne breakfast in Messrs. Samuelson's moulding loft, where several complimentary toasts were made to Martin Samuelson by the Earl de Grey and Ripon.' Following the breakfast the Earl attended a ceremony at which he was made a brother of Trinity House and later still that morning was made an honorary brother of the Humber Lodge of Freemasons. He then proceeded for lunch to the Town Hall and took upon himself the office of Lord High Steward of the Borough, succeeding the late Marquis of Normanby. That ceremony over a procession was formed at the People's Park, where a statue of Queen Victoria was unveiled. A remarkable day for Hull, the Earl de Grey and Ripon and Martin Samuelson.

On a single day the following year, 1864, the yard almost repeated the same feat, launching two iron barques and a steamer. The launches were celebrated with a banquet attended by the directors, the Mayor and both the Borough members, one of who was a large shareholder in the firm.

Martin Samuelson believed it was his duty to play his part in the public affairs of the town and served as alderman and Mayor with distinction, showing a particular concern for improving sanitation. Rumours began to spread later in 1864, that all was not well with the company and that, despite having launched over 100 iron ships, Samuelson was overreaching himself through accepting too much work with insufficient capital to carry it forward. In modern parlance, the company was crippled with 'cash flow' problems. Put simply, the firm was paying out for wages and materials before it had received payment from those for whom it was building the ships. His situation was further damaged by the bankruptcy of Zachariah Pearson, a ship owner and shipbuilder, who was bankrupted in his attempts to run the Union blockade of the Cenfederate states.

Martin Samuelson was also made bankrupt. He was forced to resign as Managing Director of the company and as an alderman of the town. At the end of 1864 the company was sold to the Humber Iron Works and Shipbuilding Company. At a Board Meeting held in January 1865 the directors minuted 'that they trusted that the company would prosper now that the hindrances to the progress of this business, which have hitherto existed, have been removed'. Be that as it may, the workers at the shipyard paid him a touching tribute when they presented him with 'a silver and coffee service, two silver salvers and a beautiful timepiece', as a token of their esteem.

The new company also struggled and in 1865 desperately tried to raise more capital. By February 1866 they were forced to the conclusion that liquidation was the only course left open to them. The ensuing liquidation lasted for many years.

Samuelson himself, however, continued to be regarded as one of the principal men of Hull. It was he who was responsible for the design of the 1870 North Bridge which spanned the River Hull between Bridge Street and Great Union Street until replaced by the present North Bridge. He continued working for the Humber Conservancy until he died in 1903 at the age of 78.

The Hull firm of Bailey and Leetham finally purchased Sammy's Point from the liquidators in 1872. Founded in 1854, they were the second largest shipowners in Hull, until their principal rivals, Thomas Wilson and Sons, absorbed them in 1903. Prior to the takeover Bailey and Leetham continued to operate the shipyard to carry out repairs to their own ships as well as contracting work for other shipowners. When Thomas Wilson and Sons took the yard over in 1903, they found it surplus to their requirements, as maintenance of their fleet was undertaken by Earle's shipyard to the east of Victoria Dock and so they disposed of the site.

The land at Sammy's Point is shown in the 1912 *Port of Hull Annual* as being in the ownership of the Humber Warehousing and Transport Company, shipbuilding on the site having ceased.

In 1998 it was announced by Kingston upon Hull City Council that Sammy's Point was the preferred site for the new tourism flagship proposal, The Deep. There can be little doubt that Martin Samuelson, with his sense of innovation and deep love of Hull, would have been very pleased.

Sources:
Fowler, *East Hull*.
Ketchell, *Victoria Dock*.
H. Philip Spratt, *Transatlantic Paddle Steamers* (1967).

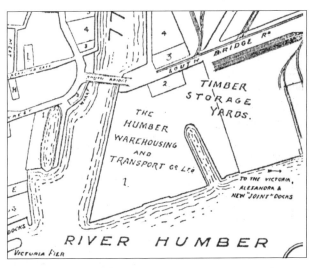

Sammy's Point. (Port of Hull Annual, *1912*).

Chapter Eleven
A Ha'penny Bridge Way: The South Bridge

As the newly opened Victoria Dock developed and trade increased, storage space became increasingly critical. Thus the dock estate expanded beyond the boundaries originally seen as necessary. Expansion occurred, firstly, to the east, in 1863, by the acquisition of a further eight acres, and later in the same year, to the west, with the acquisition of the area to the north of the Citadel, formerly the moat, which was levelled to provide storage space for timber. In 1864-5 the Citadel itself was demolished and the site levelled and proposed to be laid out into streets by the Department of Woods and Forests, as shown in the 1869 Goodwill and Lawson plan of Hull. It may be that this was the precursor of some earlier housing scheme but it was never developed as such, becoming timber storage grounds, which were let out under tenancies as shown by the Goodwill and Lawson Plan of Hull 1869

Apart from the dock, other industries had also become established on the east bank of the River Hull. For example, Martin Samuelson had built his shipyard at the western tip of the area in 1857, which in 1864 became the Humber Ironworks and Shipbuilding Company, and timber storage became a feature of the site. Other businesses were established along Garrison Side, and Earle's shipyard, further to the east, was well established, having opened in 1851 employing large numbers of workers. The increase in industry and hence jobs to the east of Hull was matched by the development of new roads and an increase in the population of Drypool, as skilled workers and labourers moved to be near to the new enterprises.

Those workers who had to travel from the west to the east bank of the River Hull, faced a particular drawback, in that travel between the two banks of the river could only be made via a long and circuitous route, using the North Bridge to cross the river. This not only made life difficult but also affected the supply of many small goods to the east bank. A more direct route giving access to the Old Town was clearly needed.

The problem was addressed in 1863, when work started to build a South Bridge across the river, in approximately the place where the old south ferry had previously operated. To enable the work to be carried out, the old south blockhouse, which still remained standing in Martin Samuelson and Co.'s shipyard, had to be demolished as well as the southern end of High Street.

The new South Bridge was a massive iron structure, opened to traffic in December 1865, and primarily intended for use as a footbridge, although carts could be taken across. It was a sideways-swinging bridge and closed up to the east bank when opened for river traffic. It connected Garrison Side on the east bank with Humber Street on the west bank

Brown's Illustrated Guide to Hull, 1891, described the bridge as follows: 'We have now arrived at the South Bridge, opened in 1865. The bridge – the southernmost connection with the opposite side of the River Hull – is of iron and of massive proportions. A small toll is charged for both foot and vehicular traffic.' The toll was a half-penny and so the alternative name of 'Ha'penny Bridge' as a means of travelling into town became popular and passed into the folklore of Hull.

The bridge was well used until the new road bridge at Drypool, built by Samuel Butler and Co. of Leeds, opened in 1889 at a cost of £17,000. Although this new bridge had a carriageway of only 15 feet 9 inches, it was later strengthened to take trams, at which time access to the east bank became less arduous, so the numbers of people using the South Bridge declined and it was left mainly to casual pedestrian use. The South Bridge closed in 1934, three years after the opening of the new North Bridge, and was finally demolished in 1944.

When plans for The Deep were first mooted in 1998, the Residents Association were consulted and asked to comment on the proposals. One of their comments was that a foot passage over the River Hull should be provided, which, they suggested, should be sited at the mouth of the river in roughly the same position as the former Ha'penny Bridge. This proposal would re-connect Victoria Dock with the Old Town and provide a safe alternative route into the City for the residents of the Dock. The planners accepted this proposal and, when The Deep is complete. A fine new Millennium Bridge will be in position to replace the former Ha'Penny Bridge.

Sources:
Wrigglesworth, *Guide to Hull*.
Ketchell, *Victoria Dock*.

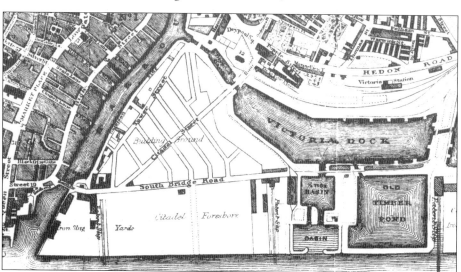

Ha'Penny Bridge, South Bridge Road.
(Goodwill & Lawson, 1869).

Chapter Twelve
Fever Pitch: The Citadel Isolation Hospital

Although it is not generally realised, Hull in the mid- and late 1800s was one of the principal ports engaged in receiving the many thousands of emigrants from Europe who were escaping from revolution, famine, religious persecution and poverty to a new beginning, in the main, to North America. Ports throughout Europe were thronged each spring with those seeking passage to the new world. They arrived in Hull by ship, often after an appallingly unpleasant passage through the Baltic, followed by a stormy North Sea crossing. When the immigrants disembarked, the main object was to process them as speedily as possible. They were taken first to reception centres, one of which was sited at Victoria Dock, for documentation and health checks, needed to avoid the spread of typhus and cholera. The disease which appeared most frequently was 'ship fever', or typhus. It was among the most loathsome of diseases, highly contagious and often fatal. Associated with poverty, filth and overcrowding, it became rampant when conditions favoured the spread of the lice that conveyed it. When it broke out in the steerage of an emigrant ship it ran through the passengers like wildfire. Therefore, those who were lice-infested were taken immediately to the Disinfecting Station at Scarborough Street. After clearance, the majority were taken in open transport, (usually followed by jeering crowds of children), a few for embarkation on a ship bound for America at Queen's Dock; but most to the onward transportation centre at Paragon Station. (which opened 8 May 1848).

From there they travelled by train, some to Leeds or Manchester, but most to Liverpool. Here they awaited a further ship for the Atlantic crossing to their new land. The majority travelled from Liverpool in 'steerage class', so-called because the accommodation was originally around the rudder of the ship, although it later came to mean any below-deck accommodation. It was cramped, airless, smelly and dark. In the 1840s many contemporary writers compared the conditions under which emigrants travelled to those which had prevailed on the Middle Passage during the days of African slave trading. Although this was a blatant exaggeration, the horrors of steerage were real enough, where hundreds of people were crowded together for weeks on end in cramped, dimly lit and poorly ventilated compartments.

The numbers of emigrants involved increased from a steady number in the mid 1800s to a flood by the late 1800s. In particular, the Jews in Russia were subjected to a reign of terror following the assassination of Tsar Alexander II in 1881, in which they were falsely implicated. As a result, thousands left their homes in Russia and Poland and walked with what they could carry to the nearest port and paid the £1 fare to travel in unimaginable misery to Hull. This flood of emigrants carried on for a number of years. For example, in a six-month period during 1888 over 41,000 emigrants from Gothenburg, Oslo, Copenhagen and Hamburg passed through Hull on their way to America. An examining officer in Hull

thought that German Jews were the most numerous but he also saw Hungarians, Romanians and some Polish Jews. They had no luggage and only a little bread and fish. He thought them dirty in their persons and in their habits generally, though some who came from Rotterdam appeared slightly better.

J. S. Fletcher in his *Picturesque History of Yorkshire* (1899), who describes the dockside scene, where 'Parties of the emigrants huddled together under the sheds, strangers indeed in a foreign land,' Another description is: 'They are for the most part singularly dirty and particularly picturesque. Some of such groups chatter volubly, others preserve a stolid silence, keeping a strict watch over their miserable belongings. Now and again the observer comes across what is evidently a family party – a group of three and sometimes four generations, represented by an ancient white haired, bowed and broken man at one end of the scale, and by a baby in arms at the other.'

The migration continued until the outbreak of the First World War. Some of the emigrants got no further than Hull and thus the foreign population of the town increased. Of those that settled in Hull, some later became among the best-known names in the city, making an invaluable contribution in many walks of life and enriching the cultural business and public life of their adopted town.

But, unwittingly and despite rigorous screening on their arrival, the emigrants often brought with them Asiatic cholera. This is an even more malignant disease than typhus, being extremely infectious and often fatal, resulting in violent diarrhoea of a watery nature, severe and violent vomiting, cramps, collapse, rapid dehydration and usually death within hours. The victim becomes wizened, with features shrunken and eyes depressed. The blood thickens causing discolouring to the skin like bruising. This is accompanied by a high fever and sometimes cramps and spasms of the arms and legs. After a few hours the patient becomes very weak and feeble, the pulse rate drops and becomes barely detectable, and death may follow. In some cases the patient lingers on in this state for some time before recovering or expiring. Starvation was the one factor most likely to lead to an attack. Thus, inevitably, whenever cholera raged at the ports of departure it would be carried on board by infected emigrants, and, after a period of incubation, would break out during the passage. The first pandemic originated in India in 1817, reaching Europe in 1830. The second began in 1840 and reached Europe in 1847, lasting until 1864. The third pandemic began in 1863, reached Europe in 1865 and lasted until 1873.

An outbreak of cholera in 1831-2 killed over 60,000 people in the British Isles, carrying off some 270 in Hull. There had been few sanitary reforms carried out, either in cleaning the streets or in relieving the chronic overcrowding, between then and the next outbreak, which occurred in 1849. The excuse was made that the Council were worried that any steps they might take would alarm the public. As a result of their lack of action and due to the fact that many inhabitants of Hull had lived under poor conditions for some time, the Asiatic cholera epidemic that year was so severe that Hull was regarded as the worst affected town in Britain. By 13 July 1849 there were 49 cases in the Mill Street area of Hull, where the worst slums were situated, and there were 20 deaths. Cholera was also reported to have broken out amongst the girls employed in the flax and cotton mills. Their living conditions were very bad.

The Groves, an area on the east bank of the River Hull just to the north of Drypool where most of them lived, was full of rats, stagnant pools, sewage and rubbish. In one of those houses, a man, his wife and child died, and, in addition, all the girls who had attended them. In the week ending 6 September, 491 people had died from cholera, and in the following week 608.

Cemeteries were overcrowded and conditions were particularly bad when bodies were placed in vaults beneath the churches. At St. Mary's, Lowgate, coffins had to be removed so that more bodies could be buried whenever a funeral took place. In churchyards large mounds of earth were thrown up. When it rained the soil was washed away, exposing the bodies and giving off 'the characteristic graveyard odour'. Such was the demand for burial space for the victims 'that coffins had to be piled one on top of another, with no earth between them'. That month proved to be the peak of the 1849 outbreak.

Several 'miracle' cures were offered and one, published in the *Hull Advertiser* in 1849, was for Reinhardt's Anti-Cholera mixture – 'the only genuine remedy'. J. G. Reinhardt was a chemist and druggist in the Market Place, Hull. He sold his remedy in two sizes, bottles priced 1s. 0d. or 2s. 6d. (5 or 12 pence) each, 'with full directions.' The same advertisement stated that he was the sole agent for Bigg's Sheepdipping Composition, and this leads to speculation that they were one and the same! Doctors prescribed their own favourite remedies, including calomel, rhubarb, castor oil, laudanum and chalk. Acetates of lead, nitrate of silver, opium, ammonia and citrate of potash were all used. Sometimes, hot air baths were recommended and also the use of mustard plasters.

In fact, mustard seems to have been a favourite medicine and 'Kingston Mustard', manufactured in 'a new and scientific manner' by Simpson, Hall & Co. of Hull, was sold in jars of 1 lb, ½ lb and ¼ lb. Dr. Fleischman advertised his cholera drops, reputed to

A familiar sight during the cholera epidemic, 1849.

have been administered to 150,000 people in Vienna, and Sir William Burnett's Patent Disinfecting Fluid – 'sealed with a cork' – was highly recommended. There was even a money back offer from one Thomas Sleighty who offered to pay £5 to the Infirmary for anyone taking his Herbal Bowel Mixture and not recovering. Some of the 'cures' were more likely to kill, but their inventors probably did not stay around for long enough to face any consequences. On 3 October posters were put up around the town to declare the epidemic was ended, at a cost of 1,834 lives, or one in every 43 of the population.

In his *Recollections of Hull* the Reverend James Sibree, Chaplain to the Hull Cemetery Company, left a gruesome account of that awful period and the never-ending series of funerals he conducted at the Spring Bank Cemetery: 'The men employed in digging the graves had no respite, but pursued their doleful task both night and day. At first single graves were dug for the reception of eight or nine bodies; but the demand for room became so urgent that double graves were constructed, in which coffins were piled one upon the other, without any earth between them. Only two of these, however, were opened; the sight was so appalling that the men refused to dig any more. The cemetery hearse was in constant requisition to remove the stricken poor from all parts of the town, and the common phrase of the men was about "fetching another load." The cholera plot presented the appearance of a quarry, or a ploughed field. There was no time to make the graves neat. Persons were seen crowding the entrance gates early in the morning, long before the wearied Superintendent was up, to order graves for friends or relatives who had died during the night; and, sad to relate, these informants were themselves, in a day or two, called to pass through the "dark valley," so short was the summons. Sometimes as many as five or six mourning trains were crowding the gravel walks of the Cemetery at the same time, while during the day, at some periods, the trains occupied the entire space between the Beverley Road end and the Cemetery gate.'

The Directors of the Cemetery Company erected by private subscription, a large obelisk to commemorate the epidemic. The inscription states that during the months of July, August and September 1849, upwards

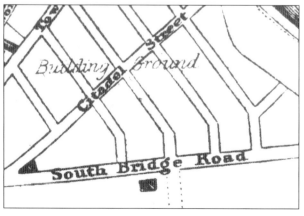

The Fever Hospital, south of South Bridge Road.

of 2,000 inhabitants fell victim to the cholera, and that the remains of 700 were deposited near the monument.

In September 1859, Sir Henry Cooper drew the attention of the Sanitary Committee to the cholera epidemic sweeping the Continent. Two rooms had been taken in the barracks of the Citadel, which by then had been vacated by the army; these were prepared for the reception of cholera victims and a staff had been engaged. One man was taken into care from a ship and recovered. The next reported case did not occur until 1865.

In 1866, the Department of Woods and Forests offered the local Board of Health an area on the disused Citadel site on which to build a cholera hospital. The area is shown at on the 1889-90 Ordnance Survey as being just to the south of South Bridge Road. The hospital was completed later in 1866 at a cost of £459. 15s. 6d. and a man was employed as caretaker. It was, apparently, a totally unremarkable building, constructed of wood over a brick base and was described at the time as 'having the appearance of a warehouse'. Initially, it provided 21 bed spaces but it was later enlarged to contain 46 beds. The Citadel hospital served primarily to isolate the victims of cholera and, later, smallpox. Conditions seem to have been primitive, a report of the time stating that it could not be used after October of each year as there was a fire in only one room and water came in at the ventilators. The report described the building as 'being more like a shed than a hospital, where persons taken thereto with cholera were expected to die'.

Hull continued to suffer throughout the middle to late 19th century with successive outbreaks of cholera, smallpox, typhus and typhoid, which claimed the life of thousands of victims, particularly in the poorest areas of the town. It is hard to imagine the crowded conditions in the worst slums of Hull and the overpowering stench to anyone not used to it. The worst smells came from the by-products of the whaling industry, because in the Greenland Yards, a mile north of the town in Sculcoates, blubber was boiled to produce oil, and offal converted into glue.

Smallpox was another disease prevalent in the 19th century and many died despite the availability of vaccination as a free service. In 1862 there was an epidemic of smallpox in Hull, during which there were many deaths, the majority of victims not having been vaccinated, through fear, prejudice or ignorance. Epidemics of smallpox broke out sporadically over the next four years. Dr. Buchanan, the Medical Officer of the Privy Council, visited the town in 1869, during which time he inspected the Citadel hospital and found that there were no means to prevent cross-infection, since it had been built for cholera cases only. The smallpox epidemic continued during 1869, about six deaths occurring each week. However, whilst the local Board of Health decided to continue using the hospital at the Citadel for cases of smallpox in the short term, they also looked at means to improve the hospital, which, since it was built of wood, was very cold. They decided a brick building should replace the wooden one, for which they received tenders, having £200 available to fund the change. In January 1872 the disease appeared again and the Sanitary Committee had £50 available to make the old Citadel hospital useable again.

Many deaths occurred in the Hull Workhouse, where the disease was in its most virulent form. By March the Citadel hospital was in a fit state to receive patients. There had been 22 deaths in the previous two weeks. The local Board of Health resolved that the Vaccination Act of 1868 should be rigorously enforced and that doctors were to give notice of all cases.

The 1882 report of the Medical Officer of Health noted that scarlatina convalescents had contracted smallpox in the Citadel hospital. This type of cross-infection could easily occur at the hospital because it was again noted that there was no real form of isolation there. During that year, there had been 84 smallpox cases in the hospital. Two years later, in 1884, there were scattered outbreaks of the disease, which were prevented from spreading by good practice and vaccination. However, the Citadel hospital was still unsuitable for use in winter and therefore a Piggot's improved hospital tent was purchased in which a constant temperature of 64°F. could be maintained.

Anti-vaccinationist propaganda had made the town vulnerable by 1899, and a smallpox epidemic which caused 144 deaths was the result. In April that year the 79 patients in the Citadel hospital and the matron contracted the disease in such a virulent form as to render their cases hopeless. During the same month a meeting of the Town Council decided that a replacement for the Citadel hospital was needed and a remote site in Sutton Fields was agreed on, despite considerable objection, which were grudgingly withdrawn. The end of the Citadel hospital was in sight.

In October 1899, the Sanitary Committee noted that there were 82 cases of smallpox in the Citadel hospital and questions were raised about the concentration of cases in the neighbourhood of the hospital. Fears had grown that the hospital itself was becoming a centre for infection. Employees of the North Eastern Railway, timber workers and slaughterhouse workers, all working on Victoria Dock, showed an unusually high proportion of cases. The 1868 Vaccination Act contained a number of anomalies, which were removed by the 1898 Vaccination Act, which also specified that only calf lymph should be used in vaccination. During 1899 a vigorous vaccination programme proved highly successful, all dockers being re-vaccinated in a shed on Victoria Dock. By November 1899 almost 40,000 people in the city had been vaccinated and the new hospital in Sutton Fields was almost complete. It opened in December as the Evan Fraser Hospital in West Carr Lane.

The last patient from the Citadel hospital was discharged on 22 December 1899. The abandoned hospital was fumigated with sulphur dioxide, soaked with mercuric chloride solution and then set on fire. The advances in public health and hygiene and, more importantly, the development of medicine into science had finally defeated these dread diseases.

Sources:
Calvert, *Hull*.
Margaret and Bob Cochrane, *Death Comes to Hedon* (Beverley, 1993).
Foster, *Living and Dying*.
Gillett and MacMahon, *Hull*.
Maldwyn A. Jones, *Destination America* (In association with Thames Television, 1978).
Markham, *Hull*.

Chapter Thirteen
A Later Citadel: the Citadel Hotel

The Citadel dominated the east bank of the River Hull for 180 years, being completed in 1685 and taken down during 1864-5. Over the next quarter century great changes took place to the area it once occupied. A comparision of the plans of the area produced in that period can best identify these changes. These are the Goodwill and Lawson plan of 1842, which shows the Citadel as it was, and the Goodwill and Lawson new plan of Hull (1869), which shows the redevelopment of the Citadel site with streets laid out. Comparison of the plans also shows, the area occupied by the construction of Victoria Dock, which opened in July 1850; the disappearance of the Citadel, which was sold by the Crown in 1863 and which was subsequently demolished during 1864-5; and the laying out of streets on the site, which are described on the 1869 new plan of Hull as 'building ground'.

South Bridge Road is shown connecting the Old Town with the new Victoria Dock, via the South Bridge, opened in 1865, and Citadel Street is also shown cutting across the site diagonally to Drypool. It has been conjectured that this street layout was the precursor of an earlier housing scheme planned for dockworkers by the Hull Dock Company. If this were ever so, it was a short-lived scheme, as the 1906 Bacon Plan of Hull, describes the area as 'Timber Yards', which were, in fact, let out in tenancies.

It seems most probable that this was the original intention for the area, as the Citadel site was bought by the Dock Company to relieve their chronic shortage of storage space. The original description in the 1869 plan of 'building ground' was possibly intended as a description of land that was earmarked for timber warehousing. A further point of note on this plan is the Citadel foreshore, which has been considerably extended to the south of South Bridge Road, which came about as a result of the 'growths', caused by the dumping of spoil excavated from the building of the New (Humber) Dock into the Humber, thus creating new land downstream.

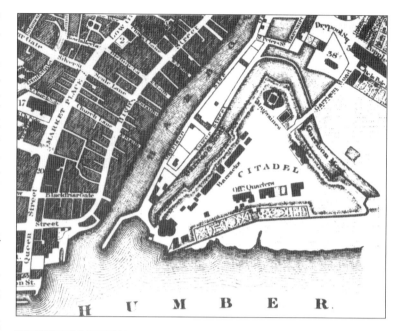

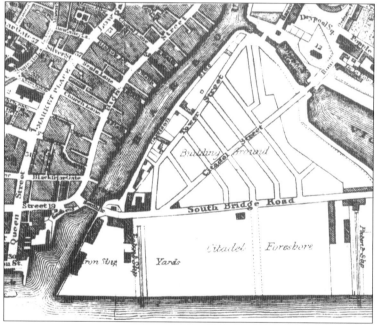

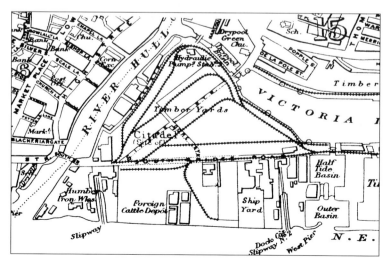

Top right: Goodwill & Lawson (1842).

Middle right: Goodwill & Lawson (1842).

Lower right: Bacon (1906).

Note the junction at the corner of Citadel Street and South Bridge Road, where a building is shown on the plan as P.H. This site marks the position of the two public houses, which were both named the *Citadel Hotel*. The first was built in the 1860s (possibly 1867) by the Hull Brewery Company, presumably attracted to this site by the hundreds of workers employed in the area, many of whom must have passed the pub daily, by crossing the South Bridge, on their way to and from work. It has been conjectured that the first Citadel Hotel was intended to replace a soldiers' canteen, known as the *Sun*, which supposedly lay within the garrison walls and which closed when the Crown sold the Citadel site.

One of the earliest documentary references to the original *Citadel Hotel* appeared in the 1867 White's Directory, where the inn keeper was shown to be William Jarman. This *Citadel Hotel* was completely destroyed during the course of the great fire on Victoria Dock on 22 April 1893. The description of the spreading blaze, carried by the *Hull Daily Mail* at the time states: 'Not so fortunate was the *Citadel Hotel*. The fire crossed Citadel Street and with astonishing rapidity destroyed a large quantity of stock in Messrs. Newsome's yard, not resting satisfied until it had taken the hotel at the corner in its merciless embrace. The building became a mass of ruins in an incredibly short period of time.' The public house was rebuilt by Hull Brewery in 1895, in the same location and again named as the *Citadel Hotel*.

Photographs of the outside of the new premises show that it was a handsome building of two storeys with dormers. The inside is said to have been unremarkable, with red leatherette bench-type seating around the walls and dark wood tables, with cast-iron bases, and chairs made of wood resting on a wooden floor. The bar was made in polished dark wood, possibly mahogany, and the mirrors behind the bar carried the Hull Brewery logo.

Sadly, there is little other information which survives concerning the pub, although it appears to have been popular at the height of its trade and photographs exist of several charabanc outings to the coast organised for the regulars.

Following the closure of the South Bridge the *Citadel Hotel* declined in popularity, as it had become 'off the beaten track' and was not sufficiently near enough to a centre of population to become a 'local'. It became essentially a workers' pub and one facing a declining trade. Following the gradual decline in trade in the 1950s, to the point where it was no longer commercially viable, the pub was closed and was finally demolished in April 1960.

Sources:
Ketchell, *Victoria Dock*.

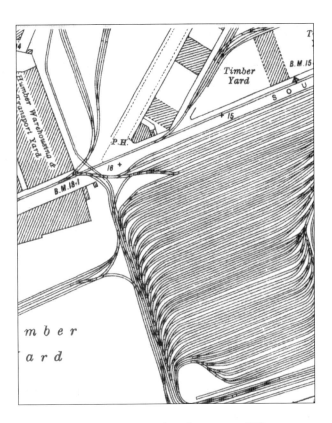

Site of the Citadel Hotel. (Ordnance Survey, 1928).

The Citadel Hotel. (Bob Burton).

Chapter Fourteen
Fresh Meat: The Foreign Cattle Depot

The Foreign Cattle Depot was built on the area shown as the Citadel foreshore on the 1869 Plan of Hull. It is shown on G. W. Bacon's Plan of Hull (1906) as sited between the Humber Iron and Shipbuilding Works and the shipyard to the west of the slipway. The depot was built in 1885, along with one on the Albert Dock, to receive imported live cattle.

The growing trade in live cattle arose as a result of the rising living standards in Britain and Europe from the mid-19th century which encouraged an expansion in the demand for meat. From the beginning, steamships played no small part in the transport of live cattle carried around the coast of Britain, initially from Ireland and, especially after 1844, from the Continent. With the advent of relatively efficient oceanic cargo-carrying steamers, a new trade was developed in live cattle across the Atlantic. in which, for a hectic period, many ships were employed. By the late 1800s great numbers of live cattle were being imported, in the main, from Argentina, although there was also a developing trade with Australia and North America. In fact, many of the cattle ranches (stocked with imported Hereford and Aberdeen Angus) and the sheep pastures in these countries were either British owned and managed or financed.

The depot at Victoria Dock was described in the Brown's *Illustrated Guide to Hull,* (1891): 'It comprises disinfecting rooms, meat market, slaughter houses and the necessary offices. In one of the slaughter houses eight beasts can be slaughtered simultaneously and there is accommodation for three hundred sides of beef. There is an additional slaughter house for pigs; and in the lairs accommodation is provided for six hundred head of cattle, or three thousand sheep.' To give an idea of the scale of the trade locally, during 1887, 52,466 sheep and lambs arrived, together with 1,954 pigs and 9,359 head of cattle. There were various similar depots at other strategic sites around the country where cattle were brought ashore and driven to holding pens prior to slaughter and distribution.

The local yard of Earle's Shipbuilding and Engineering Company also benefited from the trade. They built the liner *Otranto* for Wilson's, especially equipped for the live cattle trade. Launched in June 1877, it was one of the first vessels to use the newly developed steam-compound engines, which provided more power from a lower coal fuel burn. The liner brought live cattle from New York to Hull and had a gross tonnage of 2,353 tons with pumps, winches and steering gear worked by steam. Additional condensers were fitted to provide the cattle with drinking water and longitudinal and transverse bulkheads were provided to contain the cattle safely. To reduce corrosion, there were sewage pipes from the stables. The cattle were accommodated in what came to be known as shelter decks, which exposed the cattle to much suffering from the wide, cold and often stormy waters of the North Atlantic. The *Otranto* ended her life in February 1896, stranded on Fire Island, New York, and was later auctioned for scrapping at Long Island.

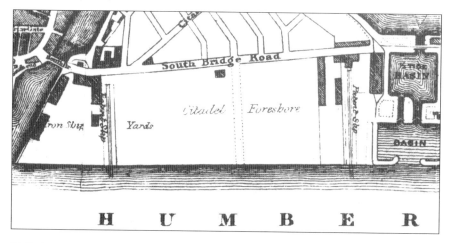

The Citadel Foreshore (Goodwill & Lawson, 1869).

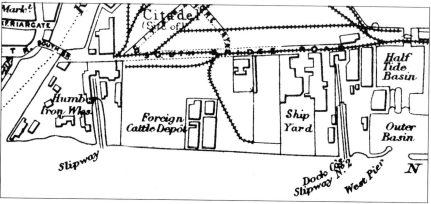

The Foreign Cattle Depot. (Bacon, 1906).

Ironically, just a few years before the boom in the live cattle trade, the first tentative steps had been taken towards the perfection of a technique which was to supplant it. Methods of refrigeration were refined, permitting the installation of refrigerating machinery on board ships for the transportation of perishable stores. Charles Tellier, a Frenchman, made some of the earliest experiments in the 1870s, when he invented an ammonia-absorption refrigerating apparatus A ship named *Frigorifique,* formerly the African Steam Ship Company iron-screw *Eboe,* built at Liverpool in 1870, sailed from Rouen to Buenos Aires with a small consignment of meat, returning to Rouen after a voyage of 104 days with a much larger cargo, not all of which arrived in good condition. However, a second Frenchman, Ferdinand Carre, who had perfected an ammonia-compression refrigeration machine, had one fitted in the steamship, *Paraguay,* another ex-British-built screw steamer, which had been built by Palmer's and Co. at Jarrow in 1864. This vessel transported a cargo of 5,500 carcasses of frozen mutton from San Nicholas consigned to Le Havre in 1877, but collision damage delayed her at St. Vincent for no fewer than four months. Despite this misadventure, the meat was in good enough condition for the guests at the *Grand Hotel* in Paris to be fed on it for a whole week.

The first refrigerated ship to be considered successful in terms of reliability was introduced about 1890, being equipped with steam-driven plant, operating on the Linde ammonia cycle. This enabled the trade to grow rapidly, and such was the pace of progress, that by December 1902 there were 147 vessels employed in the frozen meat trade, with an aggregate capacity of 8,277,400 carcasses. A further ten vessels were being insulated or built for the trade, with an additional capacity of 852,000 carcasses. The next improvement occurred in 1907, when an electric generating plant provided the power for the refrigerating plant on the newly launched *Lusitania.* By 1912, 218 vessels were involved in carrying frozen meat, with a carrying capacity of 15,963,200 carcasses, equal to 17.75 lb. of meat for every man, woman and child in the United Kingdom.

It was the success of the refrigerated trade in meat that signalled the end for the buildings forming the Foreign Cattle Depot, although they survived until quite recently, being demolished in October-November 1988. They had been redeveloped during the early 1900s into a railway dockyard building .

Sources:
Credland, *Earles*.
Ketchell, *Victoria Dock*.
The Ship.

Chapter Fifteen

Target! Victoria Dock: Enemy Action in Two World Wars

The First World War, the Great War, began on 4 August 1914. At first Hull was only affected indirectly. Posters requesting volunteers were posted around the town, as were the more sombre notices announcing the deaths of local volunteers. In the beginning the people's patriotism was high, although within a few short months their mood had become more solemn. It soon became clear that the war was not going to be the brief interlude before things got back to normal, as many had tried to hope. The lists of men and boys – many only in their teens – wounded, killed or missing, became a regular item in the local newspapers and occupied more and more space. But war was to come even closer to home

Germany had developed a fleet of large Zeppelin airships, named after their developer, Count Ferdinand von Zeppelin, with which the first air passenger service in the world commenced. Between 1910 and 1914, 35,000 people were carried safely between cities in Germany. In time of war, it was the original intention to use Zeppelin airships as naval reconnaissance vessels but as the war developed they were used instead as long-range strategic bombers. Zeppelin airship raids on Britain began in 1915 when, suddenly, those at home realised that they too, could face attack. Attempts were made to 'blackout' Hull to make raids by the Zeppelins more difficult. At first only every third or fourth streetlamp was lit, but this created an obvious disadvantage in that it left very dark patches, dangerous to pedestrians and vehicular traffic alike. The problem was overcome by painting the globes Oxford blue on the upper half and Cambridge blue on the lower half, so that little or no light was reflected upwards. This had the desired effect, and, since the lighting restrictions were so strictly enforced, Hull became known as 'the darkest city in the Kingdom'. Householders facing severe restrictions generally complied with the regulations but those who failed to do so were liable to trial by a military court.

The first raid by Zeppelins over Yorkshire occurred on 4 June 1915. The target was Driffield, although it is thought that this was due to a mistake in navigation. The airships came inland over Flamborough Head and were really aiming for Hull but managed to lose their bearings. Hull faced its first – and most serious – raid on 6 June 1915. A warning of that first raid was given at 10.00 pm by the sounding of a buzzer, sited on top of Blundell's buildings, at the corner of Beverley Road and Spring Bank, where the *Hull Daily Mail* building now stands. All the gas streetlights were turned off, public transport was stopped and other traffic was given half an hour to clear the streets. At midnight a droning of engines was heard and the sinister silver shape of a Zeppelin was seen approaching Hull from the west.

In this first attack the *Luftschiff 9,* commanded by a renowned pilot, the 'notorious' Kapitain-Lieutenant

Heinrich Mathy, a brilliant Zeppelin commander, moved east along the Humber, passing Victoria Dock, until it reached Marfleet, when it turned and made for Hull. A strange, disturbing feature of the early Zeppelin raids was that these were not impersonal attacks from a great height. The airships had named captains, had their numbers prominently painted on their sides, and approached at low level, purring menacingly as they navigated by following roads, railway lines and rivers to reach their targets. No one who witnessed the first raid ever forgot the sight of the airship with its three gondolas, 'sailing over the city' at a variety of estimated heights, or the sound of its whirring engines and clanging signal bells, Observers used a variety of familiar images to convey the lasting impression made on them. To one person it appeared 'not much longer than a cigar', and, perhaps understandingly, someone on Hessle Road remembered it as 'being as large as a steam trawler'. In fact *L9* was an 'M' Class Zeppelin, 518 feet (157.9 m) long, powered by 210 horse-power Maybach engines giving a top speed of 52 miles per hour, with a bomb load of between 1,100 lb and 1,430 lb (500-650 kg) and a combat ceiling of around 5,000 feet (1,524 m). Flying these colossal machines was almost an art form, combining the sciences of aerostatics, aerodynamics, structural and mechanical engineering and navigation. The Commander also needed to interpret and anticipate the forces of nature on his massive craft.

East Hull suffered in the raid, with several houses destroyed and some of the occupants killed. The Zeppelin dropped two bombs, harmlessly, into King George V Dock and then released part of its deadly cargo of high explosives in the area of the former Citadel, to the west of Victoria Dock. The timber yards on the Victoria Dock and Rank's Mill escaped damage, although these were thought to be the intended targets; but Hewetson's sawmill and wood yard in Dansom Lane were set on fire. The Old Town suffered the worst damage, Edwin Davis's shop premises on the south side of Holy Trinity Church were hit and the fires that raged were the fiercest of all those caused by Zeppelin raids. Besides the tragedy, there were other more bizarre happenings. The proprietor of the Fleece Inn owed his life and those of his family when his habitation collapsed about his ears to the fact that he had the foresight to seek refuge in the cellar among the barrels of beer. At the Corn Exchange Hotel a little distance away a bomb which penetrated the roof came to rest on a settee, the spring of which acted as a buffer and prevented it from exploding. As a result of the raid 40 people were injured and 19 were killed.

The fact that all of the casualties, including a number of children, were working-class people roused strong emotions, with demonstrations taking place at German owned shops, or those shops displaying a German name, even though naturalised Englishmen owned them. Great resentment was also expressed that Hull was defenceless against the German marauder, and the leading citizens of the town urged the War Office never again to leave them so exposed and vulnerable. Their concerns were heeded and the defences of Hull were improved, and searchlights and gun installations were sited within the town, which caused the Zeppelins to fly much higher. Many local people could recall for many years afterwards the beauty of a Zeppelin caught in the beams of searchlights. It was reported that Hull withstood the shock of that first raid 'most commendably and far from shaking the people's morale the raid had the opposite effect and stimulated recruiting in a marvellous way.'

A raid on the city by two airships similar to the type shown at was made on Sunday, 5 March 1916, when the buzzers sounding the alarm were operated at 8.40 am. Over 4,000 pounds (1,815 kg) of bombs were dropped on the city on this occasion, causing considerable damage to Linnaeus Street, Walker Street, Queen Street, High Street, Humber Street, Trinity House, and also in the dockland areas of Hull.

During this raid 16 people were killed and 54 injured. After the first raids there was a tendency for people in the densely populated areas to rush to the outskirts for safety. This was ultimately checked and the inhabitants reassured by voluntary street patrols who encouraged the women and children to remain indoors. The city also suffered further raids on 5 April and 9 August in 1916, the latter killing eight people and injuring 20. The following year there was only one raid, on 24 September, which caused damage in Southcoates Avenue and Dansom Lane, injuring three people. The final raid took place on 5 August 1918 when the guns were fired and succeeded in driving the airship off and thus no damage was caused to the city. There were a total of seven raids by Zeppelins, between the first raid on 6 June 1915 and the Armistice of 11 November 1918. In all 43 people were killed and 115 injured.

Those citizens of Hull who recalled the First World War must have steeled themselves for another ordeal on the declaration of war against Germany in September 1939, for they had already heard the sirens and the sound of falling and exploding bombs and had also experienced the perils of the blackout. Following the Battle of Britain in September 1940, during which the *Luftwaffe* had received a severe mauling from the Royal Air Force, the air assault switched to night bombing and was directed more and more against, firstly, London and, then, during the winter of 1940-1, against other provincial British cities and centres of industry, with the joint aims of destroying civil morale and production and supply facilities. This phase of the war, concluding in May 1941, became known as the Blitz.

It is certainly significant that Hull was so heavily bombed in both World Wars and, indeed, gained the unenviable distinction of being the most heavily bombed town in the Kingdom outside the capital during the Second World War. Hull was undoubtedly a prime target, through having extensive docks offering facilities and services to the shipping on which Britain depended in both wars, together with its large warehouses and engineering industries. Geographically, its situation close to the east coast and more or less directly opposite the German homeland, made it vulnerable. Furthermore, standing as it docs on the north bank of the Humber, it was easy to locate by moonlight, without the aid of radio assistance to navigation and blind bombing, which the *Luftwaffe* had pioneered and for which the RAF had only recently found effective counter-measures. The *Luftwaffe* declared Hull to be a primary, secondary and even tertiary target for bomber crews. This meant that Hull would be bombed when selected as the main target for a raid, or as a secondary target, if, for instance, Sheffield or Leeds were selected as the main target and the bombers were driven off by heavy anti-aircraft fire, fighters, or a heavy pall of smoke, or even low cloud. Hull could then be bombed as the secondary target on the return journey of the aircraft to their bases on the Continent. The third opportunity arose on those occasions when a bomb failed to release from the aircraft over the intended target and the crew had to attempt to release the bomb manually, as any opportunity for release was better than a return flight and landing with a live bomb on board. Hull was the last worthwhile target to aim for in such circumstances; otherwise the bomb had to be released harmlessly over the North Sea.

The *Luftwaffe* had prepared well in identifying targets in Hull. Folders were produced detailing military targets in the city. Each folder contained an accurate description of the target and the reasons for its strategic importance, together with its location and guidance in finding it and an indication of the strength of the defences. In addition to this, each folder contained a general map of Hull with the objective clearly indicated, a large scale map of the area immediately surrounding the target and one or more aerial photographs with the target highlighted. Each folder is dated March 1939 and thus were in the process of compilation until very shortly before the outbreak of war. However, some of the photographs have later dates and the folders had obviously been updated during the course of the war. Ten of these folders survive in the Imperial War Museum, London, having been brought to Britain after the end of the war. One of the folders contains the details of all the Hull docks, and one in particular contains details of Victoria Dock and the associated timber yards. The planning involved in the preparation of the documents must be viewed as a success, for virtually all of the targets identified in Hull were hit at least once during the course of the raids.

The air raids on Hull during 1940 were relatively light, but in July and August the evacuation of some of Hull's population began. Bombs were dropped on most of the docks and their surrounding installations and warehouses on at least 16 occasions and immense damage was done. On 30 August bombs caused damage to the east end of Victoria Dock. The L.N.E.R. steam hopper S.H.3 was damaged and was only prevented from sinking by the prompt action of the staff. She was subsequently pumped out and beached on the dockyard foreshore, repairs being carried out on the dockyard slipway.

At this stage in the war the RAF night fighter defences were little more than a collection of hasty improvisations. The Bristol Blenheim (designed as a bomber), the Boulton Paul Defiant (designed as a turreted day fighter) and Hurricanes and Spitfires were pressed into service as night fighters, groping around in the dark, much as their RFC predecessors had done in 1917. Nor had the German bombers much to fear

from Britain's anti-aircraft guns. In September 1940 an expenditure of 20,000 AA shells was required to down each enemy aircraft. By February 1941 the figure had dropped to 3,000, but enemy aircraft were, by and large, free to roam at will over Britain until the introduction of specialised night fighters late in 1941. In fact, Hull was defended in the main by searchlights, anti-aircraft guns and barrage balloons, which prevented low level attacks. Decoy fires were also lit on the outskirts of Hull, mainly at Sunk Island, to deceive the enemy bombers and these in fact, lured many of them away from the main target.

In March and April 1941 two heavy raids on north and central Hull destroyed homes and shelters, killing 143 and injuring 100. The most severe damage, however, was caused during the raids of May 1941. There were sporadic attacks on the first four nights of May, with damage done to the docks and the engineering company, Fenner's of Marfleet. Then, on the two nights of 7-8 May and 8-9 May 1941 came the two worst nights of damage suffered during the whole war, as far as Hull was concerned.

The map at shows the bombs which fell on and around Victoria Dock on those nights. All types of bombs were used. Incendiaries, designed to spread fire, fell in large numbers, together with high explosive bombs and parachute mines, both of which weighed around one ton (1,020 kg) and which were both designed to cause blast damage. The raids on both nights commenced around midnight and lasted for five to six hours. On the first night, 72 aircraft formed the attacking force and on the second night 20 aircraft. The usual tactics employed by the *Luftwaffe* were to send an early force of bombers armed with two types of incendiary bombs, the B1 E1 (Brandbomb, 1kg Elektron) and a derivative containing a small explosive charge, the B1 E1 ZA. These were usually dropped in canisters, each containing 36 incendiaries (BSK36), which fell apart a few seconds after release, scattering the bombs sufficiently to start large numbers of individual fires in a relatively small area. These marked the aiming points for the following aircraft, which would follow up with high explosive bombs and parachute mines, causing immense blast damage and spreading the fires which had been started earlier.

The docks were heavily bombed but many of the dock incidents were not reported during the attack, in the main for security reasons, so it is not now possible to show reliably the exact location of each explosion or fire, although those bombs that fell in the city were generally accurately reported. Reports of the damage to Victoria Dock were quite detailed and it seems that a bomb which fell on the south-east corner of the dock caused considerable damage to the quay. No. 32 Warehouse and No. 30 shed were demolished, Nos. 1, 14, 15 and 30 Warehouses were gutted by fire as were Nos. 2, 14, 31 and 32 sheds. Two lighters were sunk and six damaged. The coal conveyor and the east side of the dock were badly damaged. The east outer pier was demolished. The majority of the L.N.E.R. dockyard workshops, stores and other buildings were destroyed by fire. This loss was a serious handicap in dealing with the considerable volume of repairs necessary to restore essential traffic facilities. In fact rail communication with the dock was interrupted until 7.00 pm on 18 May due to unexploded bombs near Seward Street, Hedon Road. As a result of this raid the city centre was almost razed to the ground and much of the Old Town, an architectural mix of medieval, Tudor and Georgian buildings, was destroyed.

There were over 500 major fires on those two nights and the lights from the fires could be seen from the Danish coast by RAF bombers returning from operations over Germany. As a result of the attacks on the docklands, the Riverside Quay was burned out, and many fires and much destruction was caused in the warehouses and timber yards along the waterfront. During those two nights in May 1941, 420 people were killed and over 320 seriously injured. So many victims were unidentified or unidentifiable that on 12 May there was a communal funeral for 200. The ceremony was not made known to the general public to avoid crowds. But the tragedy and grief of those relatives present was said to be so overwhelming that it was decided never to repeat the ceremony.

During June 1941 the activities of the *Luftwaffe* decreased as units re-equipped and re-positioned eastwards in preparation for 'Operation Barbarossa', the attack on Russia. The moves were made under a cloak of secrecy and, as a cover to these movements; bomber raids on Britain were accompanied by false radio traffic to simulate larger forces. To maintain this deception the *Luftwaffe* executed heavy raids on Britain, including, on, 18 July, a large-scale assault on Hull, concentrated on the industrial area to the east of the River Hull. This area, although not neglected previously by the *Luftwaffe*, had not been the specific target of a major raid.

The map which details the raid does not indicate the extensive damage done to installations on Victoria Dock and the railways, since the itemised damage was not included in the incident reports made to A.R.P. Headquarters during the raids. This attack lasted from around 1.00 am until 4.00 am and succeeded in destroying many of the targets aimed at, including Reckitt's, Rank's Flour Mill in Drypool, Spiller's and the East Hull Gas Works. Smaller raids followed throughout the remainder of the year, causing further deaths in the city.

It was clear to the Germans by mid-1941 that the objective of the Blitz, the subjugation of Britain, had not been achieved. As further bomber unit were repositioned to the more urgent demands of the Russian front, leaving only anti-shipping units in the west, it was also clear to the British that this phase of the war was over. This, however, did not mean that bombing attacks had finished. The next major attack on the city directly affected Victoria Dock and occurred on the night of 19-20 May 1942.

The focus of the attack was once again east Hull The concentration of effort given on this night, and others to the docks and adjacent railway lines had a particular significance at this stage of the war for Hull was a major port of supply for the hard- pressed Russian armies.

Along the railway lines serving the port and from the docksides came the weapons, military supplies and food which were vital if the Russians were to hold out.

To block this vital artery, even for a short time, was a major gain for the German war effort. Several sporadic raids were carried out in the remainder of 1942 and in the early months of 1943. The next major raid was mounted on 14 July 1943. However, it lasted less than one hour. The raid centered on east Hull and, once more, Victoria Dock was bombed, with particular damage reported at the Hedon Road stables and No.14 Warehouse. A peculiar feature of this raid was the number of times phosphorous bombs were mentioned in reports.

During the remaining two years of the war, 1944/45, the *Luftwaffe were* only able to mount occasional raids against the City none of which directly affected Victoria Dock.

Despite the ability of the *Luftwaffe* to find the city with such ease, Hull became an anonymous city by official decree both during and for a long period after the Second World War. Ministerial censorship in the form of an official 'D Notice' ensured that enemy damage done to the city and its people were withheld from the British public. Reports in newspapers, on the radio and on cinema newsreels always referred to Hull as a 'North-east coast town'.

The raids on Hull during World War II were spread over four years in more than 70 separate attacks, which brought its own ordeals of long continued anxieties, tensions and disruptions to the citizens of Hull. They also brought immense destruction to the city. Some three million square feet of factory space were wiped out, 152,000 people were rendered homeless, of 192,000 habitable houses in Hull, only 5,938 escaped damage, half the main shopping area was destroyed, the docks suffered repeated damage and were out of action for three weeks after the heaviest raids.

Sources:
Calvert, *Hull*.
T. Geraghty, *A North East Coast Town* (Hull, 1989 edn).
Phillip Greystone, *The Blitz on Hull (1940/1945)* (Hull, 1991).
Markham, *Hull*.

Chapter Sixteen
A Prestigious Development: Victoria Dock Village

Victoria Dock closed to commercial traffic on 1 February 1970 and, with the exception of the half-tide basin, was completely filled in during 1971. The area was largely disused for many years following the infill, except for a few enterprises which operated in the area near to the half-tide basin and from the slipway. Among the better known concerns were Albert Draper & Sons, who used the slipway to dismantle ships in order to recover the scrap metal and other precious items. The vessels scrapped included at least one Humber ferry and many trawlers of the Hull distant water fleet. Mendham Engineering occupied a site close to the slipway; Wilson's, a transport company, occupied a former deal shed, sited between the inner and outer lock entrances at the western side of the lock pit; and a firm of caravan manufacturers used the former guano warehouse as a factory. But most other buildings were left to decay. The remainder of the dockland site lay largely derelict for several years, the uneven ground was pitted with potholes and the area flooded from time to time, creating a sea of mud, littered with rotting timbers when the tide had receded.

Construction of an extension to the A63 via Castle Street and over Myton Bridge, through to Garrison Road and Hedon Road, commenced early in 1979 and cut the former dock site almost in half. The northern side of Garrison Road was developed into the Citadel Trading Estate with access from the newly constructed Citadel Way which linked Great Union Street with Tower Street.

It was announced in November 1986 that Kingston upon Hull City Council were in negotiation with Associated British Ports to purchase the remaining 150 acres of the former dock, with the intention of developing the site through the building of 1,500 new homes. To enable their plans to be carried out, it was also announced that they intended to apply to the Department of the Environment for a derelict land grant to meet site reclamation costs. If this plan succeeded, it would be the largest housing development seen in Hull for over 20 years. It was envisaged that the project would create employment for up to 7,500 people over the construction period. During 1986, an Outline Development Brief for the scheme was drawn up by the Planning and Design Department of the Council and it was this Brief that set out the essential features to be included. The original proposal incidentally, was for 40% of the housing to be owned by the Council, 40% to private ownership and 20% for housing association homes. The total cost was estimated at £343 million.

The ambitious scheme had as its intention the creation of an urban riverside village which would revitalise the inner-city area. Like many other cities with good post-war intentions, Kingston upon Hull City Council had built housing estates on the green fringes of the city. This policy led however, to the so-called 'doughnut effect', which, although not foreseen, eventually meant that the town centre effectively closed after working hours, as the working population left for home, and, due to the increased cost of travel, became less inclined to return. A report of 1977 stated that there were only 20 people resident in the Old Town area. It was to redress this situation, through encouraging the population to move back into the inner-city, that the Council conceived and designed the Victoria Dock Housing Scheme. In 1987 Government approval of the scheme was announced through the award of a record-breaking £17 million Urban Regeneration Grant to allow for the building of a one-mile-long flood defence, incorporating a promenade, which promised to give unrivalled vistas of the Humber and which was also intended to fund the necessary programme of ground reclamation. There were two provisos to the grant: firstly, a private company had to carry out the building work, and, secondly, the homes had to be 'affordable' through the adoption of a policy of sales at market values.

In 1987 the Council selected Bellway Homes Limited as their partner, as they, through their Urban Renewals Division, had the expertise to realise the plans of the Council by completely reclaiming, renovating and ultimately transforming the disused, derelict and difficult site. Kingston upon Hull City Council put up the land as their part of the deal and Bellway Homes put up £50 million of venture capital for their part to fund the building programme. The new partners created a joint company for the development, registered as the Victoria Dock Company, in which Bellway, as the developer, held a 60% share and Kingston upon Hull City Council, as the Planning and Design Authority, held the remaining 40%. Councillor John Black was appointed Chairman of the new company and Bill Stephenson of Bellway Homes became Managing Director. The original plans called for the building of 1,200 homes of character, from compact *pieds-à-terre* to exclusive, spacious family residences. Development was to take place in 16 phases, with a planned development period of seven years. The architecture of the dwellings and the landscaping were to be carefully designed to give a mix of styles in sympathy with the surroundings. The townscape was intended to provide long tree-lined boulevards to give a strong directional feel. Behind the formal frontages would be more intimate mews and courtyards offering privacy but with a sense of community.

The plans also envisaged the inclusion of a marina, a public park, playing fields, an hotel, a public house, a community centre, a maritime museum (sited in the former Winding House) and a community school. The marina was intended to become the 'focal point at the heart of the village', surrounded by apartments and many other of the facilities contained in the brief, including a restaurant and bistro, to create a friendly fishing village atmosphere in the central area. As the houses were sold off, Bellway were to pay back Kingston upon Hull City Council for the cost of the land, with the balance paid off at the end of the development period.

Work began on building the first 39 houses comprising Phase One of the development on 11 May 1988, with a local company, Chris Moses (Building Contractors) Ltd., the main contractor both for this phase and Phase Two. The local firm of architects, Browne, Smith, Baker and Partners, were given responsibility for the design. The development of Phase One was sited immediately to the west of the original entrance to the Dock (now named Plimsoll Way). This first phase now forms The Haven, appropriately commemorating its earlier namesake, whose success formed the basis of Kingston upon Hull. The properties constructed in this phase comprised a mix of four-bedroom detached houses, priced at £61,500, three-bedroom semi-detached houses, priced at £36,750, and two-bedroom apartments, priced at £23,250. A tremendous number of people besieged the Bellway sales office, sited just off Plimsoll Way, when it first opened, calling both in person and on the telephone, trying to get a deposit secured. The unusual sight of people queuing outside the office and the show house had to be seen to be believed. The interest shown by people wishing to buy a house in the initial phase of the development was well oversubscribed, with over 500 people registering an interest, a successful launch pad for the development as a whole.

Steven Brown, then Bellway Urban Renewal project director, reported that: 'One chap from London tried to buy five homes, we've also wheedled out other speculators trying to make a fast buck, though we never thought that Londoners would go to Hull to make their profits.' Bill Stephenson, the managing director of the Victoria Dock Company, said in April 1989, after speculation that the price of homes on the development was heading into the so-called 'Yuppie' bracket': 'I am confident at the end of the day that the prices will be well within the range of the average earner, but they do have to reflect market values. No one can anticipate the way the market has gone nationally. Hull is becoming a far more attractive place and no longer is the sort of place where housing is low cost. It is called success and people have to pay for that.' Local estate agents backed up his views.

Kingston upon Hull City Council were enthusiastic supporters of the AMARC (Association of Marine and Related Charities) skills training scheme which was set up on site to help provide work for the long-term unemployed through the acquisition of skills. The scheme initially took on 20 trainees, of whom 14 found full-time employment. Soon after, a further 16 were found work placements. AMARC itself recruited a staff of 21 to manage the training project, based in the former ABP engineering offices at Sammy's Point.

Whilst the construction of Phase One was underway, the Archeological Unit of Humberside County Council carried out a dig on the site of the former Citadel, during July and August 1988, which was funded by Bellway Urban Renewals. They dug exploratory trenches in several key areas and excavated an area immediately to the south of the first phase. Much of the remains were covered by a mere six inches (15 cm) of soil, thus allowing a great deal to be discovered about the former Citadel. A report of their findings was published in September 1988.

On Friday, 21 April 1989 Bellway announced a fixed price for 70 of the 119 houses which comprised Phase Two of the new village, sited between the eastern end of Southbridge Road and the Humber. This meant an end to the anxious wait for the many prospective buyers who had put down deposits on homes before the previous Christmas, without knowing what the final price would be. Unlike most other developers of the time, Bellway put forward prices on their homes with the risk that they might have been overtaken by the time contracts were exchanged. It should be remembered that this was an era of 'gazumping', just prior to the housing boom bursting, which came at the tail end of the boom years of the late 80s, when there was falling unemployment and strong growth, topped by cuts in base-rates and income tax. The prices Bellway charged for the properties were closely monitored by the Department of the Environment. If they had been found to be overcharging or under-spending on the construction or reclamation costs, the Department was empowered to claw back an appropriate amount of the Urban Regeneration Grant. The response for all types of property was remarkable and the Bellway sales staff built up a long list of names of interested clients for future releases.

Detailed plans for Phase Three, sited immediately to the west of Phase Two, showed there was an intention to continue with the policy of providing a full range of housing to meet the needs of the market, ranging from sensibly priced apartments and starter homes up to five-bedroom houses, overlooking the Humber. Two-bedroom flats were priced at £45,750, two-bedroom semi-detached houses from £56,750, three-bedroom semi-detached houses from £52,150, four-bedroom detached houses from £112,250 and five-bedroom detached houses from £172,750.

The development at Victoria Dock began to attract national attention around this time, with many favourable comments in the national press, both about the project and the City. One report stated: 'Just ten minutes from Hull's city centre, 150 acres of derelict dock-land with the sea front extending to one mile has been reclaimed to form the setting for a mixed development of exceptional charm. The visitor will be struck by the sheer variety of design and the spacious and yet intimate groupings of the completed dwellings. Varied rooflines, broken elevations, traditional sash windows and panelled doors with stone lintels are features, which make a positive statement of individuality and quality. This impression is further enhanced by exterior detailing such as stone quoins, string coursing, decorative ironwork and balconies to some homes.'

Another national newspaper reported early in 1989: 'Bellway Victoria Dock scheme, a ten minute walk from the city centre, started building last November. In one month it sold more than 160 units – and the waiting list now has more than 300 names. People are pouring back into the Old Town in their hundreds and Hull – with employment down from 17% in 1986 to 10% today – has seen a 40% jump in property prices in a year to produce an average price for a home of around £40,000.' The *Hull Daily Mail*, in October 1989 reported: 'Imagine a warm summer evening – strolling along a tree lined waterfront walkway. Stopping to enjoy a drink in your local pub, or a meal at a local bistro bar beside a modern marina busy with vessels returning from a day on the river. Then instead of driving, or taking public transport, you simply skirt around a beautifully restored old ship slipway into an elegantly designed home in the village beside the river. But where is this idyllic lifestyle, Geneva? Paris? Or perhaps in the Lake District? In fact it's much closer to home. It is the vision which is fast developing into reality for homeowners at the new Victoria Dock, close to Hull's city centre.' These reports and several others in similar vein served to stimulate demand for homes on Victoria Dock even further.

Whilst the house-building work was being carried out there was also intense activity on the flood defences. The promenade and flood walls on the western side of the half-tide basin were the first to be improved, the work being carried out by the civil engineering and building contractors, Booth, of Riverview Road, Grovehill, Beverley. At each low tide there was a hive of activity with digging machines and cranes crawling along the bed of the Humber, putting in the foundations of the new floodwall in the limited time available. Each approaching high tide witnessed a hasty retreat of men and machines.

The promenade on the western section of the flood defences was set behind the flood wall, designed to cope with a level of one metre above the highest previously recorded tide. It has been tested several times since completion by exceptionally high tides and winds piling up the waters of the Humber, causing heavy spray across the promenade and it has passed the test with flying colours every time. It has thus so far fully justified the £2.5 million. The promenade wall on the western side incorporates some interesting wave sculptures cast into the wall panels, designed by Noel Black, in 1989.

Millions of pounds from the Urban Regeneration Grant were being spent on other infrastructure works, such as the roads, sewers and drainage of the site, as well as other particularly high costs which were site-specific. Examples of the costly difficulties can be illustrated by: the need for provision of sewage disposal from 1,400 properties, the removal of surface water (rain water and fresh water) from the 150-acre village and the reclamation of foul ground at the former timber ponds. As far as sewage disposal was concerned, matters were complicated by the fact that the east Hull sewer, which runs along Hedon Road to the treatment station and outfall near to King George Dock, was operating almost at full capacity, and increasing the size at that time was not an option. A means had to be found which would separate the provisions for the removal of sewage from the removal of ground water. The solution to the site drainage problem proved to be the half-tide basin. The groundwater drains on the site would be diverted to discharge into the basin, which would then effectively become a fresh water lagoon, the depth of which could be controlled by means of sluices, discharging the excess fresh water into the Humber at low tide. At this stage the plans to install a double set of lock gates, to replace the existing single lock gates which had fallen into disrepair were still valid and

would allow the planned use of the basin as a marina for small craft.

Work was carried out to dredge the half-tide basin, which by 1989 had become completely silted up. Major engineering work was undertaken to create two separate outfalls into the basin from each half of the site. The dock walls were refurbished following the dredging work, damaged stonework being replaced with engineering bricks. The long distance from the extremities of each half of the site and the need to create acceptable falls to the basin mean that the outfalls are set very low in the dock walls and, as they have to be above the water level in the basin, it is this factor that determined the ultimate low water level in the basin.

Bellway obtained a waiver from their obligation to provide a double set of lock gates in 1991 on the grounds that the costs were exceptional and the plans for a Marina were no longer commercially viable. They were, instead, granted permission to replace the existing single pair of lock gates with a single one piece 'flap' gate arrangement, to a design of the civil engineers, Kverner Boving Ltd. The 30-foot long, 40-ton gate was built by the Barrow on Humber construction firm, Charles Spencer. The flap gate works through being lowered, at low tide, to rest flat upon concrete support blocks; it is raised by hydraulic rams to its normal upright position. A pair of sluices sited in the breastworks on either side of the gate provides the means to control the level of water in the basin, thus creating a 'balancing system' for the inflow and outflow of water.

Work commenced in 1992, by placing sheet piling either side of the existing pair of lock gates in order to construct a coffer dam from which the water was pumped out, so allowing the removal of the old gates. Five thousand tons of concrete were poured and 250 tonnes of piles extending 130 feet below ground level were needed to form the support for the flap gate, which cost of £300,000. The associated engineering work cost £600,000 and the control room a further £100,000, bringing the total cost to £1 million, which, whilst a large sum is still a considerably smaller amount than would have been the cost of providing two pairs of lock gates. The new gates were slipped into place in late September 1992 by means of a 200-ton crane. Although Bellway continued to insist, even at that time, that there were no practical reasons 'why people fortunate enough to live in the village (or indeed overlooking the dock) should not moor a boat there and (subject to timing) come and go as they please'. However, the reality is that the opportunity for vessels entering the half-tide basin is now so remote as to be impracticable. This is owing to the combined factors of the construction of the new three-metre high sill and the low level of water which has to be maintained in the basin, due to the level of the outfalls, which in practice means that there is only a very small period in which to make an entry at either side of each full tide, thus dashing any lingering hopes harboured by sailors for the eventual use of the half-tide basin as a Marina for small craft.

Turning to the problem of the removal of foul ground, the areas which had formed the Timber Ponds were completely drained. The mud and clay forming the base of the ponds was heavily contaminated from the detritus of the timber stored in there over many years and this had to be removed. Once the foul material had been removed, a liner was laid over the new bed and sterile materials replaced the former contaminated soil.

This was a mammoth endeavour and was carried out over many weeks, using heavy earth-removing equipment and a fleet of lorries making continuous journeys. A further site-specific problem was how to make the entrance of the development appear distinguished, eye-catching and a fitting introduction to what was intended to become a memorable village. In part the problem was solved by placing the watchtower of the former Citadel atop a reconstruction of the walls, to serve as a focal point and as a reminder of the history of this area of Hull. In the main, however, the problem was solved through the creation of fine apartment buildings, which feature tasteful brick colouring and irregular rooflines. The developers and planners also spent many hours in discussing how to create a distinctive atmosphere for the village and the means of achieving a standard of elegance suggesting a real quality of living at Victoria Dock.

The solution to this problem was extremely elusive but there are several examples where it has been successfully accomplished. To many, it is best captured at the slipway. In its former working days the slipway was used as a ship repair and maintenance facility. Ships were hauled up from the waters of the Humber by means of a cradle and winch arrangement. The winch was powered by an engine sited within the engine house at the northern end of the slipway. The engine has been removed and is now preserved in a glass case on the east side of the Hull Marina. By 1988, the slipway presented a sorry sight, with crumbling brickwork and concrete, the cracks infested with weeds and having an overall air of decay. All that began to change in the summer of 1990 when the site was cleared. The open end of the slipway was sealed, making it a part of the promenade, new walls were constructed, a pathway was created around the perimeter, and a pool liner was put in place and covered with gravel to form the base of the new pond. Once filled, water plants were introduced, a new Ha' Penny Bridge was constructed to cross the pond at mid-point and a pump was installed which allowed water to cascade over stone steps set at the northern end, near to the engine house.

The engine house and its chimney were cleaned up and made stable and it was then offered for sale, despite having been identified as a site for a maritime museum in the original Outline Development Brief. However, to the surprise of most people it failed to sell, although it appeared to have excellent potential for conversion to a wine lodge, bistro, or restaurant. In 1997 plans were announced to demolish the engine house, which is the last remaining building of the former Victoria Dock and to replace it with an open garden. The Residents Association applied for Listed Building status in an attempt to prevent this needless destruction, on the basis that, once it had gone, there would be little left to remind anyone of the history of this site. A public meeting was held in September 1997 and the

overwhelming opinion expressed by those attending the meeting was that the engine house should be retained as a permanent symbol of the history of the site. Eventually their protest was successful.

The slipway itself has become home to several species of wildlife, including mallards, water hens and fish, including goldfish, which were introduced to the pond, and during 1996, one rather special tame white duck which survived two winters there, thanks to the many children who trooped down to feed it. The slipway is now surrounded by elegant apartments and, in the absence of anything being done at that time to make the half-tide basin more attractive, it makes a superb, if hidden, focal point in the village.

The Community Association (now the Residents Association) was formed in May 1990 with the intention that the development became and continued to grow as a village, in the real sense of the word, with a caring community at its heart. A commitment was made to address those issues which affected the quality of life of the people living at Victoria Dock and to seek improvements wherever possible. A committee was elected, with Colin McNicol elected as Chairperson, a constitution was drawn up and the decision was taken to hold quarterly meetings open to all residents. Early meetings were held in the portacabins used by AMARC as training classrooms, sited at the rear of the Associated British Ports Engineering Workshops and, despite the remoteness of the venue, meetings were well attended. When that venue became unavailable, meetings were held at the Waterbabes Day Nursery, Southbridge Road. This, a more central location, encouraged even more people to come along, to the point where some meetings had to be held outdoors. Many a lively discussion took place concerning, amongst other matters, the provision of what were seen as essential facilities for the village, such as street name signs, street lighting, a map of the village at the entrance for the benefit of the emergency services and trades people, provision of waste bins, local shopping, a bus service, post boxes, a telephone box, a school, a public house, landscaping for the site, a site road cleaning service and many other issues.

The Association decided at their second meeting to try to produce a quarterly newsletter, to be named *The Citadel*, so that people living at the dock could be provided with a reliable means of information on happenings in and around the village and also to create a sense of identity for the residents by explaining the history of the site. The first issue appeared in November 1991. At first a small charge was made to help defray the cost of production but, thanks to the generosity of sponsors and a dedicated, volunteer distribution team, the Association was able to circulate it free of charge. Unfortunately, after 12 issues spanning three years, it folded due to pressure of work. Gordon Rason, the present Chairperson of the Association, revived the newsletter late in 1999. Long may it run.

During 1990 and 1991 building work carried on at a staggering rate and property sales remained buoyant despite the growing evidence of a deep-seated recession and a consequent slump in house sales nationally. As a result the population of Victoria Dock Village continued to grow. The housing 'mix' had to change to reflect the changing market in order to maintain the 'affordability' factor, and it was local families above all others who bought the small semis and delightful apartments. Quite a few had 'traded up'; in some cases more than once, so they now occupy the best Victoria Dock has to offer.

One initiative developed fairly soon after the village began to be occupied was the plan to 'grow' a church on Victoria Dock. The Reverend Patricia Wick was appointed in 1991 by the Church of England as the church and community worker for the embryonic village to develop the initiative. She began by calling on all of the homes on the dock to talk to residents and also held a number of cheese and wine parties at her home to encourage people to mix and get to know one another. She also held several meetings with non-churchgoers to find out their views concerning the church. In mid-February 1992 she convened a meeting at her home, the *Wickerage* on Caledonia Park, for the ministers of the churches in the Drypool Parish to discuss future plans and to see what support they could offer. In an interview following the meeting the Rev. P. Wick said that she aimed to break down the barriers that exist between churchgoers and non – churchgoers. She continued: 'The churches' job is to work among people of all denominations, not just the Church of England. I am here to try to grow a church out of the local community.' Church services began in the lounge of her home and, as the congregation grew, transferred to the Waterbabes Day Nursery, in January 1993, meeting every Sunday at 10.30 am.

Since January 1996, church services have been held at the Village Hall and the congregation has steadily increased in size. In December 1995 the first carol concert, organised by the church for the village, was held at the Village Hall and was attended by the Bishop of Hull, James Jones (now the Bishop of Liverpool). Sufficient villagers came along to fill the Hall to absolute capacity. It was repeated the following year and met with similar success and has now become an annual event. Trisha left the Village in November 1997 in order to train for the post of missionary in Sudan and was succeeded by the Reverend Stephen Walker, who was inducted at a special service at the Village Hall in March 1998. He was later inducted as the Vicar of St. Columbus, Holderness Road, in September 1999, retaining overall responsibility for Victoria Dock. He in turn was succeeded by the Reverend Mark Bennett, who continues to take an active role in the development of the village.

In February 1992 there were 225 occupied houses on Victoria Dock and the Community Association was pressing hard for the provision of a bus service. Those people living on the dock who did not have access to a car faced a dangerous walk into town, having to cross six lanes of the extremely busy Garrison Road. Paul Matthews, who was then Transport Manager of Kingston upon Hull City Transport Department, was sympathetic to the arguments put forward and services to the dock commenced in May 1992, initially for a six-month trial period, through an extension to the Service 50 Marina mini-bus service, which served the Pier area. Later a Service 50 bus provided a much-needed dedicated Victoria Dock service. May 1992 also

saw the opening of the first shop in the village, the Riverside Store and News, owned by Neil and Moira Haylock, based in a portacabin on Southbridge Road. This provided villagers with one of the facilities they had been calling for most, a convenience store where they could purchase general goods such as bread, milk, newspapers, magazines, sweets, cigarettes and snacks from a local outlet. The variety of goods for sale increased once people expressed opinions as to what they would like to see stocked and the interior of the shop was like that of the Tardis: no corner of space was wasted in stocking most of life's little essentials.

One of the requirements identified in the initial Development Brief, to be provided by the developer, was the need for a Community Centre and, as the population of the village increased, the need for this provision became more pressing. Dozens of meetings between a Working Party of the Community Association and members of Kingston upon Hull City Council Department of Planning and Design were held at regular intervals, commencing in October 1991 to discuss the detailed plans for the Community Centre (or Village Hall, as the Community Association negotiators insisted on referring to it!). The Council officers then translated those ideas on to paper and held separate meeting with Bellway to turn them into reality. Eventually, through sheer persistence, the Community Association negotiating team, with the strong and much appreciated support of the Council officers, achieved in the design the requirements they felt necessary and work began on 15 April 1994 with the removal of the first earth to form the foundations. Various fund-raising efforts were carried out by a team of volunteers in order to provide a solid financial base to underpin the activities which it was hoped to run at the new Village Hall. These included car boot sales and also car washing, carried out each Saturday and Sunday, in all weathers and which proved to be the best fund-raiser of all.

By January 1995 the steel frame had been erected on the foundations: by March the brickwork had started; by early June the roof was on; and it was ready, externally at least, for the visit to Victoria Dock of H.R.H. Prince Charles on 8 June 1995. However, much of the internal work was still unfinished and so it was January 1996 before it was completed, at a total cost of £400,000. The Hall comprises a large lobby, a large function room known as Admirals Hall, together with two smaller meeting rooms and catering and parking facilities. The outside area has been landscaped and will eventually blend nicely into the entrance to the Victoria Park. When it finally did open early in January, Chris Hall, the chairman of the Village Hall Committee said, 'We are absolutely delighted with our new Village Hall as it will provide a real focus for the community.' The Reverend Trisha Wick said that she planned to hold normal Sunday Church services and Sunday school sessions as well as baptisms. But she ruled out weddings and funeral services because the Hall is not licensed for either activity. The chairman of the Residents Association, Colin McNicol, said that it was a superb building which everyone had been waiting for and had worked hard towards.

It is an undoubtedly handsome building, inside and

out, and, thanks to a very hard working committee, some of whom put in countless hours per week, the centre has fulfilled all and more of the expectations that were initially planned for it. The Civic Opening and unveiling of a plaque was carried out on Saturday, 4 May, by the Lord Mayor, Councillor John Black, accompanied by the Lady Mayoress and Fred Beadle, the chairman of the Leisure Services Committee. For the Village Hall Committee, Chris Hall officiated.

Since then, thanks to a hard-working committee and several other volunteers, many and varied activities have been carried out for the benefit of those living on the dock, including Keep Fit, American Line Dancing, a Youth Club, Girl Guides, Brownies, Boy Scouts, Cubs, indoor carpet bowls, badminton, table tennis, chess club, Judo classes, adult education classes, aerobics classes, meetings of the Residents Association and so on. The Hall has also been successfully used on a number of occasions to host wedding receptions, birthday parties, christenings, dinner-dances, craft fairs and carol concerts.

The Outline Development Brief for Victoria Dock also included the provision of two schools Plans to provide just one primary school in the village received a severe set back in February 1992 when Humberside County Council put the project on ice, claiming that it could become a 'white elephant', due to a lack of pupils. A survey carried out for the County Council in 1992 allegedly showed that only 15 children of school age lived in the village. The Residents Association had been pressing the need for a school, expressing both the concerns of families with young children and those of other residents. Everyone knew of people moving out of the village because of the lack of the school and others who would not move in for the same reason. The Association therefore carried out their own survey within weeks of the County Council survey and their results showed a figure of 105 children less than nine years of age living on the dock, which included 75 of pre-school age. The latter category had not even been considered by the County survey.

Despite the disparity in numbers, the chairman of the County's Education Committee, Councillor Maxwell Bird, said that the Committee did not wish to repeat two 'unfortunate experiences' where schools had been built and remained empty. It should be noted that both of those schools, Spring Cottage and Broadacres Primary schools, subsequently flourished. Bellway were said to be willing to put forward a substantial capital contribution towards the building costs, rumoured to be £1.6 million. Councillor Bird, however, said that the costs involved in building a school were regarded as high and that this was due to a number of factors, mostly the location, which meant that the scheme would have to include piling, secure fencing and protection from noise. He said: 'It is a prominent site, so we cannot put up rubbish buildings, they have got to be specially built. I don't doubt it will be built at some point but the question is when to put it in to the capital programme.'

As events turned out, Humberside County Council was abolished, following the reorganisation of Local Government of April 1994, and Kingston upon Hull City Council became a Unitary Authority with the responsibility for the provision of Education. An immediate difference in their commitment to provide a school was then detected. The argument for a school was repeated to the new Unitary Authority during 1994. The case essentially revolved around the fact that the population on Victoria Dock was growing rapidly and the nearest schools were sited at the far side of a six-lane highway which carried at peak times (coinciding with school attendance times) the heaviest density of non-motorway traffic in the United Kingdom. Young parents were obliged to make this horrendous and dangerous journey five days per week, quite a few on foot, and in all weathers, without so much as a pedestrian crossing to assist them or their children. The argument was also repeated that, for the lack of a school, some families were moving away from Victoria Dock, whilst others who wished to move there would not for the lack of a school. A vicious circle had developed.

The new Authority proved to be far more sympathetic to the arguments put forward, both by the Residents Association and Bellway, who were also actively canvassing the need for a school on Victoria Dock. The elected members for Drypool Ward and the Education Authority actively sought a way forward at a time when local authority budgets were being tightly squeezed.

The introduction of Private Finance Initiatives by central government became a possible, if not straightforward, means to unlocking the funds which might enable the school to be built. A meeting of the new Education Committee councillors was held on 28 November 1995 to discuss the possibility as a way forward. Under the PFI scheme private firms have to bid for public sector capital contracts. The tendering process is very complicated, and this was thought to deter many firms from bidding. However, the local authority lost no time in applying for a PFI to build the school. At a well-attended public meeting early in 1997 at the Village Hall between a forum comprising the local councillors and members of the education authority and many of the residents living on the dock the need for a school was repeated. The Council's officers reported that the Council had advertised the school project in the Office Journal of the European Community, inviting expressions of interest from developers. Those who had expressed an interest had been sent pre-qualification documents, setting out the Council's criteria for construction of the school as a PFI scheme, and from those expressions of interest the three parties who best satisfied the criteria had been invited to bid. Those three submissions were to be closely evaluated, from which a successful tender would be selected.

A provisional target date of September 1998 was set for the school to be opened. It was intended to be built in four phases, of 60 places in each phase, with core facilities for 240 pupils, dependent upon a timescale to be determined by increasing pupil numbers. The school would be built and owned by the successful tenderer and leased back to the education authority, which will supply the teaching staff. Other staff and non-teaching services would be provided by the successful company. The Planning Application for the construction of a 60-place school and a 26-place nursery, together with access road, car parking and playing field appeared on Tuesday 21 October 1997. It was announced that the Council had selected local builders, Sewell Construction Ltd., as the preferred builder, with one other selected as a reserve and it was anticipated that building work would commence in early December 1997 with a completion date of September 1998. It was noted that, when the plans were carried into effect, it would become the first primary school in the country to be built under a Private Finance Initiative, just one more pioneering step for Victoria Dock Village.

During 1992 one of Britain's top architects criticised the design of the village. Mr. Jim Monahan, who was responsible for the redevelopment of the historic buildings in London's' Covent Gardens said: 'It (Victoria Dock) is appalling, completely at odds with the rest of the city. It is isolated and has no real connection with the rest of the city. The only way you can go to and from it is by car. The council seem to hold it up as a style of building to be aspired to, but if that is the case I would be seriously worried for the future.' His remarks came at the end of a four-day workshop on possible future face-lifts for Hull staged by the School of Architecture at the then Humberside Polytechnic, now the University of Lincoln.

Residents on the dock gave his remarks short shrift. The chairman of the Residents Association, Colin McNicol, said: 'Of course he is entitled to his own opinion but the people living here like the overall design, it is meant to be a self-contained village and although it is early days we are working hard to create a community with the feel of a village, so we don't feel that the development is at odds with anything.' He commented: 'Access may be limited at the moment but this will improve and a footbridge will be provided across Garrison Road eventually and when the development is finished the facilities here will be superb.'

On 23 March 1992 the first turf was turned by the Lord Mayor, Councillor Dennis Woods, for what was to become the £2 million Victoria House complex for disabled people. The scheme was planned to provide a residential centre, to be built by Bellway, for 22 disabled people. The care support services provided within the centre would also be available to disabled people living nearby in specially adapted homes. The scheme was planned to have a staff of 50 including nurses, carers, a physiotherapist and managers, all of who were to be recruited from the Hull area. The central idea behind the scheme was to let disabled people live in their own homes whilst taking advantage of the special services available at the complex. The 'core' unit, situated at the end of Maldon Drive, overlooking the Humber, is run by the Sussex-based Disabled Housing Trust, which set up a unique scheme to encourage people to buy the homes, which feature en-suite bathrooms. In partnership with the Leeds Permanent Building Society, the Trust arranged a 100% mortgage to give those disabled people living on Income Support a chance to buy their own property.

The Chief Executive of the Trust, Norman Thody, said at the time: 'The aim is to try and give people as independent a lifestyle as is possible.' He went on to say: 'The scheme will care for the residents' physical, social and spiritual needs and we feel the involvement of community groups, service organisations, local churches and carers, who will come from the area, is very important to that.' The building was officially 'topped out' by the Lord Mayor of Hull, Councillor Dennis Barber on Tuesday, 2 March 1993. The Trust Chairman, Stephen Love, said: 'The building is a most spectacular site, looking directly across the Humber and it promises to be a great place for disabled people. The centre features communal rooms and workshops where residents can take part in occupational therapy sessions.' Mr. Bill Stephenson, Deputy Chairman of Bellway Urban Renewals Division said: 'The village itself and what Victoria House has to offer, could well induce many families with disabled people among their members to come and live here.' Victoria House opened officially in September 1993, helped by Hull Kingston Rovers player, Chris Harrison, and Hull City FC captain Greg Abbott, and other players, who greeted the first residents. The centre was full by Christmas of that year. The Head of Care, Mrs. Pat Pearson, launched an appeal for volunteer drivers willing to give up just a few hours per week to help in transporting the residents to various places, such as college, to youth clubs, or shopping.

Hull Civic Society awarded Bellway Homes its 'Good Mark' in March 1992 for the Victoria Dock Offices and the apartments which flank the offices. The Honorary Secretary of the Civic Society, Donald Campbell, said: 'We were impressed with the overall composition of the buildings which act as an interesting focal point for the development as a whole.' He added that the office block incorporated modern features but gave the illusion of a much earlier period.

The eastern section of the promenade was completed in 1992, at a cost of £1.5 million, thus completing the flood defences along the whole development. In contrast to the western sea wall, the wall at the east side is set to the rear of the promenade, giving a slightly more open view of the Humber. Dr. Abraham Peper, the Burgomeister of Rotterdam, officially opened the mile-long promenade on Saturday, 11 April 1992, in the company of the Lord Mayor of Hull and other Civic dignitaries. Dr. Peper said that he was very impressed with the regeneration of Hull's docks since he first came to the city over ten years ago. Councillor Pat Doyle, Leader of Kingston upon Hull City Council, said: 'One of the things we have in common with Rotterdam is a common interest in reclaiming dockland and in developments such as Victoria Dock. Therefore it is appropriate for Dr. Peper to be invited to open the east promenade. The promenade is a mile long and very pleasant to walk down but it also serves to consolidate the sea wall.' Both promenades have been planted with rows of trees, giving them an almost Mediterranean feel.

By mid-1992 it was clear that the housing boom had ended and the country was in the firm grip of a recession. It was also clear that different conditions would exist in the housing market from what had existed during the previous decade. It was considered, both by Bellway and the City Council, that the development at Victoria Dock would not be immune from the national downturn in the housing market. This meant that changes would have to be made to the original blueprint, both to reflect the alteration in circumstances and to maintain the 'affordability' factor of the properties offered for sale. In effect, this meant building more small homes and apartments on the site, which led to concerns in some quarters that 'ghettoes' could be created. Planning conditions specified that up to 15% of the areas set aside for housing had to be used for low-cost homes, sheltered accommodation and hostels for people with special needs. In June 1992 Councillor John Cartwright told city planners that, 'this could create a conflict between "rabbit hutches" on one side of the road and "palatial mansions" on the other.' His concerns were refuted by John Nesworthy, the Head of Development Plans, who said that the aim was to scatter the other housing among the rest of the development. Mr. Nesworthy also said that, since the original planning blueprint for the project had been drawn up, circumstances and needs had altered and certain changes were necessary. It was at this time that the decision was formally taken not to proceed with a marina since it was no longer seen as viable.

It was planned instead to provide a landing stage at the north end of the basin with the intention of attracting such sports as windsurfing and canoeing. Several changes to the original planning brief, drawn up in 1987 were contained in the revised planning brief for the development, which was issued during 1992. The new brief continued to identify the village centre as focused on the inner-outer basin areas. A report issued with the revised brief pointed out that there were some changes in circumstances since the scheme began and there were a number of factors which had and would have significant effect on the layout and programme of the scheme. Significantly, the area around the half-tide basin was still clearly identified as the site of most of Victoria Dock's social and community facilities.

It had been announced in February 1993 that plans to develop the 20-acre site at Sammy's Point for housing were being made by the Council. ABP, the owners of the land, were negotiating with several potential buyers who wished to develop the site. A report by the Town Clerk described the area as a 'key site', which would help complete the facelift of neighbouring Victoria Dock and regenerate the surrounding area. One option to develop the site could be in conjunction with a private builder, as at Victoria Dock. Councillor Jim Mulgrove, the Chairman of the Council's Economic Development Committee, said that the site could be developed in the same way, extending houses right up to the River Hull. The site was eventually acquired by the Council at a rumoured cost of £2 million and plans were drawn up for a scheme of housing and apartments which were very attractive, overlooking the entrance to the River Hull. Apparently, however, it was said not to be possible to get the right mix of housing to ensure economic viability for the proposal and the project lapsed.

Bellway Homes were voted the winner of the prestigious *What House* magazine Gold Award, in 1993, as the 'Best Urban Renewal Development' in the United Kingdom. The *What House* Awards are presented in a number of categories, designed to single out house builders and developers who had achieved excellence in their particular sphere of operation. Certain areas of difficulty overcome by the company during the course of the project played a part in the judges' decision in selecting Bellway for the award. The key to the award was the successful creation of a housing market in an area where none had previously existed. The development at Victoria Dock is recognised as an outstanding example of what can be achieved by real commitment to urban renewal. Councillor John Black, Chairman of the Victoria Dock Company, was equally delighted, by Bellway's receiving the award for the village and said: 'It's a very prestigious development and when you consider the developments it has beaten (referring to the London and other dockland developments) it is a major achievement. This means that Victoria Dock is the best urban development scheme in the country.' He went on to say: 'The development scored very highly in the range of accommodation it has provided, with houses ordinary people can afford to buy. It is very different from some of the London dockland developments, which are effectively yuppie ghettoes. To take a decaying dock in an inner city area and transform it into a pleasant village with a mile-long promenade is a great achievement.'

By January 1994 about one third of the planned 1,400 homes at Victoria Dock had been completed and the next phase was about to get underway with the construction of 26 two- and three-bedroom houses at Victoria Quays, and 27 three- and four-bedroom homes on the site. Work was also due to start on 60 apartments by the slipway.

During the same month Bellway were also given outline planning permission for the construction of a footbridge to span Garrison Road, near to the Plimsoll Way roundabout. A second more detailed plan was to be submitted for final approval, showing the design, the siting and height of the bridge.

It emerged at the beginning of 1994 that plans for the commercial development of shops, restaurants and pubs around the half-tide basin would not go ahead. The same economic conditions which had been quoted for the abandonment of the proposals for the marina were blamed for the lack of interest from potential developers, despite what was termed, 'an aggressive marketing exercise'. Planning permission was sought by Bellway to relocate a public house, shops, a medical centre and a crèche at the entrance to the village, off Plimsoll Way, with a new access, service road and car parking. To many residents this situation came as a bombshell, and a well-attended public meeting of the Residents Association was held on Wednesday, 20 July 1994, at which people angrily and vociferously argued the case that they felt cheated and betrayed, having been sold properties on the strength of promises which had not been delivered. They adopted a slogan for their protest, 'People before Profits', as it was the view of many at the meeting that the original plans for the commercial development were being sacrificed in the name of profit. Several members of the Association expressed the opinion that, whilst they accepted that

Reflective view of the Slipway pond.

Preparing the site of the flapgate entry to the Half-tide Basin.

The Village Hall. (May 1997).

Victoria House.

Snow on the promenade: looking toward Pilots Way.

Humber View, Pickering Ferens Homes.

Prince Charles visiting the Village, Thursday, 8 June 1995.

The Timber Dock.

Victoria Dock Primary School: opened January 1999.

The Deep: opened Easter 2002.

It's a Knockout, July 2001.

Victoria Dock Primary School: first birthday party, January 2000.

The Watch Tower: the last remaining part of the Citadel.

The Village Hall, March 1996, following landscaping.

The Hartley Bridge: originally spanned the opening between the Half-tide Basin and Victoria Dock.

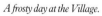

A frosty day at the Village.

the new proposed location for the commercial development was unsuitable for anything other than low-rise, lightweight development, due to the area being infill land, the previously identified area around the half-tide basin, being solid ground, was now proposed for use as four-storey high apartments. Which would deliver the greater profit? Had a truer motive for the proposal been identified?

Those at the meeting urged that the Planning Application be opposed on the grounds that the opportunity of creating a village with a distinct personality and a living centre would be lost and that the development would become a dull, featureless, dormitory estate. Residents said that they were prepared to wait for the facilities around the half-tide basin until the right economic conditions returned. A 301-name petition was lodged with Kingston upon Hull City Council, as the planning authority and 215 individual letters of objection were sent in support of the objection. A campaign was mounted to attempt to reverse the decision and many residents complained to the local press at the weakening will to carry out the original vision of a waterside village with a distinctive atmosphere, apparently because of transient economic conditions. Councillor John Black appeared before a well-attended meeting of the Residents Association on Friday, 29 July, in his capacity as Chairman of the Victoria Dock Company, with the intention of mediating in the escalating protest. He was left in no doubt whatsoever of the feelings of those attending the meeting and he promised to arrange a meeting between the developer and the Community Association. Eventually the planning application was heard and deferred until a site visit had taken place. On the day of the visit, Wednesday, 17 August, the councillors forming the Planning Committee were met by over 50 residents, many of whom had taken time off work to put forward their objections and describe their reasons for buying property at Victoria Dock, which centered around the facilities which had been promised in the outline development brief, articles which had appeared in the local and national press, the developer's publicity brochures and comments from the company's sales staff.

However, despite the support of local councillors, all was in vain, as the full Planning Committee decided to grant the application, quoting the changes in circumstances as their reason. The residents' fight was lost, leaving many of them feeling quite bitter and let down, especially as there was no right of appeal. Many expressed the view that a partnership between Bellway and the Council was such that the Council would represent the best interests of the residents who chose to live on the dock and paid a premium to do so. They felt that it had not lived up to that promise.

Councillors from Barking and Dagenham visited Victoria Dock in March 1994 as part of a two-day fact-finding tour of many of the city's housing developments and initiatives. Their council leader mounted a crane and hoisted the cupola to the top of Dukes Court, bringing the total number of completions to 550.

In spite of the national trend, sales of property at Victoria Dock had remained buoyant during 1993, as shown by home-buyers snapping up 66, two- and three-bedroom apartments in the Princes Wharf phase of the development in less than a year after they went on the market. The first phase of 41 two- and three-bedroom apartments comprising Kingston Place enjoyed a similar sales success when they were released in May 1993, eight being snapped up immediately. Kingston Place was built in four phases in a part of the development almost surrounded by water, fronting the Humber between the slipway and the outer basin. It has since been re-named Axeholme Court. The apartments were designed in three distinct styles and all were served by an intercom entry system and satellite TV link, some having balconies. Central heating and double-glazing were fitted as standard equipment. The accommodation was well designed and provided spacious apartments with excellent and uninterrupted maritime views.

The Italianate style executive two- and three-bedroom apartments overlooking the half-tide basin at the then named Earles Court, (now Sequana Court) were offered for sale during 1993, priced from £44,450, and proved to be strong sellers, due to the external design, the high internal specification, which included kitchens with fitted oven hob, filter hood, fridge, asterite sink and waste disposal, bedrooms with shower units, and their outlook facing the Humber. Other phases of the development also continued to trade strongly.

Frank Reil, the managing director of Bellway Urban Renewal Division, said in March, 1994 that Victoria Dock Village had never stopped growing because there had been no housing slump there, explaining that the market had never died at Hull even when the housing recession had gripped so grimly elsewhere. He said: 'It is really boom time at Victoria Dock. So great is the momentum of building and selling at Hull that the next hundred flats and houses, which are in the early stages of construction, have all been sold.' What a shame then that the original plans for the village were compromised. He also announced that a pub and restaurant was to be built by Cameron's brewery and a sheltered accommodation of 36 units, to be run by the Pickering Housing Association, was to be constructed at the western end of the development.

The development also continued to attract good press reports, as one of May 1994 illustrates: 'Located just a few minutes walk from Hull city centre, Victoria Dock Village is far more than just a housing development. It is a blueprint for the future, illustrating the dramatic results, which can be achieved from the careful planning and creation of a new community. The village will provide over 1,200 quality homes, comprehensive shopping provisions, school facilities, office buildings, a landscaped park and public houses – all fronted by an attractive mile-long promenade to the Humber.'

The houses at Victoria Quays were now offered for sale, as were those at Merchants Landing. At Victoria Quays the prices ranged from £43,250 to £70,550 and at Merchants Landing from £76,700 to £130,500. Merchants Landing was built in a quiet area of Victoria Dock with views either over the Humber from balconies, or facing a quiet cul-de-sac, and comprised eight individually styled executive homes of high specification, built on a generous-sized plot of land. The two- and three-bedroom apartments at Marine Basin, which boasted waterfront and river views, went on first release in May 1994 with prices from £46,950 to £66,000 for a top-floor, three-bedroom home overlooking the river. The new apartments were claimed to offer the perfect combination of quality, location and value for money. They were designed with a high internal specification, some selected properties even offering carpets, fridge, washing machine and a contribution to legal costs. The unique layout meant that almost all the apartments enjoy a waterfront view – either easterly, westerly, or the full river panorama.

On Monday, 5 December 1994, it was revealed that the city was to gain a new 22-acre public park at Victoria Dock. It was to be dedicated to the theme of navigation and astronomy in the days when the art or science of directing a ship's movement or determining its position through the use of geometry and astronomy relied on the skill and knowledge of the navigators and the sun, moon and stars, before satellite and radar. It would include a large open space, a nature area, woodland, ornamental gardens, a bowling green and a play area. The park was planned to serve all the recreational needs of Victoria Dock residents and other people living in the city centre. It was planned to incorporate a series of sculptures or a commemoration of the coming millennium. Councillor Harry Woodford made the wonderful suggestion that the Queen Victoria statue be removed from above the public toilets in the city centre to provide a focal point in the new park, which was to be named Victoria Park, and would become the first city centre park to be constructed since the turn of the century.

It was said that in providing an attractive environment the park would attract investors, raise property values and contribute to the 'Healthy Cities' programme. A 38-space car park would be built to serve the needs of motorists visiting the park. The funding of the construction costs of the park were to be met by Bellway as the developer who also agreed to fund the first two-years' maintenance costs, after which time they would pass to the Council. The original plan called for the park to be completed by December 1995. This target proved to be much too ambitious as basic preliminary work on drainage did not commence until 18 September 1995. Two days later it was announced that the project had been awarded £100,000 of Lottery money.

It was not until March 1997 that any real progress could be seen when earth-moving equipment arrived to stockpile a huge mound of topsoil which would be used to both level and cover the rough site. Real work, in the sense of actually creating the park through hard landscaping, began in August 1997, when Wrights, the Hull firm of civil engineers, arrived on site and set up their portacabins.

Site preparation and foundation work on the sheltered housing project next to Sammy's Point began in February 1995. The centre was a joint initiative between Kingston upon Hull City Council and the Pickering and Ferens Homes and would eventually provide attractive, high-quality accommodation consisting of 36 self-contained flats, of which six would be doubles, with some communal facilities, with a warden housed on site. Bellway were to build the complex and the warden's bungalow. The Burgomeister of Rotterdam, Dr. Abraham Peper, was invited to unveil a plaque to commemorate the start of building work on 10 April 1995. Councillor John Black, chairman of the City Council's housing committee, who accompanied Dr. Peper said: 'It seemed appropriate that he should be asked to mark the start of work on the development on his return visit, Rotterdam is used to riverside developments but in Hull we have had very little opportunity to develop that way until now.' He went on to say that the dockside was an ideal location for the scheme as it was started with money bequeathed to find homes for retired fishermen, their families and dependants. The building, which has superb views over the Humber and is surrounded by lovely gardens, was completed by April 1996.

Jackie Holden had been appointed as the warden for the scheme, moving from her previous position at the Christopher Pickering Lodge, where she had successfully organised many activities for her charges. The newly completed building was appropriately named Humber View and housed 41 residents when it opened. Steve Wilson, the manager of the Pickering and Ferens Homes, had the unenviable task of sifting through the list of applicants to select the successful residents. Sheltered housing is meant for people who are able-bodied and can care for themselves but need just that extra little bit of supervision and help. The job of the warden is to look after the welfare of the people in her care by visiting them daily, arranging transport; doctors' visits, the collection of prescriptions and other general care arrangements. The job doesn't stop there, as entertainment, including bingo, quiz evenings, guest speakers, live music evenings and outings, have to be organised.

It was announced in the strictest secrecy during May 1995 that the Prince of Wales, would visit Victoria Dock Village at the beginning of the following month, when he would tour the development, visit the home of one of the villagers, then plant a tree and unveil a plaque near to the Village Hall to mark the entrance to the site of Victoria Park. The visit was planned by the Palace Press Office, which expressed the wish of His Royal Highness that as many villagers as possible should be there, as he was anxious to meet them. There was much planning to be done in a fairly short space of time to make sure that Prince Charles would see the best Victoria Dock had to offer in the limited amount of time available for the visit.

The date for the visit was set for Thursday, 8 June, and he arrived on a cloudy and breezy day in his official car right on time at 10.15 am at the location chosen for the start of his visit, near to the flap gate at the centre of Victoria Dock. The crowd assembled there cheered as he alighted from his car and he smiled and talked to many of them as he walked to where the formal introductions would take place. Following a series of presentations to various members of the Bellway and Victoria Dock Company boards, the Prince was given a guided tour of the central area of Victoria Dock by the Deputy Chairman of Bellway Urban Renewals, Bill Stephenson, their Managing Director, Frank Reil, the Northern Regional Director, David Lloyd, and Councillor John Black, the Lord Mayor of Hull and Chairman of the Victoria Dock Company. Before the visit took place the Prince had made it known that he wished to visit an occupied house, so it was arranged that during the tour Prince Charles would visit, on his own, the home of Charles and June Gibson at Ocean Boulevard. This visit was scheduled to last around three minutes but actually took over fifteen, as the Prince chatted to Charles, June and their daughter, Paula, whilst they showed him around their home. Charles said that the Prince put his family completely at ease and chatted easily about all manner of things as he was conducted around the house.

After his visit, Prince Charles was driven to the Village Hall where a larger crowd which awaited him cheered enthusiastically and waved Union Jacks as he left his car. He walked across to talk to many of the people gathered there, asking them all manner of questions on subjects such as gardening, decorating, work, shopping, holidays and children. He took a special interest in the welfare of the small children, many of whom had come from the Waterbabes Nursery, asking how long they had been waiting, if they were warm enough and if drinks had been brought along for them. He was then introduced by the Lord Mayor to many of the people living in the village, including the Chairman of the Residents Association, Colin McNicol, who then introduced him to the Vicar, Trisha Wicke, the Community Police Officer, Jean Wright from Tower Grange, Chris Hall, the Chairman of the Village Hall Committee, Lesley McNicol, Chair of the Fundraisers Committee and members of the Village Hall Committee. The Prince chatted to everyone and had obviously done his homework as he asked many informed questions. He was kind enough to sign a portrait of himself to commemorate the visit, which now hangs in the entrance to the Village Hall.

The visit was rounded off by the Prince planting the first tree in an area outside the Village Hall which would eventually become a part of Victoria Park. He then unveiled a plaque, which is now sited at the entrance to the park. The Prince was presented with a framed aerial photograph of the development by Bill Stevenson and Frank Reil on behalf of Bellway. The feedback from the Palace was that the Prince had thoroughly enjoyed his visit and was impressed by all he saw.

The village featured in *The Times* late in June 1995 in an article concerning the topic: 'How does a housing estate become a community? Creating rural idylls in the heart of a city'. The feature highlighted a report commissioned by central government which had projected that there would be a need for an additional 4.4 million new households to be accommodated by 2016. In response, the Central Council for the Protection of Rural England encouraged the work of developers who were reclaiming so called, 'brown sites', those which had been contaminated, especially those in urban areas, as this approach matched their own campaign for homes to be built in cities rather than on greenfield sites. The article noted that the

British traditionally want to live in the country, or at least think they do. The problem was that present levels of greenfield house building have caused more loss of countryside than any other form of building. The solution suggested by the CPRE was to construct new homes in the 21st century by concentrating them in towns and cities in a way that counters the attractions of suburbia. One site held up in the article as an example of successful urban regeneration was Victoria Dock. Bill Stevenson commented: 'You can generate a pleasant and attractive feel without the sensation that you are in the middle of a city, at Victoria Dock there are already more than 700 homes that are occupied. There is housing for the disabled, elderly and some rented places plus owner/occupied family houses that are mixed in with more expensive ones.'

The village was once again criticised in September 1995 in a book written by London-based architect Roger Fitzgerald *(Buildings of Britain)* who described the development as 'rather crass' saying it failed to make the most of its setting overlooking the Humber. He commented: 'It could be anywhere,' adding 'there is no response to the unique character of Hull, nor to the problems and opportunities of its specific location.' Councillor John Black hit back at the criticism: 'Victoria Dock was developed to give ordinary people access to affordable traditional housing in the city, not for architects to come up with arty-farty designs which are totally impracticable. When Prince Charles visited the dock recently he was very impressed and said it was the type of traditional housing he favours. I think most people would agree with him rather than the architect.'

There was a 'Bonfire Bonanza' on Saturday 5 November when Bellway laid on a carnival day, including Viking FM Radio, Warrior, from the hit TV series, 'Gladiators', a steel band, an ice hockey demonstration featuring 'Harry the Ice Hockey Kid', the Fire Brigade and Humberside Ambulance Paramedics, and prizes including a £500 cash prize or a £2,000 discount off the price of a new house at Victoria Dock. Dozens of people turned out to see the entertainment, visit the show houses and look around the dock.

Work began on the long-awaited public house in December 1995. It was designed by Roger Evans and Associates of Birmingham for Cameron's Brewery which had invited members of the committee to examine the plans for the building earlier in the year. The design brief was to create a pub with a distinct atmosphere and identity recalling the old days of the dock. It was explained that the design of the new pub, both externally and internally, would reflect the heritage of the village to give a unique hospitality venue. The intended appearance would evoke the theme of a mill owner's house, merchant's invoicing office and a timber seasoning shed which had been taken and redeveloped.

The pub would be characterful, appealing and interesting, with due regard to authenticity balanced with a keen awareness of customers' needs. It was intended that the pub would have a timeless quality, enhancing the village feel of the development, whilst appealing to townspeople and visitors of all ages and walks of life. A competition to find a name for the new pub was run by Cameron's; through *The Citadel* newsletter and the name *Timber Dock* was selected as the prizewinner. Since more than one person had suggested the name, a draw had to be made to find the outright winner, Mrs. Dorothy Garrity of Isis Court.

The building was constructed by Street Construction of Wigan, using 'fast track' building methods, which meant that the only materials stored on site were those needed for the immediate next phase of building. This method ensured a quick build with the minimum amount of rubbish blowing about the site, a factor appreciated by the residents living nearby. The external works were completed by May 1996 and the topping out ceremony was carried out on the 23 of the month by Steve Frankel, managing director of Street, with Phil Cawood, Cameron's Free Trade Manager, and Colin McNicol of the Residents Association looking on. The building was fully completed by July and the new 'mine hosts', Brian and Maureen Doleman, worked really hard to make sure everything was perfect for the opening day, when invited guests of Cameron's were invited to be at the opening ceremony. It opened for business at 11.00 am prompt on 3 July, when the first pint was pulled by Colin McNicol, on behalf of the Residents Association Committee. He thanked Cameron's for showing their commitment to Victoria Dock through the building of a much needed facility for the community, which had been long awaited and for delivering a building of character so in touch with its' surroundings and history. Phil Cawood, on behalf of Cameron's, said they were delighted to be associated with the community at Victoria Dock and elsewhere in East Yorkshire, where they were investing heavily in a number of new public houses. The *Timber Dock* has proved popular with people both from within and outside the village from the day it opened its doors. July was a warm month and lots of people stopped to drink outdoors at the patio area and this continued throughout the rest of the summer.

Once the park is complete and has matured, there will be a beautiful view to enhance their pleasure. Inside the pub is spacious and well laid out, with a raised area and a large welcoming fireplace. A programme of evening attractions evolved, such as quiz nights, entertainers and large screen sport which proved popular and attracted large numbers. Brian and Maureen created a warm atmosphere in the pub where people can sit and relax in friendly surroundings. One important facet of the trade which the pub also developed was a growing and enviable reputation for the quality of the food, which attracted a good press. The *Hull Daily Mail* Business Correspondent, Phil Ascough, took Barrie Matterson, the CityVision regeneration manager, for lunch at the Timber Dock before they took a tour of the Village. He reported as follows: 'The walls are adorned with old black and white prints of the city as it used to look, when nothing moved very far unless it was on a ship and you could cross the docks by stepping from one vessel to another. Through the windows is an example of urban redevelopment hailed as one of the best and most imaginative in the country, where better to entertain an authority on regeneration.' The *Timber Dock* was

again featured in a report later in the year for the 'Sunday Lunch' spot. Once again, the pub scored highly in every section, which included the surroundings, the selection, the price, the service, the quantity, the quality and overall impression. Praise indeed and well deserved. Brian and Maureen moved on in July, 1998 to open another new pub for Cameron's, *The Voyager*, in Guisborough and were succeeded by Peter Clarke who remained until 2000, when he in turn was succeeded by Rob and Jill Clarke, formerly of the *Crown Inn*, Holderness Road.

Proposals for an ambitious river barrage scheme at the entrance to the River Hull, adjacent to Sammy's Point, were announced in March 1996. The project involved a revamp of the river and its surroundings, upstream of a £23 million barrage across the mouth of the river, with commercial and recreational development. Similar schemes at Stockton, Teeside and Swansea, South Wales had been spectacularly successful in breathing new life into once derelict landscapes. Land prices in both areas had surged as such plots had become prime real estate, some increasing by 100%. This is the kind of vision harboured by the planners in Kingston upon Hull who want to transform the ailing River Hull corridor into a hotbed of private investment. An economic evaluation and an environment impact statement of the region will be carried out, at a cost of almost £1.1 million and consultations with river users will take place to decide whether to formulate a bid for government cash to fund the scheme into the next stage. So, for now, it's a wait-and-see exercise.

The 22 three-bedroom Kensington house types comprising St. James Court came to the market in the spring of 1996. These were the first town houses to be built at Victoria Dock and are a very attractive design, arranged on three floors and included luxury bathroom suites, fully-fitted kitchens with oven hob and filter hood, en-suite shower rooms to the master bedrooms, cloakrooms, utility rooms and integral garages. They were priced from £63,450, which included carpets.

Bellway Homes organised a Summer Gardening Competition for August 1996, which was open to all Bellway Homes residents at Victoria Dock. The categories which were judged included 'Best Front Garden' plus two runner-up prizes, 'Best Rear Garden' plus two runner-up prizes, 'Best Small Garden' and 'Special Prizes' for best effort in a short period of time. The judges found the standard of the gardens entered to be very high and held a well attended prize-giving event in September at the Village Hall.

By summer 1996, Bellway had built just over 850 of the homes on Victoria Dock, and in August submitted detailed plans for the next phase on a nine-acre site at the eastern side of the village, comprising 102 homes and garages, together with the construction of roads and footpaths. A spokesman for Bellway said: 'The new plan represents an amendment to a previously approved scheme and will feature a mixture of homes ranging from two-bedroom to four-bedroom houses, we do not think there will be any difficulties with the new application. Work in that area should be completed by June, 1998.'

Also in the summer of 1996, Kingston upon Hull City Council publicised their bid for Lottery Funding from the Millennium Commission. The bid was to fund an ambitious scheme for a major new £30 million marine-focused tourist attraction, research centre and educational facility, to be based appropriately at Sammy's Point. The plans called for a landmark building to be designed in an eye-catching style on the scale of the Sydney Opera House, which would be immediately associated with Hull by people around the world. The project, which would put Hull firmly on the tourist map, would be a northern regional centre of the Natural History Museum and would focus on the deep seas as its theme, dealing with a wide range of issues, such as the evolution of life in deep sea trenches, life in the seas today, man's relationship with the sea, myths, legends and shipwrecks and was planned to have a 'state of the art' aquarium as the centrepiece.

Research into current and future environmental issues would be carried out by academic experts from Hull University's Humber Observation Unit, which conducts a wide range of widely acclaimed river, marine and meteorological research and which would be based at the new site. It was also foreseen that the centre would become an educational facility which could be used for programmed school visits to study the environment. Deep Sea World, operators of an advanced aquarium in Scotland, joined the partners in formulating the plan.

The final approval for the bid would come from the Council of the Millennium Commission as they would allocate the funding from the National Lottery. This source would meet half the cost of the project, the remainder coming from European grants and the private sector. It was explained that the scheme was up against many other regional and national schemes submitted for what was expected to be the last handout by the Millennium Commission. The scheme was to incorporate, as a suggestion of the Residents Association, a pedestrian crossing of the River Hull at its mouth, to offer an alternative means for those residents who walk to town, which, it was suggested, could also become a part of the successful Hull 'Fish Trail'. The bid cleared its first hurdle in being accepted and successfully went forward for further and more detailed appraisal in November 1996. Originally over 1,000 schemes were submitted and the Kingston upon Hull City Council bid had reached the final 119 schemes allowed to proceed to the next stage. Officials from the Millennium Commission came to Hull later in the year to inspect the site at Sammy's Point in order to carry out a more detailed study

Later still, during the summer of 1996, the government announced that the plans to upgrade the A1033 Hedon Road through a planned improvement scheme would be delayed indefinitely as part of their planned reduction in public spending. The likely impact on the village from this decision was discussed at the A.G.M. of the Residents Association, especially as no proposed date for an eventual start was declared.

In view of this situation the Chairman had been asked to write to the Highways Agency requesting consideration of proposals put forward at the meeting seeking local improvements in the short term. Suggestions included yellow-hatched areas at both roundabouts to prevent queuing traffic blocking the

exits, the provision of part-time traffic lights for use during peak traffic flows and pedestrian crossings. The reply was that insufficient accidents had occurred, either to qualify the areas as an accident hotspot or to justify the measures requested. The Agency pointed out that there were many schemes competing for scarce resources. Those attending the meeting then demanded that a petition be sent via the City Council to the Highways Agency stating that residents were not content to accept their reply meekly and to point out the need for action before a tragedy happened. Over 600 people signed and the petition was presented to Ward Councillors, who in turn presented it to the Director of Technical Services for the suggested improvements to be included in the bid by Kingston upon Hull City Council for improvements in access to Victoria Dock.

A Family Fun Day was organised by Bellway for Sunday, 1 September, at the Parklands, where a clown added to the festivities which included a jazz band, free barbecue and free wine for the adults and a bouncy castle and ice creams for the kids. Once again it attracted large numbers of visitors, who also took time to look at the show house and stroll around the village. Later in the year it appeared there might be another solution for funding improvements to the long-standing problem of traffic flow along Hedon Road and Garrison Road, and which would also incorporate improvements to access and exit from the village. In the autumn of 1996 the Government had announced that European Union funding could create a dual carriageway all the way to the city's docks, as the route formed part of an EU bid to link Limerick in Ireland and St. Petersburg in Russia in a massive trans-European trade route known as the E20. Mr. Kevin McNamara, the North Hull M.P., had received a letter confirming that the M62-A63 link via Hedon Road through to the ports was eligible for consideration for EU cash backing. Plans had already been drawn up by the Government for a £49 million scheme of improvement said to be just about the most important for business in Yorkshire. On a more local note, it has to be said that anything improving traffic flows at peak time past the entrances to Victoria Dock would be welcomed by everyone living there.

As background to the problem, one of the greatest difficulties with traffic flows in Hull was caused as a result of the closure of the western docks. This meant that the remaining working docks, which were increasing both in the value of trade and throughput, became isolated at the eastern side of the city. Since this situation had developed over a period of years and had not been planned for, the majority of heavy goods traffic became confined to a corridor through the centre of Hull, a route which passes the 'front door' of the village. The decline of goods carried by rail and barge made the problem worse as more goods were forced on to the road. A further incentive for the necessity to improve the east-west flow of traffic in Hull, and thereby the access to the village, was provided by the news in 1997 that Associated British Ports intended to promote a Harbour Revision Order to allow the development of Quay 2000, a new deep-water, multi-purpose, riverside terminal fronting Alexandra Dock.

The existing wooden pier, to the east of Victoria Dock Village, would be removed and replaced by a new 410-metre quay fronting directly on to the main channel of the Humber. It would be supported by a paved cargo-handling area of 7.5 hectares as well as existing development areas at the western end of Alexandra Dock. (It has now, in early 1999, become Quay 2005 and requires a £20 million investment.) The success of this scheme (and all success to it, as Hull has to develop) would mean, however, an even greater amount of traffic using the east-west axis. As ABP Port Manager, Mike Fell, commented: 'Quay 2000 is a flagship project to carry the port's success forward into the next millennium. There has been spectacular cargo growth in the 1990s and this major new facility, combined with other projects, will ensure the port of Hull remains in the vanguard of European deep-sea trade.'

Gordon Rason, who had been elected as Chairman of the Residents Association in August 1997, and Colin McNicol were invited to a meeting at the Guildhall in March 1998 to represent the Residents Association, along with Ward Councillors, the Kingston upon Hull City Council's Director of Technical Services and representatives from the Highways Agency, at which the views of residents living at Victoria Dock concerning the traffic problems along Garrison Road were explained in great detail. All the points of difficulty and the dangers people living on the dock experienced in gaining access to and from the main road were fully discussed and debated, along with the views of the City Council. The *Hull Daily Mail* also pressed hard for the improvement scheme to be given the green light through their long running 'Open the Gateway' campaign. Finally, at the end of July 1998, the Roads Minister, Dr. John Reid, gave approval for work to begin on clearing the notorious bottleneck. The Department of the Environment estimated the cost of the work at £42 million (around the cost of one Euro fighter aircraft) and a spokesman said that the work had been approved on economic grounds, claiming that the improvements would relieve the congestion on the main access route to the Port of Hull and support jobs and prosperity. The announcement was applauded by the City Council and the Council Leader, Councillor Patrick Doyle, said the news was welcome for two reasons: 'Firstly, it will improve traffic flow within the city for the people of Hull and Holderness and secondly it recognises that this is part of a major road link with the rest of the region, Northern England and Scotland. This is part of the E20 dedicated Europe route which is of local, regional, national and international importance.' Barrie Matterson, regeneration manager at Hull CityVision Ltd. said: 'The Hedon Road scheme will contribute significantly to the image of the city and CityVision's plans for the E20 corridor through Hull. In five to seven years we should see Hedon Road improved, St. Andrew's Dock regenerated, The Deep at Sammy's Point – with its own spin-offs for the River Hull corridor and many planned smaller improvements. Combined with the exciting plans for Ferensway, the image of Hull in these key areas will be transformed.'

After many rumours and seemingly false start dates had been given, work finally started on the shops and new doctors' surgery in mid-October 1996, when plant and machinery arrived on site to begin preparing the ground for the foundations and other sub-soil work. Another dispute over a Planning Application arose in November, when Cameron's Brewery submitted plans to remove a 100-foot long stretch of landscaping embankment outside the *Timber Dock* to make the pub more visible to passing traffic on Garrison Road. Residents put together a 100-name petition against the scheme, citing the loss of an amenity which was provided primarily as an acoustic barrier and which also conferred a degree of privacy and beauty as a landscaped entry to the village.

The City councillors rejected the application after visiting the site. Councillor Tom McVie said removing part of the mound would spoil the new park being laid out on the other side of the embankment. He said: 'Can you imagine going for a peaceful walk in this beautiful new park to watch 45,000 vehicles per day driving past on Garrison Road?'

Trinity Quay, a development comprising 45 three- and four-bedroom houses, was offered for sale in late November 1996 with the first sale recorded on the first day the site opened. This area has an interesting 'feel' to it as Bellway had taken great care at the design stage to offer as much contrast as possible in the three basic house styles, featuring differing brick colours and renderings on some houses. The usual high standard of specification also applied at Trinity Quay, where additionally a feature fireplace surround and living-flame gas fire were provided in the lounge, and double glazed windows with uPVC frames. The homes at Merchants Landing had also sold encouragingly, making for a good start to the year for Bellway and for the residents of the dock, as their numbers increased. Homebuyers, who realised the benefits of living so close to the centre of Hull, continued to flock to Victoria Dock, which by January 1997 had become the standard by which other dock schemes were judged. Sales continued to increase with a wide range of new homes available to suit all prospective purchasers. Within the first week of being offered, three town houses at St. James Court had been sold. At Parklands, comprising a range of 130 two- and three- bedroom semi-detached and three-bedroom detached houses, 47 were sold in just nine months. Only one three-bedroom house remained unsold by January, making this phase of building at Victoria Dock, one of the most successful.

Work which had started on the shops in October 1996 came to a sudden halt in March 1997, apparently caused by a dispute between Spar, the retail outlet which was taking two of the units and Bellway, who were building the shops. However, work carried on with the Surgery and Pharmacy, also built by Bellway, and the building really began to take shape during the summer of 1997. The village has had a medical practice for longer than most people can remember. The original practice was set up by Dr. Lyndon Stevens in 1991, using his home in Southbridge Road as a surgery. Unfortunately he was unable to register sufficient patients to make the practice worthwhile and he was forced to withdraw it in 1994. The next stage in medical care on the dock arrived with a portacabin, which was set up in Crane Road to act as a temporary surgery in early spring, 1996. The new practice was to be a satellite of the General Practice incorporating the following doctors: Dr. Bolton, Dr. Hussain, Dr. Tommins, Dr. Parker, Dr. Lees, Dr. Ellwood and Dr. Witvliet, which is based at the Morrill Street Health Centre. The satellite surgery was connected by a direct computer link to the main surgery, where patients' records were stored and from where appointments could be made. The temporary surgery was staffed by one of the doctors from the main practice working in rotation at Victoria Dock. The new surgery was opened for business early in September 1997 and incorporates a consulting room, a community health room, staffed by a practice nurse who is a part of the primary health care team, and a dispensary for medicines.

An investigation of a part of the site earmarked for The Deep was carried out in March 1997 by the Humber Archeology Partnership. In part the exploration was intended to establish the potential for display of the remains of the South Blockhouse as a part of The Deep. An excavation was carried out near to Sammy's Point by archeologists of the Partnership, funded by CityVision and with the permission of English Heritage. This area was formerly the site of the South Blockhouse, built as part of the fortifications on the east bank of the River Hull at the command of Henry VIII in 1541-3. The dig uncovered one of the largest early guns to be discovered in Britain and proved to be a find of national significance. Only a handful of guns from this period survive and close relatives of the gun were lifted from Henry VIII's ship, the *Mary Rose*, at Portsmouth. The gun, which is over two metres long and weighs over one ton, is a 'port piece', and would fire stone or other shot against hostile ships approaching the mouth of the River Hull. It may even have been used against the Royalists during the English Civil War sieges of Hull. The barrel of the gun is made up of strips of wrought iron, bound with iron hoops. The breach, or chamber, of the two-piece gun into which the gunpowder and shot were loaded, was found nearby. The tube and chamber were joined together to allow the gun to fire. Three such guns are listed as being in the South Blockhouse in 1660. The gun excavated appears to be one of them. It is intended to become a major feature of a new display at the Hull and East Riding Museum at High Street, Hull, when it has been restored. English Heritage is keen to see the presentation of the 16th- and 17th-century defences of Hull alongside The Deep, as the massive walls of the South Blockhouse remain in excellent condition a mere two feet below the current land surface. Features uncovered during the excavation, such as gun ports for the hand-held cousins of the big guns, were clearly identifiable. Hull would have a unique opportunity to place one of Henry VIII's most distinctive buildings on permanent public display, and this could form an integral element of a city centre amenity area.

More details concerning the background of the bid to the Millennium Commission for The Deep were revealed by Councillor David Gemmell and Kingston upon Hull City Director of Leisure Services, Colin Brown, in April 1997. They said that the bid was the result of a tourism strategy document which highlighted the growth in tourism – especially in short breaks in the UK – and identified the city's weakness in not having a major attraction. Colin Brown said: 'We looked at two options, this major attraction and a small aquarium, but the figures only made sense if we invested £40 million. There is a relatively low catchments area around Hull, so if it was planned as a modest development you would only get people from the immediate surrounds, but if we build something on the scale of The Deep, people will come to Hull for a day out.'

Early forecasts predicted that the project would create 200 jobs, with £2 million coming in from the 350,000 visitors going through the doors every year. Since the intention is that The Deep will not cost the taxpayers of Hull a penny in subsidies, it will not be owned and operated by the Kingston upon Hull City Council but by a charitable educational trust which would licence an operator. Profits will be invested in research, or in the facility itself.

The mission of The Deep is to tell the story of the seas and the creatures within, using the latest technology to bring long-gone marine life back to virtual reality, recreating the lost city of Atlantis, studying the mysteries of mermaids and the Kraken in an X-Files of the sea. Initial plans were that visitors would be invited to enter via a lift, to give the illusion of descending 20 fathoms below the sea. They would then enter the centrepiece, which would be a dome with portholes and connecting tunnels surrounded by a massive tank filled with ocean life, revealing the secrets of the sea floor. They would then be able to enter a virtual reality area where massive screens would enable viewers to visit Atlantis, travel below the Polar ice cap, visit the Great Barrier Reef, or, perhaps, even visit the Titanic in its watery grave. They would then enter another lift for the simulated journey back to the surface. There will be features which help the University's scientists with the studies of such threats as oil spills, and everything will be geared to helping schoolchildren by close links with the National Curriculum. Over 26,000 schoolchildren are expected to visit the facility every year. Councillor Gemmell said: 'The Deep will be a hook to get people to see what we already have in Hull. We know we have a good product but we need this development to get people here.'

The scheme won the praise of the Millennium Commissioner, Sir John Hall, when he met the officials behind the ambitious plan in May 1997 but there was a change of Government that month which later, during July, prompted a scare about the future of The Deep. It was thought possible that it might be sacrificed through the Government raiding the Millennium Fund in order to pump more money into health and education nationally, in line with their election promises. The *Hull Daily Mail* ran a campaign to 'Keep the Deep', inviting readers to complete messages of support for the project. North Hull MP Kevin McNamara also lent his support, saying: 'It would be outrageous if not one scheme in Yorkshire gets money. If one does it should be Kingston upon Hull. I would urge the public to contact Tony Blair's office and express their views.'

By the end of the month it was clear that the project was back on course, as the National Heritage Secretary, Chris Smith announced that a new Lottery-funded £1 billion package for education and health would not hit the Millennium Commission's budget. The ambitious plan, therefore, remained on the short-list being considered by the Millennium Commission. Plans submitted to the Millennium Commission in September 1997 detailed expansion to the facilities for The Deep project and included a 60-bed youth hostel and a business park. The provision of a youth hostel was supported by the Youth Hostel Association, which had identified the city as a potential site for a new hostel development. Sufficient land at Sammy's Point has been set aside for the hostel to double in size if the demand for extra beds made it necessary. Officials at the City Council believed that Hull would be an ideal hostel location because of its strong links with Europe via P&O North Sea Ferries and as a starting point for several regional walking and cycling routes. The 30,000-square-foot business park would be promoted as the Maritime Institute of Hull Business Centre. It is intended to be a flagship building aimed at attracting small and medium sized companies specialising in marine science and technology activities.

Confirmation that the bid put forward by the City Council had been successful was announced in November 1997. The Millennium Commission had awarded the grant, which would allow the scheme to go ahead more positively. However, the grant only covered 50% of the total £40 million cost of the project and access had to be gained to European funds. Other funds were available to encourage the development of small business units: English Partnerships, who would assist in the development of the 'brown field' site and CityVision who would assist from the private sector. At the end of July, 1998 there was a £7 million shortfall, £5 million of which was expected to be funded from European funds. The remaining £2 million could be raised in cash or in kind and a start had been made in raising this amount. Three of the top architectural firms in Britain were commissioned in 1998 to design a landmark building which was eye-catching, innovative and functional to house The Deep, with the winning tender announced in August 1998. Car parking spaces for 250 cars and a number of coaches were to be provided, although the main aim was for people to use pedestrian access to the site by following the extended 'fish-trail' across the footbridge over the River Hull.

Meanwhile, building work re-commenced on the shops during September 1997, when it was announced that two of the units would be operated by Spar and managed by Neil and Moira Haylock, who had pioneered shopping at Victoria Dock and spent many a long and cold winter's day in their unheated portacabin and a few hot days in summer trying to stop chocolate confections melting. At that time it was anticipated that one of the other units would be used for take-away food and the remaining unit was still to be let, although several people were said to have expressed interest. The roof timbers were in place during October and it began to look as if the Spar shop might just make the hoped-for opening target date of Christmas 1997. However, this date proved to be optimistic and, due to various delays, which included re-siting the shop entrance to the south-side, the actual date of the shop opening was Friday, 17 March 1998. It was a long awaited and greatly needed facility for residents and has deservedly proved popular. The third shop unit was opened as the Riverside Hair and Beauty salon on Friday 15 May 1998, and the final unit was opened in July 1999 as the Victoria City, a quality Chinese and English take-away food shop.

The Water's Edge and Admiral Court developments at the eastern side of the village had been released for sale in September 1997. Water's Edge was a select scheme of large four-bedroom detached houses enjoying a riverside location. Priced between £109,950 and £159,950, the superb new properties boasted a particularly advanced specification, including en suite facilities, luxury kitchens with fitted appliances and sumptuous lounges with a wide choice of gas fire and surround. Both of the new phases included uPVC double-glazing. Security and convenience were two of the chief considerations in the design and the houses at Water's Edge featured remote-control electric doors fitted as standard to their double garages. The neighbouring Admiral's Court scheme comprised an impressive selection of two- and three-bedroom family houses in a wide range of styles, all offering spacious accommodation in a secure environment. Prices for the three-bedroom houses ranged from £46,995 to £52,995, while the two-bedroom houses were priced from £39,995. Both phases demonstrated the continuing commitment of Bellway in offering affordable new homes in a wide variety of styles to suit all sectors of the market, from young singles, through families of all sizes, to the newly retired and elderly.

The company offered a number of incentives to tempt first-time buyers, including 5% deposit paid, help with legal fees, and free carpets and the chance to move in for just £100 down at some properties. For those seeking to move from an existing property, Bellway offered an attractive, home- exchange programme, where they made a full market-value offer for the buyer's property within seven days, saving the purchaser time, money and trouble in arranging a sale of their own property.

The danger of accident at the Plimsoll Way roundabout was demonstrated in September, when an articulated lorry overturned at the crossing point on Garrison Road. The lorry slid along on its side for several yards, demolishing the lamppost and throwing the driver through the windscreen. The vehicle came to rest on the verge, fully across the dropped curb which marks the road crossing. Fortunately no one other than the driver was injured but the need for a proper and safe crossing for pedestrians at this point, as a part of the Hedon Road Improvement Scheme, was reinforced.

In mid-September 1997 tenders were invited by Kingston upon Hull City Council to construct 300 metres of flood defences and to create a 3-metre wide promenade at Sammy's Point. The scheme involved the construction of both vertical sheet-pile walls and a concrete block revetment along with the promenade.

Bellway announced record company profits in October 1997, unveiling a 56% jump in full year profits to £50.3 million pre-tax. Profits included a £1.2 million exceptional gain, from the sale of Bellway's investment in Wainhomes. The report noted that prices for the groups homes had increased by about 12% in the South and by about 5% in the North of the Country. The overall average price of their houses had increased from £70,700 to £77,200, mainly fuelled by the surge in southern house prices. It was also noted that the Yorkshire area was the most difficult for sales, although this was not peculiar to Bellway, as all builders were experiencing similar difficulties in this area.

A planning application for the erection of a single-storey building to form a 60-place primary school and 26-place nursery including car-parking-service area and playing field on the north side of Southbridge Road was advised to residents by the Council towards the end of October 1997. Thus, it began to appear that the school would go ahead and the dangerous journey across six lanes of traffic on Hedon Road made by many mums and their young children could be coming to an end.

A pre-Christmas sale of new properties on Victoria Dock was held in December 1997, a particularly slack period for house sales, and some remarkable inducements were offered to people who were willing to reserve a property at that time. First time buyers were offered a £100 deposit and move-in deal. Move-up buyers were offered a full valuation part-exchange deal, together with other deals. The year 1998 also saw further remarkable offers as incentives for homebuyers to purchase a property on Victoria Dock, as Bellway continued to market the village aggressively. 'Homestarter' was billed as a deal too good to miss. They offered 5% deposit paid, carpets and curtains, £500 toward legal fees, a fridge and washer/dryer, a furniture pack which included two sofas, coffee table, TV unit, dining table and four chairs, double bed and headboard, two bedside cabinets and wardrobe: all subject to certain conditions, of course. In addition they also offered the 'Bellway Mortgage Buster', whereby Bellway offered to pay £150 per month mortgage subsidy for 12 months, again subject to certain conditions.

The latest phase of properties in the St. James Court development, which overlooked Victoria Park, were released, ranging from £39,995 to £46,500. These properties came equipped with top-class facilities which included full uPVC double glazing and which have a white Victorian bathroom suite with gold-effect fittings, a fitted kitchen with oven, hob and hood, a telephone door-entry system, communal gardens, private car parking, a viewing patio with grill and satellite TV facility.

A sales offer on properties on the Dock, more remarkable than the previous December's offer, was made by Bellway in the June 1998 'End of Financial Year Sale', when prices on some selected properties were greatly reduced, and on other selected properties the usual offers of fittings applied, with the alternative of up to £5,000 cash back. The special deals applied to buyers who could complete more or less immediately and who could move in before August 1998.

The Public Notice for building the primary school appeared in the press in February 1998. The historic

agreement to allow the proposed primary school to become a reality was signed by Sewell Construction, the builders and Kingston upon Hull City Council's Learning Services in July 1998. Thus, Victoria Dock Primary School would become the first in the country to be built under a Private Finance Initiative, the complex partnership agreement between the public and the private sector. In this case the authority rents the school from Sewell Facilities Management, who have financed the project, over a 25-year period, when the contract will be renegotiated. It is expected that the arrangements for the Victoria Dock PFI will form the model for other schemes to follow. The £1.1 million school was designed by using a state-of-the-art virtual reality computer system which allowed the designers to 'fly' around the site, 'drive' up to the front entrance and 'walk' around the classrooms, even before a brick had been laid. The system also helped the choice of the most suitable bricks, tiles and carpets. Building work began immediately after the signing ceremony, as an extremely tight deadline for completion by January 1999 was called for. The school was to be maintained by the newly created, Sewell Facilities Management, and managing director Paul Sewell said: 'We have designed and will build the school and equip it with desks, chairs and computers. All the local authority have to do is provide the children, pens, books and education.' Councillor Mima Bell, the Chairperson of Learning Services said: 'This scheme proves PFI can work for small projects and not just for major projects like hospitals and roads. It opens the possibilities of more projects in the future, where left to its own resources, the city council could not afford to respond to changing needs.'

Work on building the Waterbabes nursery commenced at the same time and progressed rapidly. Even so Wendy Oliver and her business partner, Jacky Whittaker, had to wait until Tuesday, 3 November, before they could host an open evening for parents and it was to be Monday, 9 November, before the doors opened for the children to enjoy their new building. Since then it has proved to be extremely popular with parents and guardians. The children now have the space to play and learn in lovely surroundings and Wendy and Jacky have developed strong links with the primary school.

A real milestone in the life of the Village was reached in July 1998 when Bellway announced the sale of the 1000th property in the development. The celebration was not confined to Bellway, as Paul Coates and Hayley Cable, who unknowingly bought the 1000th property, a Kensington three-bedroom, three-storey town house at St. James Court, received a surprise visit from Jim Cropper, managing director of Bellway Urban Renewal (North-East). He brought with him the congratulations of the company, flowers and champagne and a cheque for £1,000.

The temporary governing body for the school was appointed in late July to make the necessary arrangements which would allow the new primary school to open in January 1999. The new team of Governors comprised Colin McNicol, David Shortman, David Woodcock, Angela Sizer, the Reverend Stephen Walker, Cheryl Walster and Stan

Pickering. Their work began immediately and, in the absence of a school, meetings were held at the Village Hall. Problems had to be solved and decisions had to be made on many aspects, such as the admission arrangements, the name of the school (Victoria Dock Primary School), provision for a budget, estimation of start-up costs, carrying out interviews for the appointment of a head teacher and the teaching staff, deciding on equipment levels for the school and a hundred other things. Great progress was made, thanks to the dedication of the governing team and the unfailing co-operation from officers of the Council and the Drypool Ward councillors.

The Government's Office for National Statistics produced census figures at the beginning of September 1998 which revealed a distinct decline in the number of people living in Hull. Figures showed that around 8,000 people had left the city, most, seemingly, to move into the East Riding of Yorkshire. Councillor Pat Doyle, the Leader of Kingston upon Hull City Council, said that part of the problem was caused by the fact that Hull suffered from extremely tight boundaries which limited the amount of new development that could take place within the city. He went on to say: 'There is a great deal of debate, nationally, about green field sites and in the south as to whether new town developments should be built and the Government is stressing the need to build on brown field sites within cities. Victoria Dock is a prime example of this kind of development where we have taken a brown field site and we have sold a lot of houses there and it is a pleasant place to live.' Asked to comment on the development of brown field sites, John Larard of Hull and East Yorkshire-based Larard's Estate Agents said: 'The problem with trying to develop brown field sites within the Hull boundary is that small developments can be overshadowed by nearby estates that have bad reputations. It is hard to think of a site within Hull, which would be suitable, although the Victoria Dock development has been a success because it is not particularly near any of the big estates.'

Two new pillars forming the entrance to Victoria Park were lifted into place in late September 1998. Crafted in white Portland limestone, capped with bronze spheres, the pillars are inscribed with the names and tonnages of some of the vessels that were made in Earle's Shipyard. The facets of the columns with alternate straight and jagged edges running down their length make visual reference to traditional decking or planking.

As you pass through the gateway you see a symbolic representation of the night sky and its constellations incorporated into the floorscape as a marble mosaic. The constellations depicted are those that could have been seen from that spot at the point of the summer equinox in 1998. The eastern path giving access to the park also incorporates, in the form of several mosaic panels by Susan Disley, details from Galileo's notebook of 1610, showing the positions of Jupiter and its satellites. His drawings trace the movement of Jupiter and its satellites over a 12 month period. At this time, the giant sundial had been clad with Nuovalata marble from Carrara in Italy, and the time segments had been installed and it looked impressive. The sundial is a

'corrected' horizontal dial designed to work at a latitude of 54 degrees. Its gnomon rises like the prow or sails of a ship, and from behind it affords views south across the Humber. A simple sculpture by Paul Mason, in the form of a curved bench with a symbolic representation of ships in the estuary, was placed at the junction of the newly completed paths with the inscription: 'This Humber be broad about this town, some two miles or better'. By early autumn the grass was showing through the soil and the bowling greens were finished, indeed the whole area had begun to look like the landscape designers' dream when it was first expressed on paper. The artists, Susan Disley and Paul Mason, were appointed to work closely with the City's landscape design team, focusing on the form and layout of the park and investigating ways in which 'public art' and symbolic or historical references to the site's former use could be integrated into the park. Also in the park, at the rear of the Village Hall, the children's play area with new and brightly painted play equipment was completed and it soon became a safe and popular attraction for young children and their parents.

In October 1998 Bellway once again announced record profits for their previous financial year, amounting to around £60 million. They were going from strength to strength on a policy based on aggressive marketing techniques and the ruthless elimination of unnecessary overheads. The sale of properties on Victoria Dock continued to progress impressively, as more and more people became aware of the benefits of living in close proximity to the city centre. Advance sales of properties at the new development known as Wren's Court, at the extreme eastern end of the Village, went well during the latter part of 1998, ten being sold during one week. This phase consisted of two- and three-bedroom starter homes and included uPVC double-glazing, gas central heating, a fitted kitchen with oven hob and hood and a Victoria style bathroom suite. The price for a two-bedroom terrace house started at £40,995 while the two-bedroom semi-detached houses on this phase started at £44,995.

The 22 three-bedroom town houses, built on three floors, and the 94 two-bedroom apartments, comprising the latest phase of St. James Court, released for sale in October 1998, also sold well, with the majority of the three-bedroom houses and about half the apartments having been sold by early 1999. The specification for these properties included an electronically-controlled door-entry system and electric heating. Prices for these properties began at £39,995 for the two-bedroom apartments and £69,995 for the three-storey three-bedroom town houses without river view, and £70,995 for those with a river view. Sales for properties in Admiral's Court were even more impressive, all 46 properties having been sold in just 11 months. The latest phase of the site, known as Trinity Quay, opened in November 1998 and consisted of 45 high quality three- and four-bedroom detached houses. These properties included a feature fireplace surround with log-effect gas fire in the lounge, a traditional chimney, which is an unusual feature in a modern house, and uPVC double-glazed windows. The three-bedroom houses were priced at £69,995 and at £97,995 for the four-bedroom houses. Again, these houses sold well, and by early 1999 only seven remained unsold.

The Sewell Group had pulled out all the stops and the long awaited Primary School on Victoria Dock was ready at the beginning of January 1999, just as had been forecast only a few months previously. Initially, to the layman at least, it had seemed an impossibly tight time schedule, but as work progressed all the loose ends came together and the school, bright and cheerful, and the staff, eager and expectant, were ready to receive the first pupils. In the first phase the school has been built to take 60 pupils aged between five and eleven in mixed-age classes with a 26-place (full-time equivalent) nursery. However, the flexibility of the design is such that new classrooms can be added without disruption to the existing unit to take up to 240 pupils. Will Jones, the architect for the project, whose firm, Hull-based V A Architecture, designed the school, said he believed that it had achieved what people wanted it to be – a flagship for Hull. The firm was approached in mid-1997 with a fairly open brief to design the school, which nevertheless had to fit in with the area and be a showcase as a PFI project. He said: 'The open plan design and roof windows make great use of natural light . . . The concept was really to get the idea of an internal street so that as you walked through, you would get a lot of natural light. The design also incorporates a great west window, which sounds rather grand, but it means that you get light coming through the building for most of the day.' Mr. Jones also explained: 'The bright yellow colour schemes have been introduced to give the building a fresh and friendly feel and the light brickwork fitted in with Sewell's style.' Security has also been made a key feature, with automatic steel shutters on windows and closed circuit TV cameras at the entrance. A preview opening was held on 5 January to allow parents and children to visit the new school so that they could meet the staff and help the children to become familiar with their new surroundings. Other villagers were also welcomed as they had previously only been able to see the outside of the new building. The managing director of the Sewell Group, Paul Sewell, attended, as did the architect, ward councillors and governors. Without exception there was praise for what had been achieved by the Council, the builders and the staff.

The classrooms were furnished with bright new tables and chairs, books were on the shelves and bare walls awaited the children's work. The fully equipped nursery stood ready for action, and in the cloakroom bright yellow empty pegs awaited hats, coats and scarves. Mrs. Susan Roach, the Head of School said: 'There is obviously great excitement through the staff. I am really looking forward to making it look like a school. We have a beautiful building, but a vital ingredient is missing and that is the children.' She added: 'I think we have gathered together a wonderful team to work here, who are totally committed to its success.' In an interview Mr. Sewell said: 'We are very proud that this is a UK first. The completion of the construction is only the first stage achievement of the partnership. Now we have to work together to maintain this new facility to the highest standards over the next 25 years, and most importantly, allow the teachers to concentrate on teaching. I'm delighted that I will be able to be present when the doors open to welcome the first pupils across the threshold.'

On Thursday, 7 January at 8.30 am prompt, the doors were opened for the first time to admit children to the school for lessons. They were welcomed by the Head and staff, together with Ward councillor, John Ranby, and Mr. Sewell, to symbolise the unique partnership. Children and parents, warmly wrapped on a cold morning, were equally excited and the *Hull Daily Mail* was there to capture the first day, along with Radio Humberside, Yorkshire TV and the BBC's 'Look North'. Councillor Ranby said: 'This is a brilliant day. We have been fighting for the school for ten years. This school will create a real community here as parents will meet with each other and we will see the community develop further.' The Chair of Learning Services, Councillor Mima Bell said: 'We are delighted to see the completion of this project to give the community a real focus and heart. This pioneering project allows us to deliver the best we can and continue with our strategy to raise achievement in the city. The process (in building this school) has been problematic, and there were a lot of hurdles to get over, but now that it is finished I think it is a beautiful school and I think that parents who take their children there must be really pleased.'

Mrs. Elaine Njie, of Appledore Close, the mother of Ellis, aged four, said that she was really impressed with the school when she went to register him there: 'He was so excited when he saw his classroom. He just said "Wow!" Several friends of ours have moved off the dock because there was no school and people began to think that there would never be one. But now it is here I think we have to support it, the building is lovely and the staff are really nice.' As the children settled into their new classrooms they began to get to know their teachers and their new classmates Mrs. Roach commented: 'Everything has gone well and it's a real credit to the children, who have managed to stay calm despite all the excitement going on around them. We are all looking forward now to settling in and getting to know each other and starting the work.' Paul Sewell added that it was a proud day for all who had been involved with the school. 'It is a proud day for Hull. As we celebrate 700 years, we start January with a UK first, which demonstrates the pioneering nature of this city.' The staff who opened the school were Mrs. Sue Roach, Head Teacher; Mrs. Kathryn English; Secretary; Miss Suzanne Williams, teacher; Miss Katherine Hastie, nursery teacher; Mrs. Lynda Winfield, nursery assistant, Mrs. Julie Bland and Mrs. Yvonne Year, supervisory assistants, Mrs. Carol Whittaker, kitchen unit manager, and the school Facility Manager, Carl Sarel.

The school was officially opened by Deputy Prime Minister and East Hull MP John Prescott on Friday, 29 January. He was welcomed by the Chair of Governors and the Head teacher and escorted into the Hall, where an invited audience of civic dignitaries and representatives from the builders awaited him, together with the children of the school, who had written their own poem for the Deputy Prime Minister, which they recited. Two of them presented him with gifts to mark his visit. Mr. Prescott said: 'It's marvellous that time and time again we see Hull leading the way with Government initiatives. We should be proud that the children of Hull are set to benefit from the UK's first privately built school.' He also commented that the opening of the school marked a major step for the area, which has been turned from derelict dockland into an urban village and went on to pay tribute to former Councillor John Black for the work he had put in to achieving the transformation. He went on to say: 'The school will be a real focus for the community. Victoria Dock Primary School is the first of its kind, let's make sure it is one of the best.' He then unveiled a special plaque to mark the partnership between Sewell's and the City Council. Paul Sewell, Managing Director of the Sewell Group said: 'It makes me proud to be part of such a pioneering project which stands up as an example to the whole country.' He went on to say 'The requirements on us were very tough and to get approval in the first place we had to prove to the government that this project would cost the council less than if the council had the funds and built it itself. However, we do have extensive experience of building and maintaining schools in the city, and through planning and co-operation with the council we completed the project within the deadline and to budget.'

By the end of January, 1999 Bellway had sold 1,101 properties at Victoria Dock, a number excluding the people living at Victoria House, those living at Humber View and the 24 sheltered-housing bungalows which were then under construction. The total number of properties would amount to 1,302, again taking into account the exclusions. All work on the whole site was estimated then, to be completed at spring 2000. The number of properties sold is impressive by any standard but especially so when the changes and fluctuations in the housing market over the years are considered. It is often said that the three most important factors in choosing a home are location, location and location. It has also long been said that you can change the appearance of a house but not the location. And the riverside location is precisely the reason why so many people moved on to the dock, both because the site of the village is close to Hull city centre with good connections and because of the magnificent views over the Humber gained from the promenade. In fact there are many living there who consider Victoria Dock to be Hull's best-kept secret.

But there are many other factors which account for the success of Victoria Dock Village. As examples, the village has been well marketed throughout the building programme and the amenities such as the community centre, the shops, the public house, the primary school and public parks and gardens, have all come along at points where they could be sustained as the village has developed. The village is visually attractive and well laid out and there has been a good blend of properties on offer, from affordable houses and apartments for first time buyers through to luxury housing for those buying at the top of the market. The energy efficient properties on Victoria Dock have been built in differing styles to a high specification with a good range of appliances and amenities to choose from. Finally, there are also good bus links to the city centre, which was considered as an important factor for many people.

A MORI poll carried out in early 1999 into attitudes to house construction confirmed that house buyers are overwhelmingly in favour of traditionally built houses. Over 90% of those surveyed said they preferred the advantages offered by houses built of bricks, blocks and concrete floors. Houses have historically been bought as a long-term investment, and even in today's economic climate are expected to keep pace with inflation. Nearly all said that they required a home whose structure helped to maintain an even temperature in winter and summer. Traditional materials achieve this because of their thermal mass, allowing the house to act as a giant storage heater which absorbs heat from within the house when the sun is out or when the heating is on, and radiating it back into the house when the temperature starts to drop. The survey also revealed that the majority of those surveyed believed that traditionally built homes offered a long property life and the most easily re-sold of modern housing types.

There was another unveiling early in the year, when plans and a scale model showing the stunning design of The Deep were revealed to a specially invited audience of civic and business leaders at the Ferens Art Gallery on Wednesday, 3 February 1999. Guests who gathered around the model looked in awe at the pointed visitors' centre which juts out over Sammy's Point. The unique futuristic design, described by many in the audience as inspirational, was created by world-renowned architect, Terry Farrell, who said he was delighted to have been able to produce a symbolic building to house the ambitious project which helped to boost tourism, attract international recognition and bring Hull forward into the next century. The project consists of four elements housed in two buildings: a visitor attraction, the European Maritime Learning Centre, the European Research Facility and a business centre intended to foster new companies.

The architect said that he felt the design of The Deep was more original than any other he had designed and went on to say: 'I believe Sammy's Point has great potential as an area to encourage regeneration and the design of the building had to be iconic to ensure this. I was delighted to have been given the opportunity to design The Deep, with the main inspiration coming from the site itself, with the point being the focal point. I feel The Deep is an exciting project with great possibility for recognition internationally.' The Leader of the Kingston upon Hull City Council, Councillor Pat Doyle said: 'The design is splendid and one which will have a tremendous impact on the city. With this project I feel we can look forward with confidence to the next century and the next millennium ... The project will not only attract tourists and jobs, but will also be crucial to the regeneration of the River Hull Corridor and provide an exceptional educational asset.' A charitable company, EMIH Ltd. (European Maritime Institute in Hull), has been established by the City Council and the University of Hull to deliver the project. The Deep exhibition remained open to the public for the next ten days at the Ferens, attracting thousands of visitors. It then moved to the Victoria Dock Community Centre so that people living on the dock could get a closer and less interrupted view of the new complex.

In design the building is intended to look like a huge piece of rock being forced up through the ground The most prominent aspect will be the glass observation point at the apex of the roof (originally planned to be the same height as the tower of Holy Trinity Church), which will provide visitors with wonderful views along the Humber from this high vantage point. The walls will be designed to resemble an exposed rock face, with separate layers of titanium tiles, pre-fabricated steel and concrete studded with pieces of metal, glass and ceramics. The materials are planned to last for at least 20 years. The interior of the centre is intended to be broken up with three-dimensional crevices and cracks, allowing visitors to explore the exhibition spaces within.

Contractors began clearing the site for The Deep on Thursday, 25 March, the first real sign that the project was actually going to happen. The extensive preparation work was carried out by Charles Brand Ltd., a company well experienced in this type of work, which involved steel piling, to improve the river defences, removal of the huge concrete slab that formed the base for the former ABP shed, and others which formed factory floors, filling in the many holes on site and recycling the waste where possible.

By May 1999 piling work to form the sill for the new extension to the promenade was well underway and throughout summer the land was sloped back, using crushed concrete from the former bases on the site, to form the revetment for the river defences. During the month of June a note of caution was sounded when it was announced that councillors had called for more details on the design of The Deep, before granting planning permission. Particular reference was made to the emergency exits for disabled visitors, the car park layout and demonstration of a firm commitment to building the new pedestrian/cyclists Millennium Bridge over the River Hull. There was also some disappointment noted with the news that the size of the building would be around 20% smaller than originally envisaged, due to revised budget forecasts for the project and the wish to retain the existing slipway at Sammy's Point. It was pointed out that most of the reduction in the size of the building was reflected in the proposed height although the new height would still be around 90 feet (30m.)

On site work continued, over 40,000 interlocking hexagonal basaltic blocks were delivered from Holland, which were laid on the embanked slope to stop the river washing the land away, and in August work began on casting poured concrete to form the top of the promenade. During this period a parcel of land on the west bank of the River Hull was donated by the Bonus Electrical Group for just £1 (to secure the footing for the Millennium Bridge), which enabled the remainder of the Millennium funding to be released. By the end of October the site had been levelled and was almost ready for construction work to begin. The new access road for construction vehicles was complete, In late June it had been announced that the construction group, Bovis, had been awarded the building contract for The Deep and it was hoped that up to 100 full-time jobs would be generated during the building phase.

On another positive note, the enthusiasm of children involved in Hull's Education Action Zone Summer School in the project was raised by The Deep's Learning Manager, John Lawson, and PR Manager, Linda Martin. The project had featured heavily in a feature on the regeneration of Hull by BBC2 in their programme, 'Working Lunch', and many VIPs visiting the City have been given a presentation of the flagship development. The Deep also featured in the Millennium Commission's space age vehicle, 'Voyager', which criss-crossed Britain with its showcase of Millennium projects, and interest was shown in the project nation-wide.

Late in July the architect of The Deep, Terry Farrell, unveiled plans he had been commissioned to produce by the CityVision for the Hull 2020 Master Plan, an aspirational programme of development aimed at raising ambition and development. One of the particular targets of the Master Plan was to identify possible solutions to the traffic congestion between the eastern docks and the Humber Bridge. One solution was create a new northern ring road, another was to build a tunnel under the River Hull, but the most eye-catching and radical proposal was the creation of a 'Humber Highway' which would shift docks traffic on to a raised motorway over the Humber. All three options would then allow the Marina to integrate with the rest of the city centre, Castle Street could become a tree-lined pedestrian walkway and the proposals would also facilitate plans for a facelift for the Old Town. Will it happen? Let's hope so!

At least one section of the 'Humber Highway' seemed likely to be realised when it was announced, early in October 1999 that the planned improvements to the A1033 Hedon Road, the so called 'Highway to Hell', had finally moved into gear, with the announcement from the Highways Agency that work was to start within the next six months on insulating homes along Hedon Road, demolishing buildings, including the New Inn, the New Grange Club and Saltend Filling Station and moving subterranean services such as water mains. The cost of the actual roadworks had risen by £10 million to £50 million since 1996. The Agency forecast that actual road digging would commence in April 2001 and would take an estimated 30 months to complete.

In late summer, Bellway began to prepare the foundations for the four-storey apartments, which would be built around the eastern side of the half-tide basin. This phase, which would be completed during the winter of 1999-2000, represented the last major building work on the site, and people living in the Village were asked to think about and report on the factors that required resolution before Bellway moved off the site in the new year.

Since its opening in January 1999, the Victoria Dock Primary School had gone from strength to strength. The staff and governors had worked very hard and had shown great commitment in enabling the school to meet the high expectations placed on it and as a result, the numbers of pupils had increased steadily. A new teacher, Mike Smith, had been appointed to start at the beginning of the autumn term and a Classroom Support Assistant, Mrs. Jean Nelson, had also been appointed. Once the school had opened, families began moving on to the Dock and the numbers of children forecast to attend the school over the next two years meant that it had become necessary to bring forward the 60-place classroom extension, from September 2001 to January 2001. A meeting with officers of the City Council was successful and they agreed to press forward in negotiations with the Government and the contractor to bring forward the effective date. A great deal of interest had been shown in the school by other authorities planning a similar PFI route to fund new schools in their own areas Many of them had visited the school and all left impressed with what they had seen.

In September the school playing field was officially opened, with the PTFA holding its first fundraising event by staging a balloon race and a sponsored walk by the children. Paul Sewell, who opened the field, announced that the special company set up to own and manage the school had recorded such financial successes in the first year that he planned to plough the extra cash back into the school and the surrounding community. The company had set up a Community Dividend Fund, and further surpluses achieved over the course of the 25-year partnership would be added to the fund. One of the most tangible benefits would be the creation of a Heritage Nature Trail, which would be formed along the northern perimeter of the school field. A scheme for the Trail had been drawn up by the City Council landscape architect, and provisionally costed at £35,000. The intention was to create a 'Green Classroom' formed by a woodland area, a bark path nature trail with seats and bins along its length, a fenced-off pond and wet area for newts, frogs and toads, which would also incorporate a timber boardwalk viewing platform, an arboretum and an informal natural play area with vertical log walling.

The benefits were allowing them to be taught practically about conservation, nature and wildlife and enhancing their appreciation of the countryside. The PTFA agreed that this project would form a significant part of their fundraising objectives over the next few years and a special fundraising committee was also set up to explore grant availability and to raise funds solely for this purpose.

The official ground-breaking ceremony at The Deep was performed on Tuesday, 9 November, by Miss Charlie Dimmock, the presenter of the TV gardening programme 'Groundforce'. She was accompanied to the site by our own 'groundforce' team, the pupils from Victoria Dock Primary School and was greeted on site by the Lord Mayor, Councillor Brian Wilkinson and the Lady Mayoress, Jennifer Dearing. Canon John Waller of Holy Trinity Church then blessed the ground at Sammy's Point. The children from the school were asked to perform a special tribute rap-song about The Deep, for the many invited guests, following which they helped Charlie to bury a Millennium time capsule which contained plans of the project, the words to their song and a school uniform. Miss Dimmock said that she had been shown the plans of the project, and found it absolutely stunning and hoped to come back to Hull to see The Deep when it was finished.

In mid-December the *Hull Daily Mail* announced that house prices on Victoria Dock were increasing at

a rate that defied the local trend, where prices had either remained static or had fallen. It seemed that the village was becoming one of the most desirable addresses in Hull. Homebuyers with a taste for modern city centre living were providing a boom for property on the dock and helping to breathe new life into the City. It was reported that estate agents had waiting lists of people wanting to buy houses on the Dock and so desperate for properties that they were targeting homeowners in an effort to persuade them to sell. Some buyers became so desperate for a house on the Dock that they advertised in the local Spar shop on Plimsoll Way for anyone interested in selling a house to contact them directly. Steven Smith, director of urban and infrastructure projects said: 'Hull has suffered de-population but areas like this are encouraging people to come back and appreciate what the city can offer.'

Later in December, the main construction firm building The Deep, Bovis Lend Lease, signed up to the Hull Local Labour Initiative Code of Practice, whereby employers agree to recruit workers from the Hull area form their projects wherever possible. The company announced that they were to recruit for 100 construction positions and would take on local labour in line with The Deep's funders – Hull City Vision Ltd. and the Government Office European Secretariat.

The old year closed with hundreds of people gathered in the streets of Hull to say goodbye to the last century and the last millennium and to welcome the next. The sky as lit up as thousands of fireworks exploded in an early evening public display and midnight was greeted with the ships in port sounding their sirens. As the public greeted the new day, thousands of private fireworks illuminated the city. What a difference from the dawn of the last millennium, where we started our journey.

The primary school held their First Birthday Party, organised by the PTFA, in early January 2000. It proved to be a resounding success with over 90% of parents and children attending. The Deputy Prime Minister and East Hull M.P. John Prescott was invited to formally open the Victoria Park and braved wind and rain to perform the ceremony in late February. The Waterbabes Nursery won one of three prestigious Millennium Awards at the Humberside Training and Enterprise Business Awards evening held in early March. Training had remained a vital part of the nursery's culture. In addition to the training needed to meet legal requirements, staff were also encouraged to keep abreast of childcare issues and development.

Early in March new plans for The Deep were unveiled and passed by the Council's Development Management Committee. The new design looked strikingly different from the original conception and was helped by an extra £1.7 million injection from the Council. The amended plans included a dramatic change to the original proposal for the pointed tip of the building: the re-design would see the tip constructed in a mixture of clear and blue coloured glass. There would be an extension for a new ground-floor entrance, incorporating a gift shop, tourist information point, ticket office and queuing area. An area previously set aside on the third floor for the gift shop would now be used for a café and lobby area to the exhibition entrance. The fourth floor would include a sheltered terrace to provide views across the Humber and the City and a wider choice of materials to be used externally on the building, including aluminium.

The proposed pedestrian link on the west side of the River Hull, opposite the new visitor attraction was also passed at the same committee meeting. The walkway is planned to run from Humber Street, near to the Tidal Barrier, alongside the Central Dry Dock and then on to Nelson Street and Victoria Pier. It would link up with the proposed new footbridge over the River Hull to provide easy access to The Deep from the Old Town.

In the meantime real progress could be seen on site as piling work was completed and the structures began to take shape. A giant concrete bucket appeared, surrounded by steel girders and formed the first stage of a huge tank which will become one of Europe's deepest tanks when completed. It will eventually stand nine metres high and visitors will be able to watch the sea creatures behind glass windows measuring six metres wide by three metres high. The provision of the Millennium Bridge across the River Hull (to succeed the Ha'penny Bridge) came a step nearer reality in June 2000 when the City Council Cabinet Committee agreed to accept responsibility for the proposed swing bridge. The council have a general responsibility for the maintence and operation of the River Hull bridges, consistent with the authority's function as highway an navigation authority, and a report to Committee suggested that it would be inconsistent and detrimental to those functions if the Millennium Bridge were not to be adopted. The crossing, provided for pedestrians and cyclists, is intended to link the ocean discovery centre with the Old Town.

During the summer of 2000, work on the first extension of the Primary School went on at quite a pace, as the Sewell Group worked towards a deadline of January 2001 for the opening. The extension would incorporate two new 30-place classrooms, a library area, a new staff-room and a state-of-the-art Information Technology suite, containing 15 computers. The new extension was needed to accommodate the growing number of children attending the school. During the summer, as building work continued and the school continued to grow, some children were accommodated in a temporary classroom in the hall without any adverse effect on their academic achievement. It said a lot for the ability of the children to adapt and of the ability of the staff to plan and manage the situation.

The village successor to the Drypool Feast, 'Knockout 2000', was organised by the Village Hall Committee to take place on 12 August 2000. The long hours and hard work put in by the committee were blessed by fine weather and a real fun day was supported by over 2000 people, including many residents from the village. The objective of drawing the community together and making a real celebration to mark the year was achieved. Dozens of stalls surrounded the park, together with fairground rides and bouncy castles for the children and water-based fun games and competitions for those teams of

enthusiastic adults prepared to make fools of themselves.

The school was given a rigorous inspection by a Local Authority Inspection Team during the summer term, and during the three days of the inspector's visit every nook and cranny of school life was delved into. The school was given an excellent written report following the inspection, praising the ethos of the school and the behaviour of the children, pointing the way ahead and confirming the good work carried out by the staff, pupils and governors of the school.

A disturbing development re-appeared once more, in December 2000, when it was announced by Associated British Ports that permission was being sought from the DETR (Ports Division) to realise plans for the major £35 million roll-on, roll-off riverside terminal. The terminal was initially planned for 1996. However, over the years, a number of other projects had been given priority and the ro-ro terminal had been put on the 'back-burner'. In the intervening period Victoria Dock had been fully developed to its eastern boundary and thus a number of residential properties would be sited only metres from the proposed jetty. Residents nearby were angered by the proposal on several grounds, not least because, as the development is planned to be built in the river, it does not require Council planning consent and, as a result, land searches by their solicitors had not revealed the project. Many other concerns were raised: visual impact, the possible collapse of house prices, the potential risk, noise levels, dust and general disturbance, the possible 24-hour operation of the terminal, potential lighting nuisance during the night hours, the possible hazardous contents of the containers, the increase in road traffic along Garrison Road, the potential environmental damage consequent on that and also the possible environmental damage that might be caused to the river and the residential development. Nevertheless, ABP applied to the Government for a special order to allow initial construction work and, though the Council was not required to give formal planning consent for the proposal, they did have to be consulted, as a public right of way would need to be diverted. In January 2001 they replied that, whilst supporting the economic benefits of the development, they objected to the proposal on the grounds of potential noise levels.

The delivery of some of the key components of The Deep arrived on site at Sammy's Point, in December 2000. They were the windows which will hold back the waters of the huge tank; they provided everyone with a better idea of the shape of the building when it is completed. The specially made acrylic tunnel and lift shaft were made by Reynolds Polymer Technology of Colorado and were shipped over from America in sections. The tunnel needs to be exceptionally strong as it will be below nine metres of water and also needs to be exceptionally clear to enable the public to see the wonders of the ocean as they walk through the tunnel.

The new extension to the school opened on time at the start of January 2001 and the children and staff were highly delighted with their new classrooms and other facilities. Councillor Tom McVie performed the opening ceremony later, in February, and the Reverend Mark Bennett from the Victoria Dock church then blessed the school and its new extension. Head teacher, Sue Roach, said that the school was going from strength to strength and thanked the governors and parents for believing in it and helping it to move forward. Councillor Gordon Wilson, the cabinet member with responsibility for compulsory education, congratulated everyone at the school for upholding the pioneering spirit of the city through such a successful project.

Later in the month it was announced that the opening of The Deep would be delayed until February 2002, due to early design and development delays. Colin Brown, Chief Executive of The Deep said: 'It is a unique building. No-one has ever built anything like this before. It has taken a few weeks longer to get the plans and the steelwork sorted out. The design team has done tremendous work, as can be seen by anyone viewing the site of this complex, even unique building. If it means we have to wait another month or so before we are fully operational then I know it will be worth the wait.' In the same month, it was also announced that several key derelict sites near The Deep would be targeted for a major cleanup to improve deteriorating parts of the Old Town. It was intended that secure, attractive and accessible pathways would be created to and from The Deep, the Old Town area, including the museums zone and the Fruit Market. This was to be achieved through 'Gateway' features, such as better lighting, improved paving, painting, fencing and landscaping.

Several key appointments were made at The Deep in early 2001, as the business centre began to take shape and an aggressive marketing campaign to find tenants got underway. Freya Cross, The Deep Business Centre Manager, had given presentations in the summer of 2000 to representatives of principal property agents in the City outlining the facilities and services on offer in the state-of-the-art centre, which was also designed by Terry Farrell, the architect responsible for The Deep. Indeed the architecture of the Business Centre had been designed to complement the visitor attraction, with the main theme carried through by the use of the same materials used in The Deep. As the Business Centre neared completion the consultations and the subsequent marketing campaign began to pay off, as a considerable amount of interest built up and new tenants began to sign up for space in the high-profile development. A mosaic-tiled circular core, housing a spiral staircase, marks the front entrance of the centre, which was designed to provide a mixture of up to 38 incubator units for start-up and embryo businesses, with total office sizes ranging up to 238 square feet, as well as four anchor units for more established enterprises, with floor area of up to 4,380 square feet. It was intended that companies identified as local growth sectors, i.e. in the marine, marine science, high technology, IT, environmental and knowledge-based areas, would be housed in the building. By the summer of 2001 it was clear that the Business Centre had become extremely successful, the building was filling rapidly as businesses from all over Britain relocated there and inquiries were coming in thick and fast.

A strong demand for houses on Victoria Dock continued throughout 2001 and most did not stay on the market for long. The demand was fuelled in part by the widely acknowledged success of the primary school, as parents with young children of school age snapped up houses almost as soon as the 'For Sale' notice went up. Another factor was the community spirit that exists on the dock and the fact that it is considered a low crime area by the police. Bellways worked to complete the east end of the village, with landscaping and a view-point over the Humber at the end of Corinthian Way. This feature was used by many visitors to the development during the summer of 2001 who enjoyed a stroll along the promenade.

The school became a victim of its own success in 2001. It had become so popular that some children living on Victoria Dock who had applied to join the reception class had to be turned away to prevent the admission limits being exceeded. Five families were forced to appeal after their children had been allocated places at Estcourt Primary School in east Hull. This, of course, entailed them making the horrendous journey across the A63 Hedon Road up to four times per day. The eventual appeals hearing found in favour of the parents and their children were admitted to the school.

Another successful 'Knockout 2001' was held in August and proved to be even better than the previous year. Once again fine weather blessed the day and hundreds of people enjoyed a really good day out, whilst others got soaked in the fun water competitions. It is events like these and the hard work that goes into them that make a community tick.

As the futuristic lines of The Deep rise above Victoria Dock, we might pause to ponder what else may come along during this next millennium. Well, who can say? It is almost impossible for us to predict the changes that will take place in this small area of Hull during the next 1000 years. Just as difficult in fact, as it must have been for those few shepherds who lived in their turf huts and gazed up into the starry sky above Drypool 1000 years ago. It would have been impossible for them to predict the changes which have taken, place in this area over the last millennium, so we can only wonder. Perhaps it is as well that we have left our successors a time capsule to tell them who we were, of our hopes and aspirations and the way we lived. Hopefully, Kingston upon Hull will still be here, safe above the rising tides of global warming, still celebrating the past and pioneering the future.

Sources:
Threshold (Bellway Group house journal).